THE OXFORD GUIDE
TO FAMILY HISTORY

David Hey is Professor of Local and Family History at the University of Sheffield. His books include *The Oxford Companion to Local and Family History* (OUP, 1996; paperback 1998) and the *Oxford Dictionary of Local and Family History.*

Please return this item by the last date shown.

You may renew the item unless it is required by another borrower.

SANDWELL *Community* LIBRARIES

♻ 100% recycled paper.

The Oxford Guide to Family History

DAVID HEY

Oxford   New York

OXFORD UNIVERSITY PRESS

1998

Oxford University Press, Great Clarendon Street, Oxford OX2 6DP
Oxford New York
Athens Auckland Bangkok Bogotá Buenos Aires Calcutta
Cape Town Chennai Dar es Salaam Delhi Florence Hong Kong Istanbul
Karachi Kuala Lumpur Madrid Melbourne Mexico City Mumbai
Nairobi Paris São Paulo Singapore Taipei Tokyo Toronto Warsaw
and associated companies in
Berlin Ibadan

Oxford is a registered trade mark of Oxford University Press

Published in the United States by
Oxford University Press Inc., New York

British Library Cataloguing in Publication Data
Data available

Library of Congress Cataloging in Publication Data
Data available
ISBN 0-19-285305-8

1 3 5 7 9 10 8 6 4 2

Typeset by Alliance Phototypesetters, Pondicherry
Printed by Book Print, S.L.
Barcelona, Spain

Acknowledgements

I would like to thank the members of the 'Names Project' group, who have been meeting as a class organized by the Division of Adult Continuing Education at the Centre for English Cultural Tradition and Language, the University of Sheffield. They have helped not only by their individual projects but by their contributions to the shape of Chapter 2. Our work has been supported by grants from the University of Sheffield's Research Fund and from the Leverhulme Trust—support which is gratefully acknowledged.

The members of the 'Names Project' group are Valerie Answer, Denis Ashurst, Bill Beet, Vera Edwards, Margaret Furey, George and Margaret Gee, Mavis Greaves, Richard Newsam, Margaret Oversby, David Sissons, George Stoddart, Harold Taylor, Derek Tingle, Peter Wilkinson, and Michael Williams. Further help has been provided by Jos Kingston, Roy Newton, and Andrew Walker.

I am also grateful to Dr Ralph Houlbrooke of the University of Reading, who saved me from errors and made many helpful suggestions on points of detail. I am, of course, entirely responsible for the final text, warts and all.

Finally I would like to thank Sandra Assersohn, the picture researcher, and the editorial and production staff at OUP, who have made working on the book such a pleasure.

D. H.

CONTENTS

I would have you know, Sancho, that there are two kinds of lineages in the world: those which trace their descent from princes and monarchs, and which little by lit-tle time has diminished and reduced to a point, like a pyramid upside down; and others which derive their origin from common folk, and climb step by step till they achieve the dignity of great lords. So that the difference is between those who were and are no longer, and those who are but once were not.

Cervantes, *Don Quixote*
(translated by J. M. Cohen)

HOSTESS. A pair of socks, you rogue
SLY.   You're a baggage. The Slys are no rogues. Look to the
           Chronicles—we came in with Richard Conqueror ...

Shakespeare, *The Taming of the Shrew*

CHAPTER ONE

THE STUDY OF FAMILY HISTORY

FUTURE historians will look back with some astonishment at the extraordinary growth in the popularity of family history during the last few decades of the twentieth century. Throughout the ages and across the world people have had a natural curiosity about their ancestors, but only recently have amateur historians begun to trace their forebears with such fervour and delight. In Britain, in the United States of America, and in many other countries the growth of interest has been phenomenal. In Britain alone, tens of thousands of family historians, from all walks of life, are now actively engaged in this type of research and are members of one or more of the numerous family history societies that have been founded in every part of the land.

Why should this interest in our ancestors have mushroomed so spectacularly in recent years? Is it, as some cynics maintain, a reaction against the pace of change in the modern world, a search for roots in a supposedly more secure age when the traditional family was the unquestioned unit upon which society was built? If this is true, it is only part of the explanation and more positive points need to be emphasized. In the late twentieth century, for the first time in history, a great number of people now have the leisure and the means to pursue an interest that has always been a human concern. Books, adult education classes, conferences, and meetings of local societies provide the know-how that was unavailable to previous generations. Even more importantly, however, a door has been opened that allows access to the many and varied records that shed light on our ancestors. Throughout Britain, record offices and libraries now offer the general public the opportunity to use original sources and to see microfilm or microfiche copies of central records; moreover, they provide trained staff to give advice and assistance. The sheer bulk of the archives in national and local repositories gives English people and those of English descent a decided advantage over the inhabitants of most other lands. These immense collections are now available for everyone to consult.

It has been said that family history is England's fastest-growing hobby. Many family historians would reply that 'hobby' is far too mild a word to describe an overriding passion. Knowing one's ancestors is not a matter of mild curiosity; it is often part of an attempt to explain life and to understand how we have come to be what we are, not just physically through inherited genes, but how we have come to believe in certain principles or to have acquired the attitudes, prejudices, and characteristics that mould our personality. For very many people, tracing a family tree and discovering the lives of their ancestors is not a task that is undertaken lightly.

The modern emphasis on family history rather than the bare bones of genealogy represents a break with past interests. The search for roots is, nowadays, largely the concern of ordinary people who are discovering the identities and life experiences of their undistinguished forebears. The aim of family history is to satisfy a natural curiosity about one's ancestors, whoever they may have been. The modern researcher is little concerned with aristocratic pedigrees and vain boasts. His or her aim is the honest discovery of the names and, hopefully, something of the lives of all those who can be placed on a family tree, male and female alike.

The earliest genealogies were preserved by oral tradition long before they were written down. They were constructed to bolster authority by purporting to trace royal descents from gods and heroes. This ancient tradition of compiling fictional family trees to legitimize power was still flourishing in the sixteenth century, when the visual and performing arts were enlisted in support of Queen Elizabeth I's authority. At Hatfield House, where the famous Rainbow portrait of the queen shows her dress embroidered with eyes and ears that signify her ability to see and hear everything that was going on in her realm, a pedigree on view in the Long Gallery depicts innumerable coats of arms and heraldic devices, painted in colour on a parchment roll. It purports to trace the queen's ancestry all the way back to Adam.

The construction of fanciful family trees that bear no relation to the truth is an ancient vice. The Elizabethans have a particularly bad name in this respect, but the subjects of the second Queen Elizabeth are often equally credulous. The majority of English people are unlikely to be able to trace a continuous line beyond the sixteenth century, yet how common it is to hear the unfounded boast that a person's ancestors fought at the Battle of Hastings and how frequently one has to listen to assertions of descent from some famous figure in even more remote times. We deceive ourselves if we allow our self-esteem to be inflated in this ridiculous way. The pursuit of a family's history is sufficiently interesting not to need these hollow props.

In earlier centuries the establishment of a pedigree was often of practical value in an unscrupulous world, when a challenge at a court of law might deprive a family of its inheritance. The fifteenth-century Paston Letters show how a family had to be constantly on guard against the plots of its adversaries. The first pedigrees of families below the level of the aristocracy were therefore made, not as a matter of family pride, but for individual legal purposes. No collections of such pedigrees were made before the fifteenth

PEDIGREE OF THOMAS
CORNWALLIS (1560)
In Elizabeth I's reign it became the fashion amongst
the nobility and gentry not
only to construct an elab-
orate family tree but to display it as a work of art. This
pedigree was commissioned
by Thomas Cornwallis of
Brome Hall, Suffolk, and
Anne Jerningham his wife.
Their portraits in miniature
are shown towards the bottom. Amongst the branches
of vine, oak, honeysuckle,
and rose are sixty-two coats
of arms.

century. Genealogy became a sophisticated interest during the next two centuries, when it was catered for by the heralds and county antiquarians. From
that time onwards, a large number of pedigrees of rural gentry and wealthy
urban tradesmen appeared in print. The pedigrees of ordinary families were
passed on only by word of mouth.

Sufficient evidence survives to show that some poorer families were
equally interested in their origins and connections. When Robert Furse, a
Devon yeoman, wrote an account of his family in 1593, he was able to record
ten generations of it before his own. Richard Gough's *History of Myddle*
(1700–2) shows that Shropshire farmers, craftsmen, and labourers were
equally interested in their ancestors and in the family histories of their

neighbours. Such accounts were not normally written down, but were passed on orally. Some of Gough's genealogical information was obtained from the families concerned, some of it from other inhabitants of the parish. He looked at every documentary source that he could find, but much of what he knew was from what today we would call oral history. He frequently says in passing, 'We have a tradition', 'I have heard by ancient persons', and 'I have been credibly informed by ancient persons'. Country folk then, as now, delighted in talking about the family history of their neighbours, recounting their triumphs, dwelling on their misfortunes, and attributing common characteristics to successive generations and even to distant cousins.

Thomas Bewick, the eighteenth-century artist, spoke of this interest in family history amongst the old inhabitants of the cottages scattered around the edges of the common on the south bank of the Tyne in the 1750s and 1760s:

After I left the country, I always felt much pleasure in revisiting them, and over a tankard of ale to listen to their discourse. It was chiefly upon local biography, in which they sometimes traced the pedigree of their neighbours a long way back.

The length of communal memory within a local society was remarked upon by the Revd Francis Kilvert in his diary for Friday, 14 October 1870:

I turned in to old Hannah's and sat with her an hour talking over old times, and listening to her reminiscences and tales of the dear old times, the simple kindly primitive times 'in the Bryngwyn' nearly ninety years ago. She remembers how, when she was a very little girl, she lived with her grandfather and grandmother, old Walter Whitney (who was about ninety) and his wife. In the winter evenings, some of their old neighbours, friends of her grandfather, used to come in for a chat, especially old Prothero, William Price and William Greenway, contemporaries of her

A BEWICK WOODCUT
Six years before he died Thomas Bewick (1753–1828), the Northumberland wood engraver, wrote a memoir of his life in which he recalled rural scenes such as this. The church that is now Newcastle Cathedral can be recognized in the background.

PUDDLETOWN, DORSET IN
VICTORIAN TIMES
Thomas Hardy knew
Puddletown well, for many
of his relatives and some of
his ancestors lived there.
A new landowner rebuilt
much of the village from
1861 onwards, but the
centre, seen here, was hardly
affected.

grandfather, and all men born about the beginning of the eighteenth or the end of the seventeenth century. These old people would sit round the fire talking on the long winter evenings, and Hannah then a child of 8 or 10 would sit on a stool by her grandfather's chair in the chimney corner listening while they told their old world stories and tales of 'the Fairies' in whom they fully believed.

Thomas Hardy, of course, drew extensively on the stories that he had heard from grandparents, parents, uncles, aunts, and cousins scattered around the Dorset countryside. These family memories were as long as those recorded by Gough or those mentioned by Bewick in earlier times. In 1879, for instance, when he was working on *The Trumpet Major*, Hardy walked over to Puddletown and talked with his cousin James Sparks about their great-great-great-grandfather, who had lived in Puddletown in the seventeenth century and had built the cottage which had remained in the family ever since.

Describing field-work undertaken in South Cardiganshire between 1958 and 1961 for his fine book *The Agricultural Community in South-West Wales at the Turn of the Twentieth Century*, Dr David Jenkins wrote,

When I was asking informants (now aged about 80) just who had occupied partic-ular farms in the past, it was necessary to enquire carefully what period they were re-ferring to, for on several occasions I found that they started with people who had occupied those farms during the early nineteenth century. On another occasion a newspaper containing an account of the opening of a nonconformist chapel in 1832 was, in my presence, showed to a man who was in his sixties. The account named 21 people; the informant identified 19 of them as 'so-and-so's' great grandfather or whatever else the connection was, and disclaimed knowledge of the other two. I asked one informant about 80, who had spent his whole life in one locality, what people had occupied each of the 108 holdings in his parish in or about the year 1900. His information was checked against the parish electoral list for that year, and found correct in respect of 106 of the holdings.

It is interesting to ponder on what sorts of places retain strong communal memories of local families and to wonder whether or not these memories are weaker now than they were in earlier times. Were Gough and Bewick describing an interest that was shared by people all over Britain or were these rather remote communities in the Welsh Borders, Northumberland, Dorset, and Cardiganshire different from the rest? At the moment we cannot speak with certainty on such matters. A recent study of over a thousand autobiographies written by working-class men and women whose lives span the years 1790 to 1900 and a further thousand between 1900 and 1945 has concluded that although many authors began by describing as much of their own ancestry as they knew, it usually went back no more than a couple of generations. Can this apparent lapse of memory in more modern times be the result of industrialization and urbanization, the tearing-up of rural roots as families moved to the towns? When the majority of people moved only within the restricted area of their neighbourhood or 'country' and when the population was so much smaller, perhaps the pedigrees of local families were easier to remember? Perhaps there wasn't much else to talk about in some of the remoter rural areas?

An interest in and knowledge of the personal histories of one's neighbours is not merely a rural characteristic, however; it is possible to find it in many of our largest towns and cities. In Sheffield, Leeds, and Manchester, and no doubt in other great urban centres too, it was common to find, only a generation or two ago, that grandparents, uncles and aunts, and an assortment of cousins lived in the same street or just round the corner from one's own home. Extended kinship links within a restricted geographical area were as common in the towns as they were in the countryside. In such situations, family history was a natural and frequent topic of conversation.

Although the opportunities for the family historian are greater now than they have ever been, many researchers do not get past the first stage of constructing pedigrees. Assembling a family tree is merely a beginning of the task, however. The pleasures of knowledge increase substantially once we start to discover the life-styles of our ancestors and become interested in the places where they lived. We need to take the widest possible view of the subject if we are to understand properly the history of a single family. Though it is tedious to listen to all the details of another person's family history, the broad story of that family's experience may often be instructive. At its best, the study of family history should be concerned with the origin of families at the time of the formation of hereditary surnames, with the spread of the various branches and sometimes their disappearance, and with the social and geographical mobility that has brought about their rise or fall. All this needs to be considered against the wider background of British social and economic history and the patterns of emigration to new worlds overseas.

The history of the Gostwick or Gostick family may be taken as an illustration of these themes. I became interested in them when I discovered that my wife's great-great-grandfather was James Gostwick, who at the time of the 1851 census was a 64-year-old clerk living at 52 George's Grove in the parish of St James, Holloway, in north

London. He had been born in Bedford, but had moved further south to obtain one of the many clerical posts that were on offer in the capital city. Other Gosticks had travelled the same route before him, but most members of his family did not venture far. His surname has been shown to have originated near to his place of birth in Bedfordshire. The senior branch of the family was the subject of an article published in 1956 by Professor H. P. R. Finberg, who wrote, 'It cannot be said that the Gostwicks were ever distinguished by marked ability, but for a long period they were typical of many families in the upper-middle stratum of English life. Beginning as solid yeomen, they entered the ranks of gentry under Henry VIII. Sir John Gostwick was the first to bear a coat of arms.'

The earliest record of the surname is dated 1262, when a William de Gostwyc was listed among the jurymen of Stanford, Bedfordshire. Gostwick appears to be a lost hamlet that has never been identified. A tentative pedigree of the family can be constructed for the eight generations stretching from William to the early sixteenth century, after which we are on firmer ground. John Gostwick (c.1460–1512) and his brother William are the undoubted ancestors of all the Gostwicks who were seated at Willington (4¼ miles east of Bedford) until the death of William, the fourth baronet, in 1720. William's extravagance forced the sale of all the Gostwicks' Bedfordshire properties, on which they had resided for perhaps seventeen generations. The family disappeared in their native county, but did not become extinct, for a younger brother took up a post in Boston, Lincolnshire.

Meanwhile, collateral branches must certainly have been founded at various dates, for other Gostwicks have occasionally been traced elsewhere, especially in London. Professor Finberg noted that

Gostick is a variant of the name which occurs very frequently in connection with undoubted members of the family, and no doubt represents the usual pronunciation. Parish registers and other records in Hertfordshire, Bedfordshire, Northamptonshire, Suffolk and London contain many references to persons named Gostick, who probably represent offshoots thrown off by the Willington family centuries ago.

The knightly Gostwicks were the only ones bearing this unusual surname when the whole of Bedfordshire was assessed for the hearth tax in 1671; the others were either too poor to pay the tax or they had moved out of the county. The ancestors of Joseph Gostick, the Victorian clerk, have not yet been traced, but all the indications are that he was descended from a junior branch of this ancient Bedfordshire family. The fortunes of these junior branches were very different from those of the senior line at Willington. They became more and more removed from the knightly Gostwicks, who remained on their estates, both socially and physically. Their story is one that is paralleled in the history of numerous other families throughout the country.

The rise and fall of families and the contrasting fortunes of different branches are themes to which we shall return. Throughout the ages, English men and women have grasped their opportunities to rise from lowly status to the top positions in the country. Spectacular rises are much better documented than gradual falls, but of course slight movements up or down the social scale were much more common. If a rise or a fall continued in the same direction for three or four generations then the consequences for a family's fortunes could be considerable.

An example of upward social mobility through the Sheffield metal trades is provided by the Mappin family. The city has its Mappin Art Gallery and its Mappin Street, while Mappin & Webb, silversmiths, is a household name. A count of subscribers in the current telephone directories shows that the surname is surprisingly rare and concentrated in and around Sheffield. Only 95 Mappins subscribe to the national telephone system, 60 of whom are named in the Sheffield directory. Earlier distributions of the surname point to a similar conclusion. During the first five years of civil registration, 1 July 1837–30 June 1842, only 15 births were recorded with the surname Mappin; 14 of these were in the Sheffield registration district and the other 1 was in the neighbouring district of Ecclesall. The earliest reference to the surname is from the marriage in 1593 at Sheffield of Derricke Mappin and Elizabeth Dunn, followed the next year by the baptism of their son Otho, who in time was trained as a cutler. Otho's elder son, Richard, also became a cutler, but his younger son, Otho, was described as a labourer when he was brought before the quarter sessions in 1670. Eight years previously, this younger Otho had been taken by the constable to the assizes at York, where his name was recorded as Otto Mappin, alias Dedwick. Derricke Mappin had been recorded as Dedick Mappin when he was buried in 1634. Both Derricke and Otho suggest a French or Low Countries origin. The French district, Maupin, is a possible source for this name.

Richard Mappin's son Joseph was also a cutler, but the sons in the next two generations (also named Joseph) were bakers. In 1773, when the Sheffield Assay Office was authorized to hallmark precious metals, a Jonathan Mappin registered his mark; a directory of 1787 lists him as a maker of clasps and dog-collars. Several of Jonathan's sons were apprenticed to cutlers. One of these was Joseph Mappin, engraver and fruit-knife-maker, whose son, John Newton Mappin, founded the family's fortunes by becoming a partner in a very successful brewery business. He built a church at the new suburb of Ranmoor at a cost of £14,000, and when he died in 1884 he left £15,000 and his art collection for the establishment of the Mappin Art Gallery. His nephew Sir Frederick Thorpe Mappin became Master Cutler in 1855, Member of Parliament for East Retford in 1880, and a baronet in 1886. He gave many more pictures to the permanent collection of the Mappin Art Gallery and was one of the founders of the University of Sheffield, becoming

MAPPIN AND WEBB, OXFORD STREET, LONDON (1908)

Founded in Sheffield in 1863 by John Newton Mappin and his brother-in-law George Webb, the firm commissioned the architects Belcher and Joass to erect this fine commercial building in Oxford Street in 1908. The surname Mappin is still concentrated in the Sheffield area, where it was first recorded in the 1590s.

a Pro-Chancellor in 1905. His youngest brother, another John Newton Mappin, began as a cutler and with his brother-in-law, George Webb, formed Mappin & Webb & Co. in 1863. Meanwhile, other Mappins continued as cutlers, and 2 of the 12 listed in a directory of 1856 were chimney-sweeps.

An illuminating example of downward social mobility is provided by the Wasteney family. The surname takes many forms. Its modern guises include Wastnage, Wastnidge, Wasnidge, Wastenay, Westnage, Westnedge, Westnidge, and Westney. All these names are derived (via Gasteney) from a French place-name, Le Gàtinais, formerly Gastinois, which lies south of Paris and east of Orléans. The family first appears in English records in the third quarter of the twelfth century. A Robert de Wastenays is named in the Staffordshire charter rolls of c.1165, and a William Wastineis is mentioned in the pipe rolls of 1177. During the next hundred years the surname was recorded in Lincolnshire, Leicestershire, and Cheshire, and shortly afterwards in Shropshire. By 1300 a knightly family of de Wasteneys were living at Headon, near Retford, in Nottinghamshire, and just across the county boundary at Todwick in south Yorkshire.

The unusual Christian name Hardolph has been used by branches of this family from at least the fourteenth century to the present day. Sir Edmund and Sir Hardolph Wasteneys were witnesses to a charter in 1331. The name Hardolph appears in the earliest parish registers for Headon and Todwick. It was given to the son of Gervase Wastnes of Headon upon his baptism in 1579, and seven years later the Todwick registers record the marriage of Haduphus Wastnes. Hardolph Wastney of Headon was created a baronet in 1622 (when he claimed that he was sixth in descent from John Wastneys of that place). His son and namesake had a house there that was taxed on 21 hearths in 1664. This second baronet died without issue in 1673, when the title and estate passed to his nephew Sir Edmund, who sold Todwick four years later. Headon Hall was rebuilt in 1710 by Sir Edmund's son, another Sir Hardolph Wastney, but upon his death without issue in 1742 the estate passed to a great-niece. In 1776 the hall was demolished so completely that nothing remains to be seen of it. A tablet on the church wall commemorates the last baronet: 'Here lie the remains of Sir Hardolph Wasteneys, Bart. Being the last of his family in the male line, Who how respectable soever for the antiquity of it was more so for the excellency of his virtues.'

Meanwhile, a junior branch of the Wasteneys had moved a little further west from Todwick to Lamb Hill in the parish of Handsworth. They too adopted the name Hardolph for their eldest sons. Francis Wasteney, baptized at Todwick in 1621, christened his twin sons Hardolph and Darcy at Handsworth in 1667. Fifteen years later, this Hardolph was apprenticed to Anthony Hallatt, a Sheffield cutler; he obtained his freedom of the company in 1690 and was living in the town two years later when a poll tax was levied. He was buried in Sheffield parish churchyard in 1733. Fifteen other Wasteneys are recorded in subsequent apprenticeship and freedom lists of the Cutlers' Company. Mid-nineteenth-century directories record the

THE WASTENEY COAT OF ARMS

This coat of arms was allowed by the heralds at the Visitation of Nottinghamshire of 1662–4. The arms are blazoned as Sable a lion rampant double queued Argent collared Gules, in a canton a Baronet's badge, the crest as On a wreath Argent and Sable a demi lion rampant double queued Argent collared Gules. The pedigree was 'certified by Sir Hardolph Wastneys, Bart.'

Sheffield Wasteneys as cutlers, pork-butchers, provision-dealers, and cow-keepers. Other Wasteneys elsewhere in south Yorkshire followed different trades. George Wasteneys moved from Todwick to Grenoside in 1851 and became the village blacksmith; his son took the licence of the Old Harrow pub. Tombstones in Todwick churchyard show that Wasteneys remained in the village until the early years of the twentieth century; the surname is commemorated there by Wasteneys Road. Others crossed the Atlantic and one branch now lives in Woodstock, Ontario. In England the current telephone directories list 183 subscribers with various forms of this surname. The family has gone from Nottinghamshire, but 46 per cent of the entries are from south Yorkshire. The centre of Sheffield is only 32 miles away from Headon and about 10 miles from Todwick, where the family were resident six or seven centuries ago.

These three examples show how varied the fortunes of a family might be found to be if they are followed over a long period of time. Tracing the history of a particular surname is a natural and often rewarding procedure, but it is not the only method of research. A more balanced picture is provided by identifying each of one's sixteen great-great-grandparents. This is no simple task, for the increased mobility of recent generations makes it likely that at least one branch of the family has come from far afield. The job of identifying each great-great-grandparent will often take the family historian back into the late eighteenth century, well before the period of civil registration and census returns. The frustrations associated with inadequate registration before the beginning of Victoria's reign delay and sometimes prevent the completion of this research. The attempt should, nevertheless, be made.

No single example of a family tree constructed in this way can serve as an adequate illustration of the immense variety of human experience. It is common to find that over four generations the fortunes of the different branches of one's family have varied considerably. The family historian is led into a series of different worlds, as he or she discovers more and more about the lives of each pair of ancestors. Thus, all the eight great-grandparents of Mrs Margaret Furey, former secretary of the Sheffield and District Family History Society, lived within the boundaries of the city of Sheffield, and four of her sixteen great-great-grandparents were born there. Three others came from nearby villages, four came from Lincolnshire, and three came from Nottinghamshire; the places of birth of the other two have not yet been identified. The occupations of the eight great-great-grandfathers ranged from razorsmith, filesmith, and fork-grinder to mason, tailor, shopkeeper, farmer, and agricultural labourer. The sixteen surnames include Bolsover, Pickworth, and others derived from place-names, Marriott and Wilmott, which were derived from diminutive forms of personal names, and Wragg and Ibbotson, which are widespread, but particularly prolific in and around Sheffield. This basic information provides many points of departure for further research.

Reconstructing the life-styles of one's great-grandparents and, if possible, their parents, too, is a specially rewarding task that will keep the family historian occupied for years on end. For these generations, it is usually possible to put flesh on the dry bones of dates of birth, marriage, and death, with which we often have to be satisfied when enquiring about previous ancestors. The information that can be gathered from documents is usually so much richer for the nineteenth century than for earlier times, and for some of these people we may even have photographs. Our understanding of their lives may be patchy, but it is likely to be nearer the mark than our grasp of the day-to-day existence of ancestors in the more remote past. A medieval ancestor was responsible for the surname which we bear and for the male genes that have been inherited through a Y chromosome, but all our great-grandparents, not just the one with our surname, have contributed significantly to our physique, intelligence, domestic background, and environment. Knowing their stories helps us to understand our own.

In practice, the family historian advances in stages. His or her first desire is to step back into the unknown, to go beyond family memory or to check whether or not the stories on which he or she has been weaned are accurate or not. Many quickly face disillusionment as they discover that romantic accounts of the family's origins simply do not fit the facts. Perseverance will reveal a more prosaic story, but one that is all the more satisfying for being honest and accurate. Fanciful accounts of family history are rightly treated with derision by the large and growing body of amateur historians who know that if the overwhelming majority of families in times past have consisted of ordinary people of slender means, the person who traces a family tree has to expect that he or she is unlikely to find illustrious names, however wide the net is cast.

The enormous growth in the popularity of family history has helped to change thousands of people's perceptions of the past. Not knowing the dates of the reigns of the Plantagenet kings or of the battles of the Napoleonic wars, or a failure to grasp the nuances of Castlereagh's foreign policy, need not disqualify someone from studying those aspects of human history which have most meaning for the great majority of the population. Of course, a knowledge of past national and international events helps to create a framework of understanding, and may even be crucial to the interpretation of a family's fortunes, but an amateur researcher should not be put off by the arcane mysteries of the historian's craft. The specialist techniques can be learned when and where they are appropriate.

The family historian quickly finds that he or she is following lines of enquiry that no one has attempted before. The novelty of discovery is an important element in the subject's appeal. Our ancestors may never have appeared on the national stage, but they and countless numbers like them are the real stuff of history. They are the people who have shaped our own lives far more than the famous figures who have attracted so much attention. Interest in history seen through the eyes of ordinary people has never been higher than it is now in this democratic age. That interest turns to absorbed fascination when it is linked to us through ties of blood.

This book is written in two parts. The first deals with approaches and the wider concerns of the subject, the second with records and their interpretation. Professional historians have revolutionized the study of social history in recent years. Much of their work is of great interest to family historians, for it deals with such basic matters as the size of families, the ages at which people got married, the mobility of the population, and so forth. Yet this

A FAMILY ALBUM
Many families possess albums of photographs, some of which can no longer be identified. Future generations will be grateful if we label our own photographs. This album of the Fuller-Maitland family has been deposited in the Surrey Record Office. It dates from the time of Henry Fowler Broadwood (1811–93) of the famous British firm of piano manufacturers.

work is not widely known amongst amateurs. I have therefore tried to highlight those aspects that are most germane to the study of family history and
have suggested lines of enquiry—past and present distributions of surnames, patterns of mobility, the residential stability of certain families,
etc.—that may be followed with enjoyment and profit by those family historians who have finished the task of compiling a family tree and wish to
proceed to a more advanced and fulfilling stage of research.

The second part of the book is concerned with the basics of the subject—
how to get started, where to find records, how to use them, etc. A number of
good handbooks which have been published in recent years are referred to
in the Bibliography. The records available to historians are so voluminous
and scattered and the experiences of individual families are so remarkably
varied that no single book can cover every aspect of the subject. I have described the major classes of record that a family historian should turn to
first. Only when these archives have been exhausted will he or she need to
turn to specialist works that will direct him or her elsewhere.

CHAPTER TWO

FAMILY NAMES

EVERYONE, at some time or another, has probably pondered the meaning of his or her own surname and has wondered why some other people possess such strange names as Hogg or Daft, Pennyfather or Death, Balcock or Onions. Many of us will also have wondered whether everybody with the same surname is descended from a common ancestor. That is out of the question with a name like Jones or Smith, but we may have noticed how, even after all the movement of modern times, some of the rarer surnames are found only in certain parts of England. The further back we go in time, the more we find that such names are intensely local in their distribution. Many of these surnames may indeed have a single-family origin. Given the small size of the national population at the time when surnames were formed, this conclusion need not surprise us. Tracing the geographical pattern of a surname is therefore an important task for the family historian, for it may well lead towards the original home of the name.

The Origins of Surnames

Contrary to popular belief, few English families can trace their surnames back to Domesday Book. Fewer still can go back even tentatively into the Anglo-Saxon era. While it is obvious that a large proportion of the present population of England is descended from people who lived here a thousand or more years ago, it is usually an impossible task to find firm evidence of a continuous line. Only the Ardens and the Berkeleys can prove a descent from a pre-Conquest Englishman, the Ardens from Aelfwine and the Berkeleys from Eadnoth. Despite the fact that England has one of the largest and oldest collections of public records in the world, insufficient information survives with which to test the claims of other families whose names suggest a connection with Anglo-Saxon landowners.

Sir Frank Stenton has written,

The number of thirteenth century landed families which can be traced backwards to an ancestor bearing an English or a Danish name is by no means inconsiderable. It includes some families of baronial rank, such as Berkeley, Cromwell, Neville, Lumley, Greystoke, Audley, Fitzwilliam of Hinderskelfe and Fitzwilliam of Sprotborough, and many others of less prominence which were influential in their own districts.

Even though firm proof is lacking, it is likely that such families are of Anglo-Saxon or Anglo-Scandinavian descent. For example, the present Earl of Scarbrough is descended from 24 generations of known ancestors, beginning with Uchtred in the middle of the twelfth century. From that time, and probably from long before, the family have held lands in Lumley, County Durham, the place from which their hereditary surname was eventually derived. The choice of the name Uchtred, rather than a Norman French one, a century or so after the Conquest strongly suggests a descent from a native family. Even if all such claims are allowed, however, we are still dealing with only a tiny minority of the entire population of the country.

MARY ARDEN'S HOUSE, WILMCOTE, WARWICKSHIRE
This timber-framed yeoman's house is the reputed birthplace of William Shakespeare's mother. The Ardens are one of those rare families that can trace their ancestry back to pre-Conquest England. William Dugdale, the seventeenth-century historian of Warwickshire, described them as 'that most ancient and worthy family'.

A larger group of people can trace their descent beyond the Conquest into Normandy, even though in 1066 hereditary surnames there were a relatively new phenomenon restricted to some of the great landowning families. Most of these surnames were derived from the locality where the family had their chief residence. For example, amongst William I's barons at Hastings were William de Warenne from Varennes near Dieppe, Roger de Busli from Bully-en-Brai near Neufchâtel, and Ilbert de Laci from Lassy, south of Bayeux. Norman barons such as these introduced the idea of stable, hereditary surnames into England. Their example was followed by their principal retainers and, eventually, the custom spread down the social scale in all parts of the land.

During the two centuries or so that followed the Conquest most major landowning families and many knights adopted hereditary surnames, especially if they lived in the south of England, the Midlands, or East Anglia. Fashion played some part in this process, for the desire to conform is always strong, but the need to secure hereditary tenure in the uncertain period of Norman rule was probably of paramount importance. For this reason, a high proportion of these early surnames were derived from the place where the family had its main residence. In the twelfth and thirteenth centuries it was a common practice for the senior line of a major landowning family to adopt a hereditary surname of this type, while junior branches gradually acquired different surnames. It was not then a matter of prestige or status for junior branches to claim a connection through a common surname with the mightiest families in the land.

The fashion for hereditary surnames spread gradually till it was accepted by all sections of society. Richard McKinley, the leading authority on the subject, has concluded that 'The development of hereditary surnames in this country was a prolonged and complex business, not operating uniformly over the whole of Britain, but subject to marked regional variations and to differences between one social class and another.' The question of why hereditary surnames had become generally adopted by the end of the Middle Ages is a difficult one to answer. The assertion that the practice spread because of the growth of record-keeping cannot be supported. On the one hand, medieval scribes were content to enter a man's name in the form of 'Richard, the son of John' and, on the other, many surnames arose from diminutives of personal names or pet forms that do not appear in medieval documents. It seems unlikely that surnames derived from nicknames (including many obscene ones which have not survived) were coined by a scribe. It is far more likely that such surnames began as bynames that were invented by a person's neighbours. Many bynames never developed into hereditary surnames. Surviving records from the period 1250–1350 show that some people were known during their lifetime by two or three different bynames, and it is now impossible to say why one of these sometimes became a hereditary surname in preference over the others.

Between 1150 and 1300 the number of male first names in general use was

Baptised

For the year 1712 —

Males — — — 25.

ffemales — — — 27.

In all — — — 52.

1713		
April	6	Elisabeth, daughter of Willm Stapleys — Gardiner —
May	2	John son of Richard paine — Sadler —
	6	Thomas Son of Thom: Blake a Traveller —
	10	Elisabeth daughter of Edwd Steel a Traveller —
	11	Mary daughter of John Holman — Labourer
		Anne daughter of Christopher Hudson Husbandman —
	24	Christopher Son of Christopher Lambert Husbandman
	27	of Thomas Dodd — Brickmaker —
	29	Jane daughter of mr Thomas Bristow.
June		George Son of Thomas Baker Labourer —
July	18	Susan daughter of James Lee — Blacksmith —
	24	Benjamin Son of Stephen Carter — Collar-maker —
august	6	Mary Matthews daughter of mr Thomas Sanders —
	7	Richard Son of Robert Holland Labourer —
September	30	Frances daughter of Edward Wells —
	23	Edward Son of John Green — Labourer —
	27	Richard base born Son of Samuel King —
October	28	Catherine daughter of John Turner — Wheelwright —
	5	Mary daughter of John Wood —
	7	William Son of William Moorer — Barber —
	17	Margaret daughter of Robert Marbin —
November	22	Mary daughter of Benjamin Glasbrook —
	8	Jane daughter of Edward Ellis Labourer
	11	Eleanor daughter of Henry Holesworth — Butcher —
	15	Richard Son of John Edwards — Labourer —
November		John Son of mr John Hill Attorney at Law —
		William Castleman —
December	4	Thomas Son of Richard Miller — Labourer —

THE BAPTISM REGISTER OF REIGATE, SURREY (1713)

On 29 May 1713 Jane, the daughter of Mr Thomas Bristow, was baptized at Reigate. The surname preserves the original form of the place-name Bristol. Occasionally, extra information is added to the usually terse entries in parish registers. This one gives the occupations of most of the fathers of baptized children. The gentlemen of the parish were distinguished in the usual way as 'Mr'. Two outsiders were noted as 'Travellers'.

declining sharply, while at the same time a few male first names were becoming very common. This helps to explain why a man might need a byname to differentiate him from other people with the same personal name, but it does not explain why the byname became a hereditary surname. The desire of smaller landowners to ensure the continuity of their property was probably as strong a reason for the adoption of hereditary surnames as it was amongst the richer groups of society. Whatever the reason, the fashion spread slowly downwards, taking hold first in the south and in East Anglia, between 1250 and 1350. Even in these prosperous and populous parts of England, however, many people who were assessed for the poll tax in the years 1379–81 were recorded without a surname. Nevertheless, by the fifteenth century the practice had been adopted there by almost everyone. In the north of England and the lowlands of Scotland people were generally about a century behind the south in accepting such developments. The spread of hereditary surnames must therefore be seen as a long drawn-out process, varying in time between regions and also between classes. Much detailed research yet needs to be done before confident statements about the precise timing of this process can be made.

A few tentative conclusions can be reached about the adoption of hereditary surnames by urban dwellers. Some of the richer Londoners had acquired surnames by the second half of the twelfth century, and during the first half of the thirteenth century wealthy families in most of the larger provincial cities had done likewise. Within another hundred years many English urban families had acquired hereditary surnames. It is not certain, however, how many medieval townspeople were unrecorded; perhaps a substantial number of unskilled labourers without surnames escaped the attention of tax-collectors. Most of the recorded urban populations seem to have had hereditary surnames by the fifteenth century. Even so, Tudor York contained some inhabitants who were recorded without a surname.

In the countryside, where the majority of English people lived, few tenants had acquired hereditary surnames before the middle of the thirteenth century. The process accelerated during the next hundred years in the south, the Midlands, and East Anglia, but in the north many countrymen were still without such surnames by the year 1400. During the following century the majority of northerners adopted surnames, but in some parts of the north, such as south-west Lancashire, the process was not completed until the sixteenth century. Serfs seem to have acquired hereditary surnames about the same time as the rest of the farming population. If a good series of manor court rolls survives, the descent of servile families can often be traced back into the Middle Ages, for the rolls record the deaths of bond tenants and the names of their successors. Some surnames were used only by serfs, not by freemen, and even today they are most commonly found in those parts of the country where they arose. Bond, Cotman, and Thrall are amongst the surnames that are derived in this way.

The adoption of a hereditary surname was not the end of the process. Some names were corrupted out of all recognition over time, especially if a family moved to a new district. The Lancashire name Aspinhalgh, for instance, has become Aspinall, Aspinough, Asmall, Aspull, and so on. Other people acquired totally different surnames when they moved. Thus, when John Ellis built a cottage in Myddlewood, Shropshire, in 1581, his new

EDWARD HASTED

Edward Hasted (1732–1812) was the author of the monumental *History and Topographical Survey of the County of Kent*, one of the country's greatest county histories. He is portrayed here at the age of 45. Professor Alan Everitt has shown that the author's surname was derived from Highsted, near Sittingbourne and that variant forms include Haisted, Heighsted, Heysted, Haysted, Hoysted, Hysted, Hyested, Histed, and Highsted.

BLAXLAND FARM, STURRY

Kent has a number of distinctive surnames derived from its scattered farms. This fine timber-framed farmhouse at Blaxland marks the spot where one such surname originated.

neighbours called him Ellis Hanmer, after the village whence he had come; his descendants accepted Hanmer as their new surname.

The stock of surnames was greater in the Middle Ages than it is today, though it has been replenished in recent times by European and Common-wealth immigration. Many surnames of single-family origin were lost at the time of the Black Death and the other pestilences of the Middle Ages. Some became extinct because the families that bore them were never prolific and eventually succumbed in the male line. A few more rare names will disap-pear before the end of the twentieth century. The rare surnames that have survived are mostly concentrated in or near their place of origin. They give a distinctive flavour to the names of each of the counties of England. The Hogbens come from Kent, the Heathcotes from Derbyshire, the Fells from Cumbria, the Postlethwaites from Lancashire, and those who bear the sur-name Greengrass come from Suffolk. The old saying still rings true that 'By Tre, Pol and Pen ye shall know Cornish men'. Despite all the mobility of recent generations, the distribution patterns of many of our surnames are intensely localized.

The Etymology of Surnames

The study of the meaning of surnames has traditionally been the preserve of the linguist. For many years the standard works were the *Dictionary of British Surnames* and *The Origins of English Surnames* by P. H. Reaney, a for-mer professor of English language; the dictionary has recently been enlarged and brought up to date by R. M. Wilson. Another modern work is that of two lexicographers, P. Hanks and F. Hodges, *The Oxford Dictionary of Sur-names*. The scholar whose expertise is in old languages clearly has a lot to contribute to this subject, yet the explanations offered for the meaning of a name by a linguist are often unsatisfactory. The surname Broadhead, for in-stance, is normally classified as a nickname, but the geographical distribu-tion of the surname, both now and in the past, points to different origins. The south Yorkshire Broadheads appear to be descended from a family that once lived at a farm on Broadhead Edge, near Holmfirth, while the Lan-cashire Broadheads came from a farm of that name in the parish of Scaris-brick. The Yorkshire Broadheads are recorded at their place of origin in mid-fourteenth-century manorial court rolls. Even as late as a subsidy roll of 1545 for Agbrigg, Morley, and Skyrack wapentakes (a large and populous part of the West Riding), there were only three Broadheads, all of whom were living in Holmfirth. Perhaps the Broadheads in other counties ac-quired their name as a nickname, but in northern England the derivation is quite different. Local historical knowledge is therefore essential if the ety-mology of such names is to be interpreted correctly. In recent years, the work of Richard McKinley and others has begun to shift the emphasis away from purely linguistic explanations to interpretations based on detailed studies of local topography and genealogies, but an enormous amount of research throughout the country remains to be done. In the quest for the origin of surnames, the amateur family historian and the local historian are well placed to contribute.

As we have already noted, every county has its stable core of surnames which have persisted through the centuries from the time of their formation to the present day. This is especially true of those areas of scattered settlement where surnames were derived from the names of hamlets and farms in the thirteenth and fourteenth centuries. Even within their county of origin, however, some of these local surnames have remained rare while others have become common. The current Sheffield telephone directory lists only 23 subscribers with the surname Abdy, which is derived from a local farm, but 152 people with various spellings of the surname Broomhead, which has arisen from the name of another local farmstead. The separate fortunes of a family or families obviously determine whether such surnames remained scarce or became numerous. Some families had several males who survived long enough to start new branches; other families just managed to survive in the male line; and in many other cases the family surname eventually disappeared through the lack of male heirs.

Records from the thirteenth century and the first half of the fourteenth note a large number of surnames (and many more bynames which failed to become hereditary) that are now lost. Conversely, the considerable natural increase of the national population during much of the sixteenth century and the first third of the seventeenth produced a situation in which surnames of single-family origin became common in those areas where they originated. Families which had only one or two branches at the time of the poll tax returns of 1379–81 often had several branches recorded in the same locality in the hearth tax returns of the 1660s–1670s.

To interpret the meaning of a surname convincingly we therefore have to trace the name backwards over the centuries. It is unwise to depend on the modern form of a surname when seeking its etymology, for it is very common indeed for a name to have changed in such a way as to be hardly recognizable. For example, the surname that has arisen from the personal name Bernard has sometimes become Barnett or Burnett, Gascoyne has become Gaskin, and Ensor (the shortened form of the Derbyshire village of Edensor) has sometimes been changed to Answer. When a surname has been traced back to its area of origin, it may be helpful to know the local pronunciations of the name of a village. Elsewhere in Derbyshire, Bolsover has produced the surname Bowser, Tideswell has led to Tisdall, and Barlow is one possible origin for people called Barley. Some of the surnames that still baffle linguists can be interpreted convincingly by those who have detailed knowledge, not only of a region's place-names and the history of its families, but of local dialects.

One of the largest categories of surnames is that which is derived from personal names. Some of these surnames, such as Paul or Thomas, come directly from the personal name of the father of the man who was the first in that line to possess a hereditary surname. Others have -s or -son added as a suffix to a personal name, e.g. Roberts or Johnson, and yet others are prefixed either by Fitz-, the Gaelic Mac-, or the Welsh ap or ab.

Many of the personal names which have given rise to surnames are no longer in current use. These include Old English names such as Edrich or Godwin, Scandinavian names such as Thorold and Tooley, and post-

JEAKES HOUSE, RYE, SUSSEX
This surname could have been derived in two very different ways. It may (as in this case) have come from the personal name Jacques or from Middle English *geke*, meaning a fool or simpleton. The illustration shows a house built in 1689–90 by Samuel Jeake, as a woolstore. His grandfather Henry spelt the surname Jake, Jacques, and Jeakes. Four generations of the Jeakes family lived in Rye.

Conquest names such as Everard or Hammond. Some surnames (and many place-names) are likely to have been derived from unrecorded personal names that were no longer in use by the time that our first written records begin. We have records of a large number of pre-Conquest names, most of which were given to the wealthier inhabitants; we may reasonably suspect that some puzzling surnames are corrupted forms of unrecorded personal names belonging to the less well-off sections of pre-Conquest society.

The Normans introduced many masculine names which remain popular, notably William, Richard, Henry, and Roger, together with the Breton names Alan and Brian. Biblical names, such as John, Thomas, and Adam, and the Greek names Philip and Alexander also became common after the Conquest. These gradually replaced the Old English and Scandinavian names, which, with very few exceptions, such as Edward and Edmund, had either disappeared or had become rare by the middle of the thirteenth century, even among poorer families.

The evidence for female names is less full, but by the thirteenth century most of the Old English and Scandinavian names had become unfashionable, while the names Anne, Elizabeth, Jane, Rose, Alice, and a few others had become very common. Thus, a large number of personal names were disappearing and a small number were being widely used at the very time when surnames were being formed. Few new masculine names were created during the later Middle Ages. In the sixteenth and seventeenth centuries Puritan families favoured obscure Old Testament names, but this trend has had little effect on the stock of English surnames, for by then most surnames had long been fixed.

Pet forms or shortened forms of personal names have given rise to an astonishing variety of surnames. About 100 surnames, as varied as Richards, Hitchcock, Dickson, and Higgins, are derived from the personal name Richard. Descendants of medieval men named Robert may now be called Robson, Dobbs, or Hopkins, while amongst those with a medieval ancestor whose name was Nicholas are those families which now bear the surnames Nicholls, Nixon, and Collinson. Pet or shortened forms of personal names are not easy to trace, because they were rarely recorded in medieval documents. It has been suggested that many of these forms were not used until the thirteenth century, by which time they were necessary to distinguish people, for the number of male personal names in general use had been considerably reduced. Pet or shortened forms of a personal name were not usually turned directly into surnames, but they were commonly used with the suffix -son. The addition of -cock, or of -kin, -et, -ot, -mot, -on, and -in, to a diminutive form of a personal name has given rise to numerous other common surnames.

Although surnames derived from personal names without the addition of suffixes or prefixes were not restricted to a particular social class or confined to certain parts of the country, some individual surnames of this type nevertheless retain a regional flavour. Thus, Batty (from Bartholomew) and

Parkin (from Peter) are mostly northern forms, while Jenkin (from John) and Perrin (also from Peter) are found most commonly in the south-west. Surnames ending in -son are both numerous and widespread, but they are particularly plentiful in northern England. Examples can be found in Yorkshire and Lancashire during the last third of the thirteenth century and the first half of the fourteenth century, then after 1350 they become very common indeed. Originally, -son names were largely confined to small tenants and were hardly ever used by wealthier landowners. Such names were also common in Lowland Scotland and were sometimes used in the Midlands and East Anglia, but in the south the suffix -s was preferred if such forms were used at all; many people in the south had acquired hereditary surnames by the late thirteenth century, before the fashion for -s and -son forms began. Subsequent social and geographical mobility has blurred these old distinctions, but the basic pattern can still be observed.

The tendency for certain names to acquire a final -s or -es that they did not have originally complicates this pattern. It is a common experience for the genealogist to find that the name he is tracing changes in this way. A Sheffield family that was consistently named Crook in sixteenth- and seventeenth-century sources eventually became known as Crookes, no doubt because this was already a common local surname that had been derived from a village a mile or two from the town centre. Many other examples could be cited, however, where there is no such ready explanation for the change; it seems to have been a natural tendency for English people to add -s to certain names, especially to short ones.

Surnames ending in -s were commonly used in Wales, but this form was also used in parts of England long before the Welsh began to adopt English-type surnames in the sixteenth century. Names such as Edwards or Roberts are often English rather than Welsh in origin. The Welsh seem to have favoured this form of naming because it was already popular in those English counties that lay immediately across the border, especially in Gloucestershire and Herefordshire. Before the sixteenth century Welsh-speakers did not normally have hereditary surnames, unless they moved to England. Emigration from Wales occurred at an early date; some of the border counties, such as Shropshire, had attracted many Welsh immigrants even before Wales was united with England under the Tudors. The unification hastened the process whereby the Welsh population took surnames that were either shortenings of the ap or ab forms (the Welsh equivalent of the suffix -s or -son) or new creations from Anglicized forms of Welsh personal names, with the possessive -s added. Thus, ap Howell became either Powell or Howells, and ab Evan was adapted to Bevan or to Evans. In the more remote parts of Wales, English-type surnames were not adopted until the late eighteenth or early nineteenth centuries, by which time the evangelical revival had made some Old Testament names such as Habbakuk fashionable.

In the Gaelic-speaking parts of Scotland, Ireland, and the Isle of Man the prefix Mac- was used in place of the suffix -son. Most surnames in the

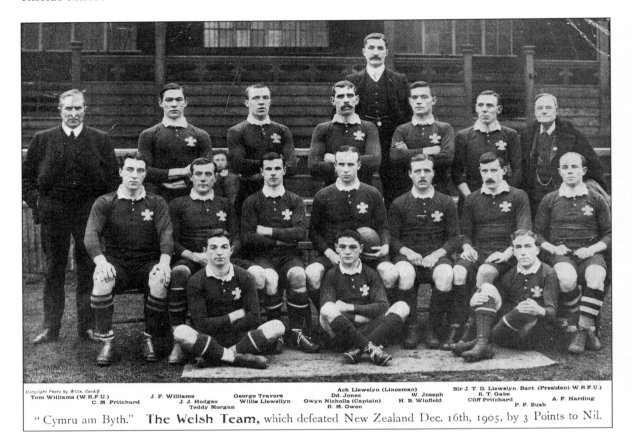

Copyright Photo by Wills, Cardiff

Tom Williams (W.R.F.U.)
  C. M. Pritchard
J. F. Williams
  J. J. Hodges
    Teddy Morgan
George Travers
  Willie Llewellyn
Ack Llewelyn (Linesman)
  Dd. Jones   W. Joseph
Gwyn Nicholls (Captain)   H. B. Winfield
    R. M. Owen
Sir J. T. D. Llewelyn. Bart. (President W.R.F.U.)
  R. T. Gabe
Cliff Pritchard   A. F. Harding
    P. F. Bush

"Cymru am Byth." **The Welsh Team,** which defeated New Zealand Dec. 16th, 1905, by 3 Points to Nil.

Scottish Highlands, including those which were not prefixed by Mac-, long remained those of clans rather than of individual families. The considerable amount of movement between Scotland and Ireland makes it difficult to determine whether a particular surname has a Scots or an Irish origin. Gaelic surnames are very rarely found in England before the nineteenth century, however. When such names did eventually migrate southwards, they were often changed into forms that English tongues could manage. Sometimes, as with the change from MacShuibne to MacQueen, the relationship between the old and new names is barely recognizable. The alteration of this and other Scottish names in relatively modern times alerts us to the possibilities of equally dramatic changes to imported names in the past.

The prefix Fitz- was used in Norman England in the same way that Mac- was used in Scotland and Ireland. It was derived from the French phrase *fils de* and was in limited use before about 1300 among the wealthier landowners. The widespread, but mistaken, belief that Fitz- implies illegitimacy arises from the much later practice, started by Charles II, of naming royal bastards in this manner. Nor do surnames derived from a female personal name necessarily come from an illegitimate line. We can only speculate on the reasons for choosing a mother's personal name rather than the father's;

THE WELSH RUGBY UNION TEAM (1905)
The names of the members of this victorious side include many that are instantly recognizable as being Welsh in origin. English surnames appeared in the valleys when migrants came in search of industrial work.

perhaps the father died when the child was young, perhaps the woman was a strong character, perhaps the family's property had been inherited through a female line. As Richard McKinley has written, 'The processes by which surnames arose are generally difficult to follow and often seem to be haphazard.' During the twelfth and thirteenth centuries there were no fixed rules about married women's surnames. The convention that women took their husband's name when they married arose gradually, spreading downwards from the landowning classes, during the period when surnames were becoming hereditary.

A related group of surnames are formed from nicknames (a word which

PORTRAIT OF SIR MUNGO MURRAY, SON OF THE 2ND EARL OF ATHOLL (1668–1700)

The surname Murray is derived from Moray in north-east Scotland. Mungo was an alternative name for St Kentigern, a sixth-century prince and missionary in Strathclyde. Though men of Murray's social class spent part of their time in England after James VI of Scotland became king of both countries, Highlanders rarely migrated south of the border before the nineteenth century.

is derived from an eke, or alternative, name). Some of these—Long, Short, White, Grey, Fox, Wild, Blessed, Welbeloved, and so on—are common and obvious (except that they sometimes referred to qualities opposite to those which are implied), but many others are rare and obscure. Even if it is clear what the literal meaning of a nickname is, the reason why it was originally bestowed cannot now be revealed. We can do no more than guess why a man living in Tideswell, Derbyshire, in 1381 was known as Richard Snowball or why 10 heads of household in the county of Bedfordshire in 1671 were called Mouse. If nicknames acquired in modern times at school or at work are often given for the most trivial or contradictory reasons, then clearly we shall never know how such names started back in the Middle Ages. Large numbers of nicknames occur in medieval records, but a lot of them are now extinct. This is hardly surprising; it is more difficult to explain why so many nicknames did become hereditary surnames. We may note, however, that this is a widespread phenomenon in other European languages.

Another large group of surnames is derived from occupations or from an office, rank, or status. Long before surnames became hereditary, bynames were derived from Old English words for occupations; some are found in the folios of Domesday Book. By the beginning of the thirteenth century, the more common occupational surnames were already numerous. The reason why Smith or Taylor or Wright became such popular names was that normally there would have been only one such craftsman per village and he would thus be readily distinguished by his occupational name. Many surnames that are derived from occupations are restricted in their distribution. Mariner is an obvious case, but others are less straightforward. In the cloth trade, for instance, fullers were known by a variety of dialect words whose usage is reflected in past and present distributions of certain surnames; thus, Walker was the preferred term in northern England and Scotland and in the West Midlands, while Tucker was usual in south-western England and Bowker was common in south-east Lancashire.

Some surnames that end in -er were derived from obscure trades that are no longer practised. The surname Flather is largely confined to the West Riding of Yorkshire; indeed, in the poll tax returns of 1379 it was found only in Morley wapentake and for the next 200 years was restricted to the Leeds–Dewsbury area, before a branch of the family moved a little further south. In the current UK telephone directories, 100 of the 148 subscribers are found in the West Riding and all the rest are scattered thinly. The most plausible explanation of the name is that a flather was a flayer of skins, but this is not certain. And for reasons that are far from clear, some of the common occupational names are feminine forms, e.g. Webster (weaver), Baxter (baker), Brewster (brewer), Dempster (judge), and Dexter (dyer). Not all surnames that end in -er are derived from occupations, however; some, e.g. Downer, are topographical in origin.

Certain occupational surnames, which were not originally confined to a particular region, became common in restricted areas because individual families with these names had numerous male descendants. On the other hand, some rare occupational names, such as Palfreyman, are scattered thinly but widely. Even though such names are rare, their distribution shows that they could not have had a single family origin, nor could they have started in just one part of the country. In this, they contrast sharply with rare surnames that are derived from minor place-names.

Names taken from an office, such as Bailey or Butler, often have a clear meaning, but those that apparently denote a rank may well be nicknames. Thus, no one with the name of King can prove royal descent, even in an illegitimate line. Twelfth- and thirteenth-century records provide many examples of serfs with such nicknames as Pope, Knight, or Squire. On the other hand, the exact status of a serf is often signified by surnames such as Bond or Cotman, which were particularly numerous in the south and the Midlands. Later, social mobility has obscured these origins; even in the thirteenth century freemen with surnames derived from the unfree status of their ancestors can be found. Amongst this group of surnames are to be counted most of those formed from a personal name with -man added. Some such names, e.g. Bridgeman, may be topographical in origin, but most were originally the names of servants or other dependants. Examples include Bateman, Coleman, Jackman, etc. Though widespread, they are particularly common in the north. The Mathewmans, for instance, are still strongest in Yorkshire, where the name seems to have originated.

Topographical names, by which we mean those derived from features of the landscape, either natural or man-made, are one of the most numerous categories of surname. They are common in the south-east, especially Sussex, and are relatively rare in the north, except in Lancashire. In the Middle Ages most topographical terms had a precise meaning, so that there are, for instance, several different words for marshland. Thus, the surnames Kerr and Carr refer to marshy ground covered with trees (often alder) or scrub. Some of these words are dialect terms that are confined to a particular region. Moreover, as the English language developed, some topographical terms acquired slightly different meanings. Unravelling the etymology of such names is therefore fraught with difficulties. However, it is often possible to point to a limited distribution, and thus a regional origin, for some topographical names. For example, families with the surnames Booth, Clough, Moss, or Rhodes must have northern origins and those named Costedel, Wister, Stanstreet, Soundry, and Forebench must hail from Sussex.

Some names that are topographical in origin may appear at first sight to belong to other categories. Names such as Weller or Wellman are not derived from occupations or from servants, nor have names such as Mills or Banks acquired their final -s from the personal name of a father. Many of the topographical surnames that are recorded between the twelfth and fourteenth centuries are preceded by a preposition, signifying at, under, over, by, etc., or by French prepositions and articles, such as 'de', 'de la', or 'del'. In some parts of the country these forms were used by scribes as late as the sixteenth century. In most cases, the preposition never became attached to the surname, but a group of distinctive names that includes Atwell, Bywater, Overend, and Underwood have been formed in this way. Examples of shortened forms are numerous and include Nash (from atten Ash), Danvers from de Anvers, etc.

Occasionally, topographical surnames can be traced back to their point of origin. The topographical name Coldwell has arisen in many places that are far apart. People bearing that surname today may be descended from any one of a number of different families. Nevertheless, those Coldwells who can prove an ancestral line that takes them back three centuries or more into one or other of several localities within Agbrigg or Staincross wapentakes, in south-west Yorkshire, are probably descended from a family that lived at Coldwell farm in the township of Austonley in the fourteenth century. John de Coldwelle was living there in 1376, and three years later he and Thomas de Coldwell were assessed at the basic rate of poll tax. Within the next hundred years the family had moved elsewhere, so that in 1481 the 'messuage called Callwell' was held by William Brodehede. Two hundred years later, six branches of this Coldwell family were living within a few miles of their place of origin.

Surnames that can be identified with particular places rather than with general features of the landscape are classified as locative. They are perhaps the most interesting group of all for the family historian, for in certain parts of the country it is often possible to pinpoint the exact origin of such a surname. There are, of course, many problems to overcome in the process. At least some awareness of the pitfalls in interpreting place-names is required. It is always necessary to go back to the earliest recorded spellings of both the surname and the place-name, for either one or both may have been substantially altered over the years. Matching a modern form of a surname with a modern form of a place-name is a dangerous business.

A basic problem is to decide whether a surname has been derived from a place because a family was long resident there or for the opposite reason that a family left, never to return, at the time when surnames were being formed. Many major landowning families acquired surnames from their principal estates and numerous small farmers adopted surnames from their holdings. Equally, however, many families sought their fortunes elsewhere at a very early period of surname formation. Speaking generally, it seems to be the case that if a surname is derived from a farmstead or hamlet and if past and present distributions of the name are concentrated in the neighbourhood of that place, then we may assume that the surname has arisen from the residence of the family in that spot when surnames were being formed. If, however, a surname is that of a large village, town, or county, or of a district such as Craven or Gower, then it is likely that an emigrant has assumed his surname upon leaving the place and settling elsewhere. Certain families moved considerable distances in the early Middle Ages during the period when surnames were being formed. The various tax returns of the fourteenth century provide numerous instances of surnames that indicate long-distance migration. If a family moved a considerable distance shortly after the surname was formed, the present cluster of the name may not indicate the place of origin, but rather the place where the migrant settled.

Another obvious problem is that a surname may be derived from any one of a number of place-names. Nothing can be done about surnames such as Norton, Sutton, Aston, Weston, etc., or about which Houghton or Wells is the most likely home of a particular name, but there are other traps for the unprepared. Thus, a researcher may be unaware that Norfolk has a village called Ripon or that south Yorkshire has a village called Wales. Another problem is that many villages from which surnames have been derived have completely disappeared. About one in every six of the Leicestershire villages that were recorded in Domesday Book no longer survives and therefore is not listed in gazetteers. If deserted village sites are difficult to locate, the problems of identifying them are minor compared with the task of tracing those lost farmsteads which are the source of surnames. The starting-point for such a venture is to determine the present and past distribution of a name by the methods which will be outlined in the final section of this chapter.

The surname Ramsker provides an apt illustration of a name which has arisen from a small place that no longer exists. Until the eighteenth century it was almost entirely confined to the Sheffield area. The knowledge that this was so led Mr C. A. Ramsker to the discovery of records of the lost place-name Romesker, a farmhouse situated on the south escarpment of Bradfield Dale, only a few miles north of the city centre. The place-name was first recorded in 1295, when Adam Heggar de Romeskar obtained a grant of land nearby. The hereditary surname had not yet been formed, but in 1379 Robert Romesker, a webster, and his wife, Cecilia, paid 6d. poll tax. As they were the only people in the West Riding with this rare name at that time, it is likely that everybody who now bears the name Ramsker is one of Robert and Cecilia's descendants.

Locative surnames that are derived from farmsteads or hamlets occur in those parts of England where settlements are scattered over the hills or amongst the woods. Devon names such as Chugg or Lobb and Lancashire names such as Broadbent or Laithwaite, and numerous others, are still characteristic of the districts whence they came and, even now, many of them have not spread very far, except perhaps where a few migrants have ventured further afield, perhaps to London. In Lancashire and the West Riding of Yorkshire many locative surnames that were derived from Pennine farmsteads increased greatly in numbers during the sixteenth and seventeenth centuries, but remained concentrated in the same area as before and continue to do so to the present day. The large numbers of people who now bear such a surname are all likely to be descended from a common ancestor. Conclusive proof cannot be obtained because surnames were formed before the

JOHN GALSWORTHY
(1867–1933)
The famous novelist was
deeply interested in his family's origins and in their
long history as Devonshire
farmers before they left for
London in the 1830s. He
found their names in
the parish registers of
Wembury and Plymstock,
not far from Plymouth. The
surname is derived from a
remote farm in the north
west of the county, whose
name means 'the bank or
slope where the bog-myrtle
grew'.

period for which firm genealogical evidence is available, but it is nevertheless often possible to show that sixteenth- and seventeenth-century families
bearing the same surname were related.

Surnames which have ramified greatly form only a minority of the present stock of names and an even smaller proportion of the surnames and bynames that were in use in earlier times, some of which have since become
extinct. Most locative surnames have not ramified greatly, but have remained scarce even near their place of origin. The families that did ramify
tended to belong to the lesser gentry and substantial tenants, whose economic standing made them more likely to raise children successfully.

Genetic factors no doubt played a part; it is noticeable that the most prolific families had already produced different branches by the end of the fourteenth century.

Although locative names are a distinctive component of the stock of any region's surnames, they are not amongst the most common ones. If, for instance, a count is made of all the surnames beginning with the letter B in the current telephone directory for Sheffield, Brown heads the list with 1,287 subscribers, followed by Barker, Booth, Bailey, Bennett, Bell, Baker, Bradley, Briggs, Brooks, and Barnes. This group includes surnames derived from personal names, from occupations, and from northern dialect words for topographical features, but only Bradley is a locative name and even that is one with multiple possible origins. The locative surnames Bradshaw and Barlow (19th and 21st in the list, respectively) also have more than one possible place of origin. It is not until we come to the 36th name, Broomhead (144 and a further 8 with alternative spellings of the name), closely followed by Bagshaw (134 and 6 variants), that we arrive at surnames that are undoubtedly derived from minor place-names in the locality and which are probably of single-family origin. Other surnames which local people will recognize as being distinctive to the district come way down the list. For example, Bullas (and its variants Bullos, Bullous, Bulloss and Bullus), which was derived from Bullhouse, 14 or 15 miles north of the city centre, and which features largely in the earliest register for the parish of Sheffield, occurs only 50 times. The rare name Blanksby, which comes from a deserted medieval village site in the grounds of Hardwick Hall, less than 20 miles to the south, is noted only 12 times.

Another rare name that occurs in and around Sheffield is that of Ronksley. The home of the surname was a farmhouse in the uppermost part of Derwent Valley, 12 miles or so west of Sheffield, in the chapelry of Bradfield. The farmhouse was destroyed when Howden reservoir was constructed earlier this century; the last occupant of the farm left in about 1909. The name survives nearby in Ronksley Moor and Ronksley Wood. This was 'Ranc's clearing', so-called from an unrecorded personal name or perhaps a nickname meaning proud or insolent. A John de Ronkeslai was here in 1366, but the original family had left by 1546, when Thomas Barbur de Ronksley was the tenant. The first mention of the surname in the neighbouring parish of Sheffield was in 1596, but the family was never prolific. During the reign of Charles II no Ronksleys were recorded in the hearth tax returns for Derbyshire and Nottinghamshire and only 4 families were listed in south Yorkshire: James Ronghsley had three hearths in Bradfield, Francis Rongsley had one hearth in nearby Stannington, and across the border in the parish of Sheffield, William Ronkesley had one hearth in Brightside, and George Ronkersley had one in Upper Hallam. Three centuries later, the surname is still as restricted in its distribution and the name remains a rare one. The current UK telephone directories list only 35 Ronksleys, 23 of whom appear in the directory for Sheffield, Rotherham, and the Hope Valley, the district where the surname originated. Another 5 are recorded nearby in Greater Manchester, 3 are found in neighbouring parts of Yorkshire, 3 live on the Lincolnshire coast, and just 1 example of the name is found far away, in Surrey.

Many more examples of locative names with precise points of origin such as this might be quoted. We shall return to the techniques of locating the homes of family names in the final section of this chapter.

Early Immigrants' Surnames

The stock of native surnames that was formed during the Middle Ages has been added to at various periods in the past by new names brought in by immigrants. Naturally, many foreign names were Anglicized in the course of time and some of these took the same forms as old English surnames. For example, the French names Hervé and Charpentier were readily turned into the English forms, Harvey and Carpenter. Moreover, some immigrants consciously adopted an English name that did not necessarily relate to their original one. It is therefore impossible to gauge the extent of particular phases of immigration by the survival of foreign names. People today are well aware of past immigration and they are often persuaded that if they bear an unusual surname then their ancestors must have been immigrants, preferably Huguenots, who have popular appeal. Migration within England, rather than entry from abroad, is, however, the usual reason why a name might sound unusual. Some surnames have strayed a long way from their original home, others have been changed considerably in the course of time. It is a sound rule that the origin of a surname cannot be determined merely from the present form of the name.

France has been a persistent source of new surnames, even from before the time that most surnames became hereditary. Between 1066 and 1200 a considerable number of landed families took surnames that were derived from French place-names, but which were gradually modified into the forms now in use. Names such as Boon, Boswell, Dangerfield, and Manners arose in this way. A steady trickle of immigrants crossed the English Channel or the North Sea during the next three centuries. Many of them acquired surnames such as Fleming or Flanders, Burgin if they came from Burgundy, Bremner or Brabazon if they originated in Brabant.

London was the destination for many of these early migrants, especially the foreign merchants. In the sixteenth century immigration occurred on a larger scale and for different reasons. In particular, many Protestant refugees from France and the Low Countries sought refuge in southern and eastern England. Records from the reign of Henry VIII provide a broad picture of the nature of these movements and the composition of the places where the 'aliens' settled. They show that from 1546 many Dutch and Flemish families were driven from their homes by the Duke of Alva's persecution of Protestants. These refugees from the Low Countries were soon followed by French Protestants (Huguenots), who were driven abroad by persecutions that began in the 1560s and which reached an infamous climax at the massacre on the eve of the feast of St Bartholomew, 1572. The Huguenot Society has published numerous volumes which contain the names of those who sought freedom to worship as they wished by settling in this country.

The scale of foreign immigration during the sixteenth century was certainly significant. Between 1540 and 1600 over 50,000 men, women, and children crossed the sea to settle in this country. The government welcomed the refugees for the craft skills that they brought with them. By the middle years of Elizabeth's reign, foreign refugees were well established in the capital. Elizabethan London had Dutch (or Flemish), French, and Italian Protestant churches in the midst of the hundred or so parish churches that served the native population. Though most of the foreigners headed for London, 'alien settlements' were established in Sandwich in 1561, in Norwich in 1565, and by the end of the decade in Stamford, Southampton, Maidstone, and Colchester. In Norwich and Canterbury, the scale of immigration was so considerable that at one time foreign immigrants formed a third of the total population. The contribution of the refugees to the national economy was considerable. Their skills were particularly appreciated in the textile industry, where they helped to establish the 'new draperies' that provided so much profit and employment, and also in the iron and glass industries which they helped to transform.

In some of the places where they settled, the immigrants founded their own churches. At St Julian's Church, Southampton, for example, the registers begin in 1567 and continue for 230 years. The first list of communicants reveals a congregation of just under 60, whose professions included a doctor, weavers, bakers, cutlers, and brewers. Their places of origin were given as Valenciennes, Lille, Dieppe, Guernsey, and Jersey. The Canterbury congregation came mainly from Lille, Nuelle (Belgium), Tourcoing, Waterloo (Belgium), Armentiéres, and other places on the borders of Picardy and Flanders. The refugees were of all ranks and professions, but many arrived destitute. The majority gravitated towards London. Large numbers made their home in Soho and the East End of London, but some settled in other suburbs such as Southwark and Bermondsey. Refugees came into England in even greater numbers after 1680, when Louis XIV began to persecute the Huguenots with renewed vigour. London was again the preferred destination, but many settled in the south-east, or in Plymouth, Exeter, and other parts of the south-west. The more adventurous eventually sailed for America.

The distinctive surnames of many of these immigrants allow us to trace their movements. For example, we can follow the progress of Lorraine ironworkers who migrated to the Sussex Weald during the reign of Henry VIII and then to other parts of England, taking with them the new technology of

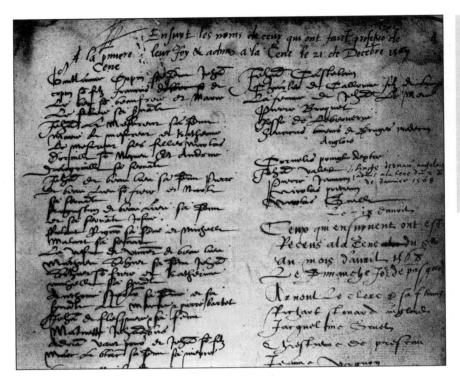

WALLOON IMMIGRANTS IN SOUTHAMPTON (1567–8)
The register of St Julian's, the Walloon church in Southampton, is a major source of information about foreign immigrants. It was edited by H. M. Godfrey and published by the Huguenot Society of London in 1890 with the title *Registre de l'Eglise Wallonne de Southampton*.

the charcoal blast-furnace. Sixteenth-century subsidy rolls for the south-eastern counties contain the names of considerable numbers of foreigners who were subject to an alien tax. Some of the immigrants, such as the Jordans and the Tylers, had surnames that were already well established in England, but others can be recognized immediately. Thus, the Lawrence Dippray who appears in the Sheffield parish register between 1573 and 1580 was no doubt the Laurens Dupre who contributed 4*d.* as an alien to the subsidy levied in the Netherfield hundred of Sussex in 1560; by 1582 he was back in Sussex. The Vintins preferred to stay, working for generations as mill-wrights in the iron works around Sheffield. Eleven Vintins are named in the current Sheffield telephone directory.

Christian Names

During the twelfth and thirteenth centuries nearly all the personal names which had been popular in Anglo-Saxon and Anglo-Scandinavian England became extinct. Edward is one of the rare survivals which continues in popularity to this day. The Norman kings and barons bore the Germanic names William, Richard, Robert, Henry, Ralph, Odo, Hugh, and Walter, while their comrades from Brittany had Celtic names such as Alan or Ives. These names soon became popular amongst all classes of society and some remain modern favourites. During the twelfth and thirteenth centuries biblical names came into fashion, notably those of the apostles and the evangelists. Meanwhile, girls were being christened Joan (first recorded in England in 1189), Agnes (1189), Catherine (1196), Mary (1203), Elizabeth (1205), and Anne (1218).

Old Testament names were first given to children during the thirteenth

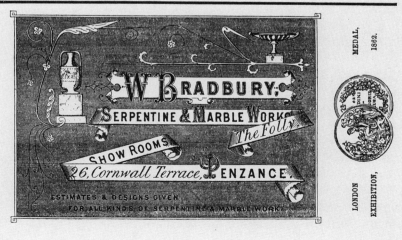

J. WILTON ASH,
COACH BUILDER,
SADDLER, HARNESS MAKER, &c.,
PENZANCE.

Saddlery & Harness Works, 1, GREEN MARKET ;
Coach Works, 52, MARKET JEW STREET.

JACOB C. W. CORIN,
"FARMER'S ARMS."

Potato, Brocoli, and Peruvian Government Guano Merchant.

FOREIGN WINES & SPIRITS,
Burton Ales and Stouts.

CAUSEWAY HEAD, PENZANCE.

W. BRADBURY,
SERPENTINE & MARBLE WORKS,
The Folly
SHOW ROOMS
26, Cornwall Terrace, PENZANCE
ESTIMATES & DESIGNS GIVEN
FOR ALL KINDS OF SERPENTINE & MARBLE WORK

MEDAL, 1862.

LONDON EXHIBITION,

and fourteenth centuries, perhaps through the influence of the Mystery plays. These names included Abraham, Absolom, Adam, Daniel, David, Isaac, Jacob, Jonah, Joseph, Noah, and Tobias, and Anna, Eve, Hester, Judith, Sarah, and Susanna. Despite the addition of these new favourites, the number of first names in common use was dwindling during the period when surnames were being formed. Names such as Austin, Basil, Bennet, Blaise, Brise, Christopher, Clement, Crispin, Denis, Fabian, Gervase, Hilary, Martin, Quentin, Valentine, and Viel became rare or disappeared, though of course some have been revived in modern times. Five names—Henry, John, Richard, Robert, and William—accounted for 38 per cent of all the recorded masculine names during the twelfth century. During the thirteenth century this proportion rose to 57 per cent, and in the fourteenth century to no less than 64 per cent.

In the sixteenth and seventeenth centuries, fervent Puritans favoured biblical names—the more obscure the better—or names of their own invention, either in Latin or in English. The biblical names Benjamin, Hannah, Jacob, Joseph, Samuel, Sarah, and Susan became established favourites. Others, such as Amos, Caleb, Ebenezer, Elijah, Noah, and Zachary, were revived in the nineteenth century, together with names which expressed such qualities as Faith, Hope, Charity, Prudence, and Patience. The contribution of the Puritans to naming-practices had even greater effect in America than in England.

A number of classical names, such as Horace or Julius, were adopted by educated families in the sixteenth and seventeenth centuries, and though they never became as popular as those derived from the Scriptures, they add to the variety of first names that can be found in early parish registers. The seventeenth-century register of the parish of Sheffield includes such distinctive names as Bertholina Anderton, Obedience Baker, Obediencia Bates, Easter Barnsley, Livinius Bingley, Silvanus Birch, Sedguicus Chappel, Quatuor Fenton, Heneage Graham, Hengiss Green, Volantine Hickson, Exuperius Ince, Boethia Jessop, Lemuel Nutt, Onesiforous Oates, Peninah Roberts, Damaris Shaw, Epaphras Spooner, Goodeth and Temporantia Stacy, Charitas and Hadassa Staniforth, Cassandra Wadsworth, Cheveril White, Temperance Yates, and three members of the Calton family named Ezra, Phebe, and Zacharias.

In the eighteenth century, Latin forms of women's names, e.g. Anna or Maria, became popular, especially among the upper classes. Some Anglo-Saxon or medieval names, e.g. Alfred, Edgar and Edwin, or Emma and Matilda, were revived later in the century. Under the influence of the Romantic Movement, Tennyson, and the Pre-Raphaelites, it became fashionable to name a boy Guy, Hugh, Nigel, Quentin, Ralph, Roger, Roland, Walter, or Wilfred, and to christen a girl Alice, Amy, Edith, or Mabel. The Oxford Movement was responsible for the revival of such names as Aidan, Alban, Augustine, Benedict, Bernard, and Theodore. On the other hand, many other Christian names which were once fairly common are now obsolete. For example, Amyas, Dionys, Ellis, and Fulk fell into disuse during the sixteenth or seventeenth centuries and have never been revived.

The use of surnames as Christian names began as an aristocratic practice in the sixteenth century. The earliest known example is that of Lord Guildford Dudley, whose mother was a Guildford. During the seventeenth and eighteenth centuries it became a common practice for the nobility and gentry to preserve ancestral names on the female side in this way; some female surnames became hereditary Christian names for the first-born male in each generation. Names such as Sir Harbottle Grimston sound ridiculous to modern ears, but other surnames that were adopted as first names have spread far beyond the family that originally adopted them. They include Douglas, Dudley, Keith, Neville, Sidney, Stanley, and Stuart. Families further down the social scale rarely followed the aristocratic and gentry practice of perpetuating the surnames of female lines in the first names of their children before the eighteenth century, but occasional earlier examples can be found. In my own family, for instance, Spurley has been used as a Christian name since the seventeenth century right through to the present time. The use of surnames as Christian names became increasingly popular in Victorian times and is still widely used in the United States of America. The practice of using hyphenated surnames to preserve that of the female line also became more popular in Victorian times. Snobbery certainly played a part in this, though in the case of certain Welsh families, and others with very common surnames, hyphenated names helped to identify particular lines amongst all the other Joneses and Williamses.

A curious feature of sixteenth- and seventeenth-century parish registers, namely the use of aliases, may sometimes be explained in similar terms. The parish register of Norton, Derbyshire, for example, records several generations of a family known as Steven alias Urton. Such aliases sometimes indicate the desire to perpetuate a female surname, perhaps because of the inheritance of property through the female line. In other parishes, an alias was sometimes used when the surname was a common one in that area, for example, where surnames were formed from Welsh patronymics. An alias could also be used to differentiate one branch of a family from another, for instance, if a man remarried, and to denote illegitimacy. The use of aliases was gradually abandoned during the eighteenth century in England, but continued later in Scotland.

A few Christian names, such as Evelyn and Hilary, have long been used by either sex. Sometimes, as with Francis and Frances, or Jesse and Jessie, they are spelt in different ways. The Normans introduced the practice of forming a feminine equivalent of a masculine name; Paula for Paul, Patricia for Patrick, etc. Some female names that were popular in the Middle Ages acquired alternative forms, such as Isobel and Elizabeth, Ann and Agnes, Hester and Esther, Marion and Mary Ann, Joan and Jane, etc., which were used interchangeably in the early parish registers. Pet forms, such as Nancy for Anne, Polly for Mary, Meg for Margaret, and Sally for Sarah, were common in more modern times. The family historian needs to be well aware of all these possible permutations. The custom of shortening names, sometimes with the addition of a suffix, or of forming nicknames by rhyming is an ancient one. A name such as Bartholomew, for example, could be shortened to Bat, Bate, Batty, Bartle, Bartelot, Bartlett, Batcock, Batkin, or Tolly, all of which have become surnames. The Normans introduced the diminutive suffixes -ot, -et, -un, -in, -el, in combination with shorter forms of names, to produce such forms as Philpot, Willett, and Perrin. The suffix -on was commonly applied to feminine names, e.g. Allison and Marion. In the thirteenth and fourteenth centuries these French suffixes gave way to the English suffixes -cock and -kin, which were popular at the time of surname formation, but which declined in use after the middle of the fifteenth century.

The medieval practice of baptizing children with the Christian name of a close relation or with a name chosen by the senior godparent remained the custom during the sixteenth and seventeenth centuries. Family historians will be well aware of the problems of sorting out which generation is which, when the same restricted group of names are constantly used. A further complication is caused by the common practice of giving a child the same name as that of a dead elder brother or sister. The task of identifying an individual is made easier once it became fashionable to christen a child with two or more Christian names, but this was a late development. Again, the fashion spread down the social scale, following aristocratic example. The practice remained rare until the middle of the eighteenth century, and even in Victorian times many parents were content to give only one name to a child.

Surnames in the Seventeenth Century in Five Counties

The hearth tax returns of the reign of Charles II have been widely used by local historians but their potential for family history is largely untapped. Collectively, they provide a useful database for assessing the distribution patterns of English surnames approximately half-way between the period of surname formation in the later Middle Ages and the present day. These returns list the householders who paid a tax on their chimneys at various dates in the 1660s and 1670s and, in some cases, they also list those householders who were exempt from the tax. No list at this time can claim to be comprehensive, but we can be confident that an analysis of the surviving returns will provide us with firm evidence of the extent to which surnames had spread across the country from their original bases or had remained close to their homes.

The returns are housed in the Exchequer division of the old Public Record

Office at Kew. They vary in quality from year to year, but the number of membranes noted in the typed index enables the searcher to make a quick judgement about which is the fullest and most useful return. A number have been printed (with indexes of surnames) either by a county record society or by a family history society. The printed returns for Bedfordshire (1671), Dorset (1664), Nottinghamshire (1674), Oxfordshire (1665), and Surrey (1664) provide a fair sample of 56,408 householders in widely different parts of the country. An analysis of the returns for these five counties enables us to assess how far the experience of each part of the country was different from that of the rest. It also allows us to make a number of general points about the distribution patterns of English surnames just over three centuries ago.

The apparently straightforward, though tedious, job of counting all the householders and then each of the different surnames in a county is complicated by the various ways in which names were spelt. It is far from easy to decide whether some of the spellings represent the same surname written and pronounced in a different way or whether they indicate names which have evolved separately. Family historians will be well aware that in the past the surnames that they are researching may have been spelt in more than one manner. In this analysis, therefore, an attempt has been made to eliminate variant spellings. A judgement has had to be made in every case. Fortunately, the margin of error does not affect the broad conclusions that can be reached.

The first conclusion is that the proportion of surnames to householders throughout our sample was roughly 1 : 4 or 1 : 4.5, but that not every county conformed to the general pattern. Dorset had 2,500 recorded surnames in 1664, that is, 1 to every 4.5 householders. The 2,134 surnames listed in the Bedfordshire returns of 1671 produced an almost identical proportion of 1 name to 4.4 householders, and the 2,833 separate surnames recorded in Nottinghamshire in 1674 represented a similar proportion of 1 surname to 4.2 householders. In Surrey, however, the 4,204 surnames noted in 1664 amounted to 1 name in every 3.9 householders, and in Oxfordshire in the following year, the 2,305 recorded surnames were in the proportion of 1 to every 3.2 householders. The experience of Oxfordshire in this respect was markedly different from that of Dorset, Bedfordshire, and Nottinghamshire.

The conclusion that Oxfordshire had more surnames per head of population than the other counties in the sample is reinforced by a count of the surnames that appear only once in each of the returns. In Bedfordshire and Dorset, names recorded only once accounted for 9.9 per cent and 9.6 per cent, respectively, of the total householders; in Nottinghamshire, the names in this category accounted for 11 per cent of the county's householders, and in Surrey single names represented 14 per cent of the householders; but in Oxfordshire names that appeared only once accounted for 17.3 per cent of the householders, even when great care had been taken to eliminate variant

THE SURNAME
HILKENE

Hilkene is a very rare surname. In the first five years of national civil registration only 5 births were recorded under this name or its variants; Lambeth and Hull each had 2 children named Hilkin and Sculcoates (a northern suburb of Hull) had 1 named Hilken. The tombstone stands in the cemetery at Norwood,

spellings. The figures can be reworked by adding together the surnames that were listed just once or twice. When that is done, the differences between the counties in this sample become even more pronounced. Names that were unusual in an individual county context constituted 1 in every 8 householders in Dorset, 1 in every 7.5 householders in Bedfordshire, 1 in every 7 householders in Nottinghamshire, 1 in every 5.8 householders in Surrey, but as many as 1 in every 4.7 householders in Oxfordshire.

The figures suggest either that Oxfordshire had always had a larger stock of surnames than the other counties in the sample or that the population of Oxfordshire in the later seventeenth century was more mobile than that of the others, in which case it must have attracted even more immigrants than Surrey, which included the urban parishes on the south bank of the Thames, opposite the City of London. This second explanation does not therefore seem very likely and is not supported by the evidence of the locative surnames which were found in the county in 1665. The high number of unusual names cannot be attributed to the University, for only a few of the members of the colleges were recorded in the returns. Oxfordshire's position in the south Midlands, not far from the capital, no doubt made it likely that the county would have had more of a floating population than did remote Dorset, but it is not immediately obvious why nearby Bedfordshire should have been so different to Oxfordshire in its naming patterns, especially as Bedfordshire was the more populous of the two counties, though smaller in size. As we shall see in Chapter 3, the inhabitants of Bedfordshire were loath to migrate beyond their county boundary even in the mid-nineteenth century. Oxfordshire, too, had families that never moved very far. It seems likely, therefore, that the county had spawned an unusual number of different surnames in the Middle Ages, but this hypothesis begs the question why should naming-practice have been so different in Oxfordshire from elsewhere. Clearly, a great deal of work remains to be done before we can get a firm impression of the composition of the English population in the various regions of the country at different points in time.

Surnames alone do not give a firm indication of population mobility, for an unknown number of people with common surnames were not related to any other families within the same county and may, indeed, have been recent immigrants. Conversely, some of the rare surnames that are listed only once or twice may have had a local origin. In Bedfordshire, for example, Sir William Gostwick headed the only family in the county with that surname, even though it was derived from a minor Bedfordshire place-name and, as we have seen, can be traced thereabouts over several hundred years. Furthermore, some families that had surnames which were derived from places far away may have moved to Bedfordshire in the distant past, perhaps even at the period of surname formation. Surnames can therefore be used only as rough indicators of population mobility over long periods of time. With these qualifications in mind, we can none the less point to migration patterns and to examples of residential stability that are of great interest to family historians.

The hearth tax returns provide numerous examples from all parts of the land of families that lived close to the place where their surname had originated three or four centuries earlier. Each of the counties under consideration had a group of distinctive surnames that were not found, or appeared only rarely, in the other counties. Names of every category were represented amongst these rare groups. We may start with those Bedfordshire surnames that were derived from habitations and which can be classified either as locative or topographical. A rare name that is unfamiliar to the outsider, but which was shared by 16 Bedfordshire householders, is that of Empey or Impey; it was derived from a site where saplings had been enclosed by a hedge. The 34 households named Crouch or Croutch were descended from one or more families that had lived near a wayside cross at the time of surname formation. The returns for the other counties mention a single family with this name in Dorset, another in Nottinghamshire, and 2 more in Surrey, but in our sample the Crouches were numerous only in Bedfordshire. Other households possessing surnames of this type probably include the Faldoes or Faldows (10 examples) and the Fenshams (15), for these sound like place-names, the 11 Linfords, who may have been descended from a migrant or migrants from Buckinghamshire, and the 13 Riseleys, who probably originated from the Riseley in Bedfordshire, rather than from one of the other places of that name in Berkshire, Derbyshire, or Lancashire. Negus (15) is another name that may be topographical in origin, but such a provenance is disputed. The etymology of many of the rarer surnames remains mysterious.

The distinctive occupational surnames that were in use in seventeenth-century Bedfordshire include Brace or Brase (18), meaning a maker or seller of armour, or possibly of breeches, and Pedder (12), a variant pronunciation of Pedler. Even a few surnames which had been derived from personal names were largely restricted in their distribution to Bedfordshire in our sample. The Sibleys (17) and Tilcockes (15) each had a representative in Surrey, but none elsewhere. These surnames were derived from medieval feminine names, while Thorowgood (13) came from the Middle English name Thurgod. Nicknames which had given rise to Bedfordshire surnames included Pennyfather (6) for a miser, Doggett (11) from dog, and Mouse (10) for a timid person. None of these names had spread very far; some, at least, may have had a single-family origin.

Other surnames recorded in the various hearth tax returns stand out equally sharply, but for a very different reason. They are distinctive not of the county where they were found in the reign of Charles II, but of other places, and therefore point not to residential stability but to long-distance migration. Welsh surnames of the ap/ab form, such as Powell or Bevan, can be spotted easily, and so can certain northern names, especially the locative ones. The 7 Cumberlands, 5 Sheffields, 3 Rotherhams, and 8 Nottinghams were probably descended from men who had migrated south at the period of surname formation, but the families with surnames derived from minor place-names had perhaps arrived more recently. A Yorkshire, Derbyshire, or Lancashire origin can be attributed to the 15 Bedfordshire families with the names Appleyard (1), Bamforth (4), Bickerstaffe (1), Calton (2), Dodsworth (1), Metcalfe (2), Raworth (2), Roades (1), and Worrall (1). A few other names could no doubt be identified as having been derived from other parts of England.

These immigrant names form only a small proportion of the stock of Bedfordshire surnames and thus reinforce the impression of limited movement. How does this pattern compare with the situation in Oxfordshire? Contrary to what we might expect from its larger stock of surnames, Oxfordshire had even fewer names of undoubted northern origin than did Bedfordshire. It had no Cumberlands, Sheffields, or Rotherhams, just one Nottingham, and only a small number of names that were derived from minor place-names. The way that the Lancashire name Bickerstaffe had been changed to Biggerstaffe, Piggerstaffe, and Packstaffe (one example of each) shows how difficult it is to identify an immigrant name that has been altered over the course of time. These changes suggest that this particular name had arrived in Oxfordshire well before the period of the hearth tax returns, and indeed Bickerstaffe is found in Oxford in the fifteenth century. Likewise, the four Osbaldestons in 1665 may have been descended from the three people with this Lancashire name who were living in Oxfordshire in 1523.

In his study of *The Surnames of Oxfordshire*, Richard McKinley has commented that in 1665 it was still true that many more locative surnames in the city of Oxford were derived from places in Oxfordshire than from places in any other county. He has identified 154 definite locatives in the hearth tax returns; 21 of these certainly came from Oxfordshire and 8 more were possibly local, but only a small number came from neighbouring counties. Another 8 were derived from Yorkshire, 7 from Staffordshire, 4 from Devon, and a few from Lancashire, Cheshire, Derbyshire, and Nottinghamshire. McKinley concluded that there is no evidence from locative surnames of considerable migration into Oxfordshire from any part of the British Isles at any time between the twelfth and the seventeenth century. A comparison between the hundred rolls of 1279 and the hearth tax returns of 1665 shows a high degree of continuity at the level of the county and even of the hundred, though not of the village. Those who moved did not usually move very far.

A number of characteristic Oxfordshire surnames, of all categories, are recorded in the 1665 returns. The 4 Allnuts (a surname which is also found in neighbouring Buckinghamshire) were descended from someone with an Old English personal name, the 5 Breakespeares from a person with that nickname; both surnames were already ancient ones in the county. Another name with a long history in Oxfordshire was Quatermaine, recorded in the twelfth century as a rare byname Quatreeyles ('four ears'). The 18 Quatermaines in 1665 were probably descended from this single individual. Wild-goose was a more common nickname, which was shared by 10 households in Oxfordshire in 1665, but was also found in contemporary Derbyshire. The bird was known for its shyness and was difficult to catch—hence 'a wild-goose chase'—so the nickname was probably applied to someone noted for his wariness. Wildgust, Widgust, and Willgoss are variant forms of the name.

Some distinctive Oxfordshire surnames were derived from local places, such as Bloxham (9), Flexney (11), and Crutchfield (7). The 11 Doyleys are of great interest, for D'Oylly was one of the surnames recorded in the Oxfordshire folios of Domesday Book. As such, it is amongst the earliest examples of an hereditary surname to appear in the county. Dolly was a variant form of the name, one example of which appears in the hearth tax returns for Surrey. Another ancient and unusual name, Fettiplace, was a hereditary surname in Oxford by the twelfth or thirteenth century; it had acquired seven branches in the county by 1665. The name was formed from French words describing the activities of an usher. Another rare occupational name was that of Slaymaker (or Sleamaker, Slimaker, etc.). It was first recorded in Oxford in the late sixteenth century and in 1588 at Banbury, where Richard Sleamaker, a stranger, was buried. It remains a rare surname in the late twentieth century.

Some surnames which were spread throughout the country were nevertheless particularly strong in certain counties. Thus, the name Franklin, which denoted a rural status just below that of gentleman, was much more common in some counties than in others. It was rare in East Anglia, for instance, and in our sample of hearth tax returns only 2 examples were recorded in Nottinghamshire, 5 in Dorset, and 10 in Surrey, whereas Bedfordshire had 20 and Oxfordshire had 34. The name was already widespread in thirteenth-century Oxfordshire and must have grown from several families.

The differences between the stock of surnames of each county were clearly considerable. One would expect habitation names and, to a lesser extent, names formed from specialist occupations, to vary from one part of England to another, but the differences run deeper than that and affect every category of surname. In Staffordshire, for instance, surnames created from pet forms or diminutives of personal names, such as Danckes, Janckes, and Tonckes, are, or were, peculiar to that county. Our present sample of surnames includes many more examples of distinctive names that were, and sometimes still are, confined to restricted areas.

In 1664 no fewer than 32 Dorset householders bore the locative surname Gillingham and 15 were named Mintern; none of these families had moved far from its place of origin. Other habitation names are less obvious. The 21 Kelloways took their name from a place in France. With so many householders sharing that name in 1664, it seems unlikely that they were all descended from a single Norman family, yet the name is found once only (in Surrey) in the other counties under review. Minor place-names had given rise to the surnames Whetcombe (8), from Dorset, Clatworthy (4), from Somerset, and Bowditch (14), which is situated in Devon. Loder (28) may belong to the same category. Dictionaries of surnames suggest that this name was derived either from an occupation or from proximity to a road or watercourse. It is possible that the 3 Loders who were recorded in the hearth tax returns for Oxfordshire had surnames that were derived in one or the other of these ways, but the concentration of the surname in Dorset strongly suggests a derivation from Loders in the parish of Burton Bradstock, a place-name which was recorded as Lodre in 1086. Other habitation names listed in the Dorset returns include Orchard (22), which might have been derived from the Somerset rather than the Dorset place of that name, and Furseman (6), a topographical name for someone who lived near a stretch of furze or gorse. (The surname Furse, incidentally, is particularly common in Devon.)

The occupational surnames in Dorset include some of uncommon interest. Hellier or Hellyard (22) was a name given to a roofer, Hodder (19) was a West Country name for a maker or seller of hoods, Furmage (12) was a cheese-maker, and Mackerill (10) was a metonymic name for a fisherman who specialized in a particular catch. Surrey had 7 Mackerills in 1664 and the surname arose early in north-eastern England. Biles (20) might have been another metonymic name, for a maker of bills or pruning-hooks; on the

THE SURNAME LODER
Adam Loder stands outside his shop at Lyme Regis, a few miles from the Dorset village of Loders, where the surname originated. In the first year of civil registration (1837–8) 42 births were registered under the name Loader, Loder or Lodder; 22 of these were in Dorset or Hampshire and all but 4 of the rest were in other parts of southern England.

other hand it might have been a shortened form of a personal name such as Billa (but not William, which was not abbreviated in this way in the Middle Ages).

Dorset also has a number of interesting surnames that were derived from nicknames. Gollop or Gallop (14), Sturmy (11), and Squibb (23) arose from nicknames applied to people who rushed about, or were volatile, or who were sarcastic or spiteful. Samways (37) meant stupid or foolish. Snook (23), with its variant Seanock, may have been a topographical name applied to a projecting piece of land, or it may have been a nickname for someone with a long nose. Each of these names, except for two examples from Surrey, was confined to Dorset. The peculiarities of provincial speech must have played a major part in the formation of surnames that were derived from nicknames. A knowledge of the medieval forms of that speech is indispensable to the correct interpretation of these and other names. Such knowledge may yet lead to explanations of the surnames Lush (15) and Meech (19), whose meanings remain obscure.

It is hardly to be expected that seventeenth-century Dorset would have more than a handful of northern names, and this is indeed the case. One example each can be found of the surnames Bickerstaffe, Clegg, Ensor, and Stillingfleete. The immigrants came instead from the west, some like the Clotworthys (4) from Devon, some like Mary Trevelian (or her ancestor) from Cornwall; others bore names such as Ireland (6), Welch (14), or Gower (4), and a very few had specific names such as Fluellin (4). Alexander Appowell of Ockford Fitzpaine still bore the old Welsh form of surname, but he was exceptional. Immigrant names formed only a tiny minority of the stock of Dorset surnames. One has only to browse the pages of the hearth tax returns of this county to sense immediately that the flavour of its names is very different from that of the other counties in our sample.

Nottinghamshire, as one might expect from its position, had a considerable number of surnames which had originated in one or other of the northern counties. Three centuries or so had elapsed since most of these surnames had been formed, so their presence in Nottinghamshire represents a long period of movement. The Yorkshire names include Adwick (Addick), Ambler, Anestey, Aselby, Barnsdale, Barnsley, Barrowclife, Benbridge, Brearley, Broadhead, Broomhead, Camsall, Cawthorne, Craven, Crawshaw, Crosland, Doncaster, Edlington, Emley, Everingham, Featherstone, Flether, Fulston, Hawksworth, Hellaby, Hemsley, Heppinstall, Hepworth, Hey, Keighley, Maltby, Metcalfe, Micklethwaite, Midop, Moorehouse, Odde, Pickering, Pocklington, Ripon, Rotherham, Rudston, Scofield, Selby, Soreby, Staniforth, Stanniland, Wadsley, Wadsworth, Wakefield, Warburton, Whitby, Wigglesworth, Wombell, and Wortley, and perhaps others. Some of these names had been altered considerably since they had been coined and can be recognized only by someone with local knowledge; Barraclough had become Barrowcliffe, for instance. Those Nottinghamshire surnames which originated even further north, or across the Pennines from

Lancashire and Cheshire, form a smaller group. They include Appleby, Butterworth, Clegg, Cumberland, Duckworth, Ettenborow, Hattersley, Higginbotham, Kellett, Kendall, Lancaster, Marples, Mottram, Pilings, Pilkington, Poynton, Roebotham, Shuttleworth, Singleton, and Winterbottom.

The neighbouring county of Derbyshire naturally provided a steady supply of immigrants. Twenty-two householders bore the name Peck or Peeke, signifying their family's origin in the Peak District. Others who came down from the hills in the west bore the more specific names of Bagshaw, Bamford, Beeley, Buxton, Calton, Crowden, Dore, Duckmanton, Dunstan, Glossop, Haddon, Heathcote, Inkersall, Kinder, Matlock, Offerton, Olerinshaw, Padley, Raworth, Rowsley, Sitwell, and Wingfield. Only a few travellers entered the county from the south or the east. Their distinctive names include Blatherwick (Northamptonshire), Bristow, Buckingham, Horncastle, Maplethorpe, March, and Norfolk. Another 8 householders were named Ireland and 12 were called Welch. In all, over 540 Nottinghamshire householders in 1674 bore one of the names quoted above, and no doubt other surnames can be found to prove migration into the county at some unknown time in the past. This is a higher number than in any of the other counties in our sample, but the reason is undoubtedly because a high proportion of surnames in the neighbouring counties of Yorkshire, Derbyshire, and Lancashire were locative in origin and can thus be readily identified. Furthermore, we have to remember that the 540 or so householders bearing these particular names represented only 1 in every 22 householders in Nottinghamshire. We are still speaking of a small minority.

Nottinghamshire had many surnames that it could call its own, within our sample. Alvey (19 examples) was derived from a Middle English personal name, Bellamy (30, with 1 each in Dorset and Surrey) from a Norman French one. Surnames that originated as nicknames included Bee (11) and Trueman (36, with 1 each in Bedfordshire and Oxfordshire) and two nicknames of French origin, Blonk (4, from *blanc*) and Bullivant (7, from *bon enfant*). Flower(s) may have arisen as a term of endearment, but may in some cases have been an occupational name for a miller or an arrowsmith; Nottinghamshire had 45 householders with this name, compared to 4 in Dorset, 3 in Surrey, 2 in Bedfordshire, and 1 in Oxfordshire. The 9 households of Footits probably shared a common descent. This nickname was peculiar to Nottinghamshire and is still largely confined to the county; like Foot in Devon, it may have referred to a deformity. Dafte (14) was certainly a nickname, but one that meant meek rather than stupid. In 1664 all the 10 Nottinghamshire people who bore the surname Dafte lived in the township of Hickling; 10 years later, 12 Daftes lived in Hickling, and 1 each in Whatton and Wisall. It seems likely that all these people were descended from a common ancestor, but as Hickling lies on the county boundary the hearth tax returns for Leicestershire need to be consulted as well. Two Daftes (both of whom were exempted from payment of the tax on account of their poverty) were recorded not far away in Rutland.

BOOTS THE CHEMIST
Jesse Boot's shops have made his surname known throughout the land. It is one of the distinctive names of his native county of Nottinghamshire. The photograph shows his first shop, in Goosegate, Nottingham (1877).

The other classes of surname may be dealt with briefly. Some Nottinghamshire place-names, including Cottam (19), Elston (14), Gunthorpe (9), Hawkesmoor (8), and Keyworth (16), gave rise to surnames that were still confined to the county in our sample. Caunt (24) was a topographical name from a Norman French word, but this category of surname was not as popular here as it was in the southern counties. Certain occupational names have strong Nottinghamshire connections, though they were not confined to that county. Herring (16), Kitchen (37), and Boot (12) are metonymic names for a fisherman, a cook, and a bootmaker. Jesse Boot (1850–1931), the founder of the chain of chemist's shops, was of course a Nottinghamshire man. Finally, Nottinghamshire produced a small group of surnames whose meanings cannot yet be explained, but which were local in their distribution. The names include Gabitas (16), Musson (15), and Nettleship (14).

Our final example is Surrey. The county shared many of the characteristics outlined above, for it was still essentially rural, but it differed from the rest in that its northern boundary was the Thames and within its territory lay the borough of Southwark. Part of the rapidly expanding population of London had found accommodation across the river from the City. Surrey was by far the most populous of our five counties; its inhabitants numbered more than twice those of Oxfordshire. By 1664 immigrants had come from far afield. Lancashire names included Backstaff, Bickerstaffe (2), Broadbent, Buscough, Higenbotham, Hollinsworth, Kellett, Lancaster (5), Lankasheere (3), Manchester, Rigby, Roebottom, and Winterbottom. Names from further north included Appleby, Borradell (2), Durham, Kindall (2), and Raby, while Yorkshire was represented by Abdey, Ackworth, Ambler, Armitage, Baraclift, Beverly, Bissaker, Brotherton, Bulmer, Cawood, Cottingham, Craven, Dent, Dungworth, Featherstone (3), Fothergill, Holdernesse, Holdsworth (3), Kempsall (5), Kettleby, Mallum, Metcalfe (4), Pickersgill, Pudsy (2), Selby (10), Sheffeild (3), Wakefield, Wetherby (6), and Yorke (3). Surnames that originated in Derbyshire included Adney, Ashburne, Buxton (2), Darbishere, Duffield (2), and perhaps Lineger (4). Other migrants had moved from the west, bearing names such as Ireland (5), Welch (7), Gower (3), the Welsh names Powell (13), Fluelin, and Hanmare, and the English names Summersett (2), Cornwell, Cornish (2), Ludlow (2), and Shrewsbury. Maxey, Poltney, Rampton, Ratcliffe, Rutland (2), and Shadwell were amongst the locative names that came from Midland and eastern England. The surname evidence confirms that London was attracting settlers from all over the land.

Rural Surrey was the home of some distinctive surnames that had as yet rarely spread beyond the county's bounds and which are still thought to belong to south-eastern England. The surname Killick was borne by 24 Surrey householders in 1664. John Kyllyck, a vintner of London, whose will was proved in 1439, is the earliest known person with this name. He asked for candles to be lit for him in the churches of Nutfield and Bletchingley, both of which lie in Surrey. A John Killick was constable of Bletchingley a decade or so later. Three Killicks lived in Nutfield in 1664.

Albury (9) is an example of a surname that was derived from a Surrey place-name. Some other rare names had originated just across the county boundary. Goring (16) was a place in west Sussex. Another place called Goring can be found in Oxfordshire, but as no examples of that surname can be found in the hearth tax returns for Oxfordshire, the Sussex place is perhaps the likelier source, though one must never be dogmatic in favour of the nearer place. The surname Billinghurst (21) was also derived from a place in west Sussex, whereas Chitty (36) was derived from Chitty in Kent. A

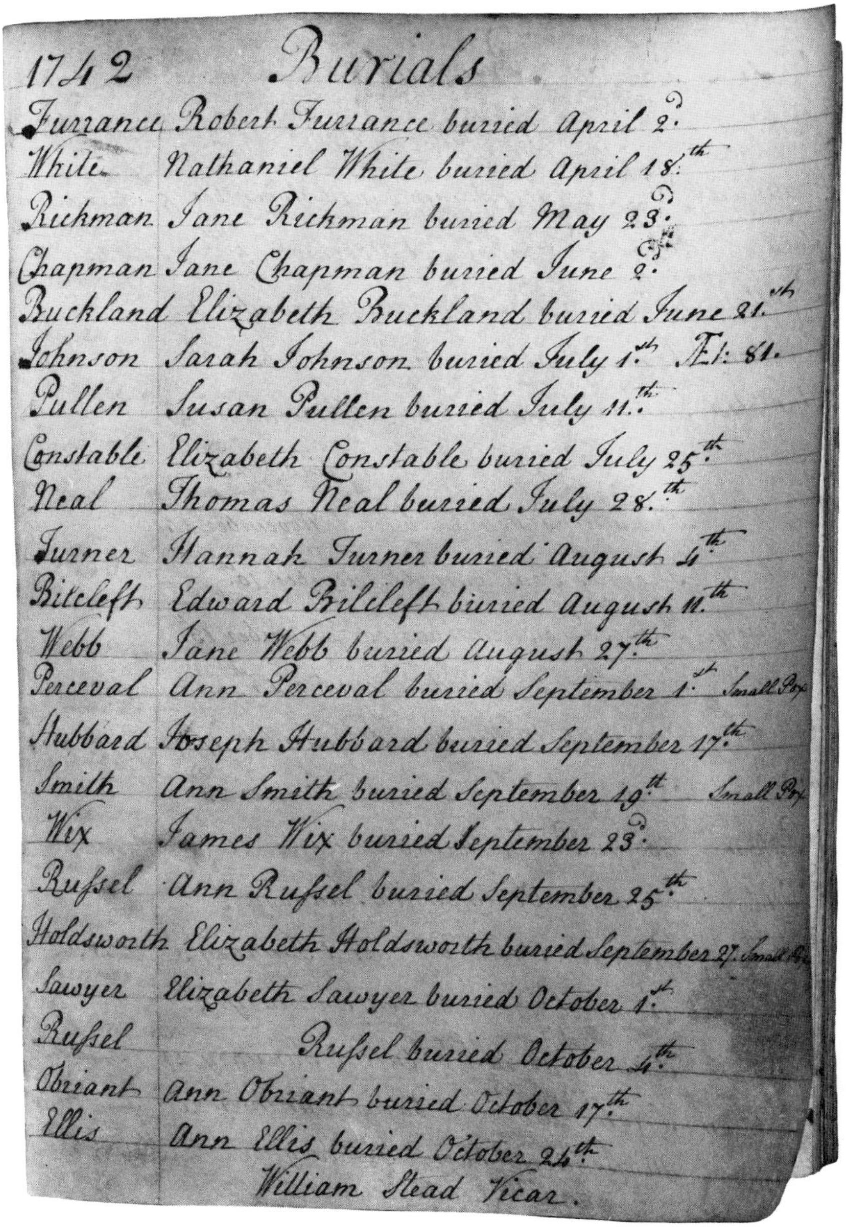
1742 Burials

Furrance	Robert Furrance buried April 2d.
White	Nathaniel White buried April 18th
Rickman	Jane Rickman buried May 23d.
Chapman	Jane Chapman buried June 2d.
Buckland	Elizabeth Buckland buried June 21st
Johnson	Sarah Johnson buried July 1st Æt: 81.
Pullen	Susan Pullen buried July 11th
Constable	Elizabeth Constable buried July 25th
Neal	Thomas Neal buried July 28th
Turner	Hannah Turner buried August 4th
Bilcleft	Edward Bilcleft buried August 11th
Webb	Jane Webb buried August 27th
Perceval	Ann Perceval buried September 1st Small Pox
Hubbard	Joseph Hubbard buried September 17th
Smith	Ann Smith buried September 19th Small Pox
Wix	James Wix buried September 23d.
Russel	Ann Russel buried September 25th
Holdsworth	Elizabeth Holdsworth buried September 27. Small Pox
Sawyer	Elizabeth Sawyer buried October 1st
Russel	Russel buried October 4th
Obriant	Ann Obriant buried October 17th
Ellis	Ann Ellis buried October 24th

William Stead Vicar.

The Burial Register of Reigate, Surrey (1742)

An unusual or puzzling surname often stands out from the rest. The surname of Edward Bilcleft, who died in Surrey, is derived from a Yorkshire farmstead which was formerly known as Bilcliff and is now called Belle Clive.

family with this name had settled in Godalming by 1371; nearly 300 hundred years later, 13 households of Chittys still resided in the parish. Others were found nearby in Aldershot, Farnham, Guildford, and Worplesdon.

Distinctive Surrey names in the topographical category include Tichener or Tickner (62), for someone who lived at a crossroads or a fork in the road, and Nash (8), for a person who lived by an ash tree. By 1664 the name was written as Nach, Naish, Naith, Nease, and Neasse. Longhurst (38) is a common topographical name of multiple origins. Mebbanke, Maybank, etc. (24), Inwood (15), and possibly Daborne (14) are also in this category. Surnames formed from personal names include May (22, with 2 examples in Nottinghamshire), which is derived from a pet form of Matthew, and Snelling (32), a patronymic formed from Snell. Tegg (14) was an occupational name for a shepherd, but no explanations can yet be offered for Stovell, Stovold, Stowell (20), Geale (15, with 2 in Nottinghamshire), and Hulliberry (6).

The hearth tax returns of the reign of Charles II are thus an invaluable guide to the distribution of English surnames three or four centuries after their formation. They show that some people had travelled long distances to set up homes far from their points of origin. Some of these migrants bore distinctive names and can be traced, but we have no way of telling how many people with common surnames were immigrants. The immigrant names stand out in each of the county lists, for in every part of England one is struck by the different regional flavour of the stock of surnames. Armed with local knowledge of naming-patterns, the reader could identify an unnamed county by glancing through its list of names. The English population had grown only slowly back to its highest medieval levels and the great majority of people had not moved very far. Ten of the 45 taxpayers in the Nottinghamshire township of Hickling in 1664 bore the surname Dafte, and at that time no other Daftes were recorded anywhere else in the county, nor in any of the other counties that we have examined. Evidence such as this points not only to the residential stability of certain families, but to the single-family origins of many of our surnames. At a point midway between the Middle Ages and the present day, the uncommon English surnames were still intensely local in their distribution.

Locating the Home of a Family Name

We have seen that a large number of surnames appear to have had a single-family origin and that many others started independently in only two or three different localities. In such cases it is often possible to trace a surname back to the district of its original home, even perhaps to identify the particular farmstead or hamlet from which it sprang. If a family historian does not restrict his enquiries to his own surname, but follows various branches of his family tree, it is very likely that he will come across surnames which can be treated in this way. Finding the home of a family name is therefore a challenge that all might face, perhaps as the ultimate quest when ancestral lines have been traced back to a time when the available records are inadequate for the task of proving all the links in the chain.

The essential first step in this quest is to establish the current distribution of the surname, for it is surprising how often family names, even after all the mobility of modern times, are still rooted in or near the places where they were first recorded in the Middle Ages. The most accessible source for this exercise is a reference library collection of telephone directories, covering the entire country. A high and increasing proportion of British households are telephone subscribers at the present time. Some rare names may not be included in the directories, but we can be confident that the general picture of the stock of surnames contained in this source is reasonably accurate.

There are 103 directories for the whole of the United Kingdom. It is not usually possible to consult a complete collection of directories that is earlier than that in current use, but ideally one would like to go back to the 1970s before the modern practice was started whereby a subscriber may be listed in two overlapping directories. A careful count of the subscribers in each volume (eliminating those who appear twice, but including all the variant spellings of the name) should be made and the results plotted on a map of the whole country. As London has acted as a magnet for migrants during all the centuries since surnames were formed, it is normal to find that some, perhaps many, people there possess a surname that is otherwise concentrated elsewhere. The distribution of the name in and around London can often be disregarded, unless of course all the other examples of the surname are from those parts. Counting common surnames such as Turner or Walker will not prove a worthwhile exercise, but it is surprising how many surnames that may be thought common turn out to be well represented in certain areas and hardly at all in others. For instance, there are 239 Staniforths in the Sheffield telephone directory, but only one each in the directories for Exeter and Portsmouth and none at all in that for Colchester. The current distribution of a surname often, though not invariably, provides our

first clue to where that name originated. The Staniforths derived their name from a lost place-name on the eastern edge of the parish of Sheffield.

The present distribution of a surname then needs to be checked against geographical patterns further back in time, for if the name is a rare one, the movement of a single family which subsequently became prolific might have had a considerable effect on the later distribution of the surname. To establish the whereabouts of people who bore the same surname early in Victoria's reign, we need to consult the indexes in the Family Records Centre, 1 Myddelton Street, London, EC1. (These are sometimes available in local libraries on microfilm.) A reasonable sample may be obtained by counting all the births entered in the indexes for the first five years of civil registration, beginning on 1 July 1837. With very rare names it may be necessary to take a longer sample, say up to 1852 when the registration districts were changed. The results can then be plotted on a map of the superintendent registrars' districts. These districts do not, of course, coincide with those of the telephone directories, but they are small enough to achieve the same purpose of showing how a surname may be concentrated in its distribution, 150 years or so before our previous sample.

The task of plotting even earlier distributions becomes increasingly difficult the further back in time we go. Unfortunately, only a few counties have a series of hearth tax returns in print. As we have seen, where such records are available, they are invaluable for plotting distributions of family names in the 1660s–1670s, half-way between the period when surnames were formed and the present day. For the previous century, we are dependent upon parish registers. The International Genealogical Index of the Mormon Church (known familiarly as the IGI) provides uneven coverage of parish register data, but is an accessible source that may well narrow a field of enquiry to a limited number of parishes. The index must certainly be consulted, even if it is far from comprehensive. Once we get back beyond the beginnings of parish registration of baptisms, marriages, and burials, the picture becomes even fainter. We can no longer hope to construct a database of names across the country. If the searcher is very lucky he might find that a set of poll tax returns for 1379–81 or the records of a thirteenth- or fourteenth-century lay subsidy have been printed for the county that he is interested in. This would take him back right to the period when surnames were being formed, though the list would be far from complete.

There are, of course, many other sources which enable the genealogist to trace a particular name back step by step, but unless there is a good series of medieval manorial records, it is unlikely that a direct line will be traced back beyond the sixteenth century. Fortunately, by the time that parish registers began, most surnames were still heavily concentrated in or near their place of origin. Armed with knowledge of the sixteenth-century distribution of a name, the researcher is well placed to discover its home. He will need large-scale ordnance survey maps and the patience to search through all the available sources for the medieval history of his area. The volumes of the English

Place-Name Society are indispensable in the counties where they are available, for they record the earliest forms of minor place-names, which were often first written down about the time when surnames were being formed. The availability of medieval records in print varies from county to county and depends on whether or not a record society has been long established.

A few examples will help to explain the procedure. J. Douglas Porteous has traced 'the history and geography of an ordinary family in an ordinary place' by seeking every reference that he could find to members of the Mell family. Mell is a rare name which appears to have been a northern dialect term for a meal-seller or meal-maker. The surname is found not only in England but in The Netherlands, the adjacent parts of lower Saxony, and occasionally in southern Sweden and Latvia. Moreover, in both Norway and Sweden the prefix Mell- is found at the beginning of at least 80 distinct surnames. All these countries fringe the North and Baltic Seas and had regular contacts with north-eastern England.

All the UK telephone directories in use in 1980 were searched, but only 82 people with the name of Mell were found. A major cluster was discovered in Yorkshire and Lincolnshire and a minor cluster in and around London, but only a few others were located elsewhere. Sixty-two of these Mells eventually replied to a questionnaire and thereby provided much evidence of family links. The information that was obtained in this way was collated with that gleaned from the indexes of births at the Family Records Centre for the whole period 1837–1979 and from the Mormon IGI for the years 1538–1850. This huge mass of data was then analysed on a county basis for Lincolnshire and the East Riding of Yorkshire, where the name has been known for over 400 years. A thorough search was made of all the parish registers of these two counties which were not covered by the IGI. Three East Riding and one Lincolnshire parish stood out as possible points of origin for the surname. One of these was Thorganby on the northern edge of Humberhead, just south of York. Here, the surname could be traced back much earlier, though direct links between the people who were recorded could not be proved. Thomas Mell was living in Thorganby in 1295, Amice Mell was there in 1339, and in 1377 John Mell, husbandman, paid poll tax there. In the sixteenth century the Mell family were still living in Thorganby, but by then other branches had begun to spread a little further afield.

This example takes us back to the village where the surname had appeared by the late thirteenth century. Sometimes it is possible to identify a hamlet or even an isolated farmstead as the home of a family name. The parish of Chapel-en-le-Frith, high in the Peak District, is the source of a number of distinctive locative names. One of these is derived from the hamlet of Bagshaw, which stands on a wind-swept hill about 1,000 feet above sea-level. Professor Roy Newton has counted 1,176 Bagshaw subscribers in the current UK telephone directories and has found that 29.4 per cent were concentrated in only four adjacent areas: Sheffield had 134, south Manchester 100, Chesterfield 58, and north-east Manchester 53; the next highest was Nottingham with 45. He concludes that after about 700 years of the surname's history nearly one-third of all the Bagshaw(e)s were still living within about 25 miles of Chapel-en-le-Frith. His next task was to count the 878 births recorded in the civil registration indexes between 1 July 1837 and 31 December 1851. Of these 310 (35.3 per cent) were listed in five registration districts: Bakewell had 119, Sheffield 96, Ecclesall Bierlow (west Sheffield) 33, Stockport 33, and Chapel-en-le-Frith 29. Further back in time, the hearth tax returns of 1670 for Derbyshire show that the Bagshaws were then concentrated in the north-western part of the county, around their place of origin. By that time, only 2 families had ventured into south Yorkshire and 2 into Nottinghamshire. The late seventeenth-century distribution of the surname points unerringly to the hamlet of Bagshaw as the place of origin.

The hamlet of Bagshaw may once have been a single farm, like Ollerenshaw Hall in the same parish. This hall took its name from a small alder wood (recorded in 1251), for oller is a dialect form of alder. When the county of Derbyshire was assessed for hearth tax on various occasions between 1662 and 1670, 11 householders bearing the name Ollerenshaw were recorded. Three of these householders were settled in south Derbyshire, but the other 8 were living in the north-west of the county, close to the point of origin of the surname. Indeed, 5 of them were still to be found in the township of Bradshaw Edge, whence the name was derived. Only 1 family of Ollerenshaws was living in the neighbouring county of Nottinghamshire at that time, and none at all had settled in south Yorkshire. The surname had not migrated very far during the three or four centuries since its formation.

The topographical name Downer has a very different distribution. Of the 635 subscribers in the current telephone directories 30.9 per cent are located in five neighbouring districts on the south coast: Bournemouth (54), Southampton (47), Isle of Wight (42), Brighton (28), and Portsmouth (25). Another major cluster (144 or 22.7 per cent) live in Greater London. Only 28 subscribers named Downer (4.4 per cent) live in the six northern counties of England and only 12 (1.9 per cent) live in Scotland. The current distribution of the name supports the suggestion that a Downer was someone who lived on the Downs in southern England. At the beginning of Victoria's reign, the Downers were almost entirely confined to this area. Between 1837 and 1842, 104 Downer births were registered. All except one of these babies were born in southern England; the odd one was born in Stoke-on-Trent. Forty-four were registered in the Isle of Wight, 21 in Sussex, 14 in Dorset, 7 in Hampshire, 1 each in adjacent parts of Somerset and Wiltshire, 9 in London, and 6 in that northern outpost, Watford. During the last century and a half the Downers have moved to London in large numbers and some have migrated in search of work to most parts of the country; it is reasonable to suppose that many of these migrants were farm labourers who left what was then a depressed area in search of a better life elsewhere.

The homes of the rarer occupational surnames can be located by the same technique. Crapper is a northern form of cropper, though what exactly was

being cropped back in the Middle Ages is unclear; it may have been iron, but it is possible that it was cloth, or something else. The Crappers appear 262 times in the current telephone directories. The name is not found in eastern England or in the Welsh borders and is recorded only 8 times south of the Thames; its distribution is therefore totally different from that of Downer. Nor have the Crappers migrated to Scotland or to the four northern counties of England, while few have moved to Lancashire. Their stronghold is Sheffield, where 110 (42 per cent) are listed in a single directory. The next highest concentrations are in adjoining districts in the West Riding of Yorkshire and Derbyshire. Two-thirds of the Crappers listed in the current telephone directories live within these two counties. The only other cluster is in Oxford (15, with a few nearby).

The evidence of birth certificates registered during the five years beginning on 1 July 1837 confirms this remarkable pattern. Of the 83 Crappers recorded, 34 were born in or near Sheffield, 24 in other parts of the West Riding, 14 in Oxfordshire, 5 in Lancashire, and 6 elsewhere. As no Crappers were recorded in the hearth tax returns for Oxfordshire in 1665, the ones living there in the nineteenth and twentieth centuries must be descended from migrants from the north. Three centuries earlier, 4 Crappers were listed as payers of poll tax in the West Riding: 2 in the parish of Ecclesfield and another 2 further north at Emley and Idle. It is likely that everyone bearing this unusual surname is descended from one of these old Yorkshire families.

Surnames derived from personal names and nicknames may also have a

SURNAME DISTRIBUTIONS FROM TELEPHONE DIRECTORIES

Downer
The southern origin of this name is still evident from the entries in the telephone directories of the late 1980s.

Crapper
The northern origin of this name is equally clear from the modern distribution.

distribution that suggests a common ancestry. An example is provided by the nickname Grubb, which was given to a small person; the smallest screw is still known as the grub-screw. The distribution of the name in the telephone directories and civil registration records shows that many families rose independently in this way. The name is common in eastern Scotland, in the West Midlands and over much of southern England. The 23 Grubbs listed in the Sheffield telephone district may nevertheless share a common ancestor, for the name is unknown in the surrounding districts. The hearth tax returns for south Yorkshire (1672) record only 2 Grubbs, Edmond and Thomas, both of whom were living in Sheffield. No Grubbs were recorded in neighbouring Derbyshire at this time, but 5 householders bore this name in various parts of north Nottinghamshire. A William Grubbe was living at Scrooby in north Nottinghamshire in 1299. The Sheffield Grubbs appear frequently in medieval records relating to Sheffield and the neighbouring parish of Ecclesfield, where John Grubbe was living in 1374, probably at the hamlet of Barnes, where the family were recorded on several occasions during the fifteenth and sixteenth centuries. He was the only person bearing this surname in the poll tax returns for south Yorkshire five years later. Armed with this information, the family historian who is tracing the ancestry of one of the present-day Grubbs of Sheffield should use his genealogical skills to see whether he can trace his line back to Edmond or Thomas Grubb, living in Sheffield in 1672 (in which case he may reasonably work on the hypothesis that he is descended from the John Grubbe of 1374), or whether the line points to an immigrant. If the immigrant came from north Nottinghamshire, in search of work in the expanding industrial city, then the researcher should look to the names recorded in the Nottinghamshire hearth tax returns and to the possibility that William Grubbe of Scrooby was his ancestor.

The methodology of tracing the homes of family names outlined above can throw up occasional surprises and unexpected puzzles. The surname Havenhand is well known in the Sheffield district today and is widely recognized as a distinctive local name. However, this name is not recorded locally before the early eighteenth century, when George, the son of Joshua Havenhand, a farmer from the neighbouring parish of Dronfield, was apprenticed to a Sheffield cutler. A search of the UK telephone directories was therefore made to see if the original home of the name could be located, but the exercise merely confirmed that Havenhand was a Sheffield name. The Sheffield directory had 83 entries and the neighbouring ones for Barnsley and Chesterfield had 38 and 13, respectively; another 39 people (many of whom were known to be related to Sheffielders) were scattered throughout England. No other district had even a minor cluster of subscribers with this name.

The only plausible explanations are that the surname was invented very late or that it has changed its form. We have already quoted examples of surnames that were altered over time. When such mysteries arise, a popular explanation (as in the present case) is that the name belonged to foreign im-migrants, usually Huguenots. However, this explanation is rarely the true one. The name Havenhand does not appear in Huguenot records and it is hard to see how or why a French immigrant should have been farming in Derbyshire in the reign of Queen Anne. The Joshua Havenhand who is the first recorded person so far found with this unusual surname died in 1747, 20 years after his wife, Gertrude. The burial register for the parish of Dronfield identified the hamlet of Stubley as their place of residence at the time of Gertrude's death. A Samuel Havenhand, who also lived at Stubley, was recorded on one occasion—the baptism of his son Benjamin in 1733—as Samuel Holland, a variant of the name that alerts us to other possibilities, including that of a Dutch name which has been corrupted. (Dutch farmers settled in south Yorkshire upon the drainage of Hatfield Chase in Charles I's reign.) In the parish of Beighton, not far away to the east, an 'intention of matrimony' was declared on 23 July 1654 and on the following two Sundays between Francis Howenhand of Beighton, labourer, and Margaret Champion of the same parish, spinster. When they eventually married on 25 August 1654, Francis's surname was recorded as Haunomd. Clearly, this was a name that caused some difficulty. It seems possible that Howenhand was an earlier form of Havenhand, but at the present time neither form has been traced back further.

A similar problem arises with the surname Elshaw, but this is explainable in a different way. It is reasonable to begin an enquiry into this name by sup-posing that it arose from a minor place-name, for 'shaw' is a word that means a small wood, but no such place can be found. Ellershaw (Lancashire) or Elsham (Lincolnshire) are possible points of origin, for Elshaw could eas-ily have been corrupted from such forms. The International Genealogical Index records some Elshams who were living in London between 1710 and 1762. Mr Geoffrey Austin of Hatfield Peverel (Essex) has extracted all the births, marriages, and deaths from the records of civil registration between 1837 and 1900 and has shown that everybody with the surname Elshaw was descended from William Elshaw, who was buried at Eckington (Derbyshire) in 1839, aged 80. The records of the Cutlers' Company of Hallamshire offer a partial solution to the problem. They note that in 1775 William Elshaw of the Foundling Hospital, Ackworth, was apprenticed to Isaac Atkin of Norton, sicklesmith, for seven years, and that three years later (presumably because of his master's death) he was apprenticed to Luke Staniforth of Mosbrough Moor, sicklesmith. William Elshaw was granted his freedom in 1791. Ten years later, William, the son of William Elshaw of Ridgeway, in the parish of Eckington, was apprenticed to Thomas Goodison, razor-grinder, for eight years six months, and in 1809 James, the son of William Elshaw of Ridgeway, was apprenticed to his father (a sicklesmith) for seven years. The line had be-come well established. The surname appears to have been coined at the foundling hospital, where William Elshaw was admitted as the three-week-old William Collins on 26 April 1758.

The rare surnames that can be traced back to their points of origin by the methods outlined above include some whose meaning remains mysterious. The surname Shemeld and its numerous variants is a case in point. It is first recorded in the poll tax return of 1379 for the parish of Handsworth (which is now incorporated in the city of Sheffield), when Robert Shemyld', a smith, and Denise, his wife, paid 6*d*. tax and Adam Shemyld' paid 4*d*. Three centuries later, the hearth tax returns of 1672 for south Yorkshire recorded 8 householders with this surname, 6 of them within the parish of Sheffield. The name had not yet spread very far, but it was already being spelt in a variety of ways, including Shemild, Shemell, and Shimmell. Across the border in Derbyshire, Thomas Shemilt paid tax on one hearth in Ashover, and in Nottinghamshire a Mr Shinwell paid tax on four hearths in Mansfield. The name had not yet taken a firm hold in these counties.

By the beginning of Victoria's reign many more variant spellings were in use, as people bearing this distinctive surname migrated from their home area. It was a difficult name to catch exactly. The 67 births which were registered in various parts of the country between 1837 and 1842 were recorded with no less than 21 different spellings. In Cheadle (Staffordshire) the family was known as Shemilt, in Bakewell (Derbyshire) as Shimwell, but in Sheffield the old pronunciation of the name was usually preferred. About half (33) of the births were registered in Sheffield or in the neighbouring districts of Bakewell and Chesterfield. Another 16 births were registered within 50 miles of Sheffield; the rest were distributed widely but thinly, with a small concentration of 5 in Woburn, and 3 in London. A century and a half later people with different versions of the name are found in most parts of the kingdom, though usually only in small numbers. The current telephone directories list 512 subscribers, of whom 35.65 per cent are listed under Sheffield, Chesterfield, and Derby. A further 7.8 per cent live in the Stoke-on-Trent district (which covers much of north Staffordshire) and 6.1 per cent live in or near Nottingham. Another 9.2 per cent now reside in Greater London, a far greater number than in the early years of Victoria's reign. Like the Crappers, the drift of the Shemelds has been towards the south rather than to other parts of the north. Nevertheless, 25 Scottish subscribers bear four versions of the name. In some places a particular variant spelling has become accepted as the norm. In Ashbourne, for instance, all 9 subscribers are named Shemilt. The 38 Shimwells in the same directory are nearly all to be found in a few parishes around Bakewell; in the country at large, 14 of the 18 births registered with the name Shimwell between 1837 and 1842 were from the Bakewell registration district. Sheffield, the original home of the name, has 31 subscribers named Shemeld, 1 Shemald, 1 Shimeld, 2 Shemmelds, 3 Shemmells, 5 Shemwells, and 23 Shimwells. Even the ones who have not migrated have sometimes acquired forms of the name that are very different from the original one.

Finally, let us return to the nickname Daft(e), which was found in only one of our sample counties in the third quarter of the seventeenth century,

THE DISTRIBUTION OF THE
SURNAME DAFT(E)

The distribution of the
surname in the telephone
directories of the late 1980s
points to its origin in the
Midlands.

and which in 1664 was confined to the Nottinghamshire township of
Hickling. Does the later distribution of the surname support the hypothesis
that all the people now bearing this distinctive surname are descended from
a single family? Indeed it does. In the first five years of civil registration
81 births were registered under the name Daft. Of these, 50 were registered in
the adjoining Midland counties of Nottinghamshire, Leicestershire, and
Derbyshire, a further 22 were from a little further afield in Lincolnshire,
Staffordshire, and Warwickshire, and only 9 others were born elsewhere.
Today, 163 Dafts subscribe to the telephone service. Of these, 57 live in the
Nottingham district and 58 live in other parts of Nottinghamshire or
Derbyshire or Leicestershire. In other words, 70 per cent of the Dafts live reasonably close to Hickling, where the name was concentrated in the seventeenth century. Few people bear this name outside Midland England and
large parts of the country have no families with this name. It is possible that
migrants changed their surname on moving—perhaps some of the Daffs
originated in this way—nevertheless, the current distribution of the name
points unerringly to the area where it was coined several centuries ago.

Family historians have much to contribute to a general understanding of
the residential stability of certain families over the centuries and the mobility of others. The number of one-name societies that have sprung up in recent years attests to the popularity of this form of enquiry. It is now over a
hundred years since Dr H. B. Guppy published his pioneering analysis of the
geographical distribution of British surnames, *Homes of Family Names in
Great Britain*, but we are still groping our way towards a true understanding
of these matters.

CHAPTER THREE

MOBILITY AND STABILITY

I T WAS once a commonplace of social history that our ancestors had limited horizons and that they remained rooted in the same spot throughout their lives. Historical research over the past 25 years or so has destroyed this view. Historians have established beyond doubt that people in the past commonly moved from their native parish, that migration was a normal stage of the life-cycle. Even in the Middle Ages much of the population was constantly on the move. In the sixteenth and seventeenth centuries, to judge from the evidence of parish registers, apprenticeship indentures, diaries, and depositions before various courts, the great mass of English people—men and women, country-dwellers as well as those living in towns—moved from their place of birth at least once in their lives. The pendulum has now swung so far that the new orthodoxy amongst social historians emphasizes mobility at the expense of stability. The evidence of continuity of surnames within the various local societies of which England was composed, however, points firmly to the persistence of core groups of families within a few miles of their origins, even if the majority of their neighbours were always on the lookout for a better life elsewhere.

BEFORE 1800

Old Patterns of Movement

The evidence for population mobility in the Middle Ages is largely that of locative surnames taken from manorial court records and national taxation returns. For example, the court rolls of the Huntingdonshire manor of Warboys between 1290 and 1353 record the surnames of tenants who had come from 43 different places in nine counties. Edward Miller and John Hatcher quote evidence from Warwickshire, Wiltshire, Tynemouth, and Cambridgeshire to show that the rural population of certain villages in-

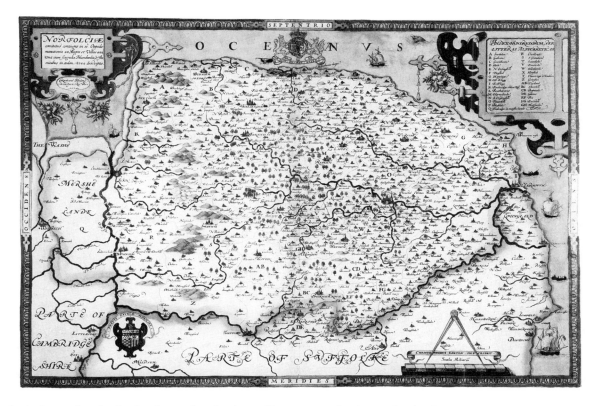

cluded people who had migrated only short distances and others who had come from far afield; the inhabitants of the Cambridgeshire village of Soham who were listed in the lay subsidy return of 1327, for instance, included those who had originated in neighbouring villages and others who had moved from Suffolk, Norfolk, the Isle of Ely, Huntingdonshire, Hertfordshire, Lincolnshire, and Derbyshire.

In parts of England, lords of the manor had the right to demand a 'chevage' payment if an unfree tenant wished to move elsewhere. The records of such payments indicate a very high rate of mobility among this class of people. The Norfolk manor of Forncett had no more than 135 servile holdings, yet every year during the last quarter of the thirteenth century about 100 unfree tenants paid to leave. Similar rates of emigration have been found on other Norfolk manors, on the Somerset estates of Glastonbury Abbey and in Cornwall. Some other manors record very few chevage-payers, however.

Some of these emigrants travelled far from their homes, perhaps to settle in one or other of the new towns that were created between the Norman Conquest and the Black Death or perhaps to set up home in some provincial city. P. H. Reaney's study of deeds and rolls for Norwich during the period 1285–1350 shows that the city attracted immigrants from 351 places within Norfolk, 73 places in Suffolk, and 77 widely scattered places elsewhere. Most

SAXTON'S MAP OF
NORFOLK (1574)

During the 1570s Christopher Saxton produced a series of maps of the counties of England and Wales. He published the collection as an atlas in 1579, the first of its kind. His map of Norfolk shows the central importance of Norwich, a regional capital which attracted immigrants from many parts of the county.

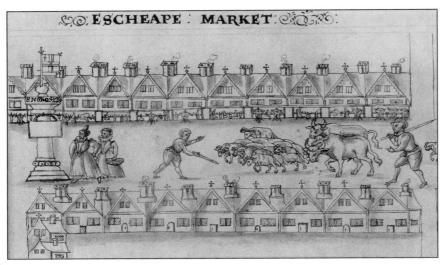

ESCHEAPE MARKET

EASTCHEAP MARKET, LONDON

Like the smaller towns, London had large spaces for market activities. Eastcheap was so-called to distinguish it from Cheap Side (to the east of St Paul's) which was the city's major market in the Middle Ages and beyond. 'Cheap' is derived from the Old English word for market; it survives in such place-names as Chipping. Eastcheap was a long street which ran from Candlewick Street to Tower Street. Hugh Alley's picture of 1598, based on 'a very old Drawing', shows Eastcheap as it was in Tudor times before the tall buildings surrounding the market place were destroyed in the Great Fire of London of 1666. Butchers lived on both sides of the street. The picture shows livestock being driven towards the slaughterhouses. In front of the butchers' shops carcasses and joints are displayed.

people who moved during this period evidently travelled only short distances, though a minority ventured much further afield. In Forncett, over 70 per cent of emigrants between 1400 and 1575 settled at places within about 12 miles of the manor, including those who headed for Norwich. Marriage partners were usually found within a radius of 10 or a dozen miles.

London was a magnet in the Middle Ages, as it was to be in later times. People of every rank came in large numbers to the capital. Professor Reaney's map of the original homes of London immigrants between 1147 and 1350, which was based on locative surnames that were only just becoming hereditary, demonstrates large-scale movement from the south Midlands and East Anglia and a thinner stream of migrants from every part of England, except Cornwall. Although these surnames cannot be regarded as proof of recent migration, they indicate the places where migrant families had originated over the last generation or two. They make it clear that from the earliest years of the fourteenth century, at least, London was attracting settlers from all over the kingdom. A little less than half of a sample of 564 names taken from a subsidy roll of 1319 were derived from places in the counties surrounding the capital. Sylvia Thrupp has commented that many of these short-distance migrants entered trades that were largely supplied from their home area, becoming butchers, dealers in corn or malt or wood, or workers in wood or leather. Likewise, the settlers from East Anglia were employed in the fish and cloth trades and such industries as the making of gloves, purses, and caps. She suggests that the relatively small numbers coming from the west and the south reflected both the lesser density of population there and also the local importance of Southampton, Salisbury, and Bristol, which probably absorbed most of the surplus population of the surrounding regions. In time, however, London became the goal of migrants from all over the land.

A list of families living in the archdeaconry of Stafford in 1532–3 names about 51,000 people, with 2,055 different surnames. These names include a number that were derived from places that lie well beyond the county boundaries. Some families had migrated considerable distances during the century or two since their surnames had been formed. Distinctive Lancashire names included Aspenall, Brodbent, Chadwyk, Greenhalgh, Higginbotham, Hollenworth, Lathom, Leyland, Loncaster, Manchester, Mellor, Mellynge, Pemerton, Pilkenton, Rachedall, Robothom, Salford, Shepulbotham, Singleton, Smethurst, Wigan, and Wolstonholme. Yorkshire names included Benbryge, Cawood, Douncaster, Pickering, Pomffryt, Ramskare, Rosynton, Segewycke, Wakfeld, Whitby, and Yorke. From further north, immigrants bore the names of Carlyll, Gatskyll, Harbottell, Kendall, and Wasshynton, and from Wales a small number of people came with the names Flewellen, Powell, Price, Rhys, ap Richard, Walch, and Wales. Other immigrants had travelled from neighbouring counties, particularly Derbyshire, and some had journeyed long distances from Brighton, Daventry, Glastonbury, Kent, Leicester, Stamford, etc. Collectively, they formed only a minority of the residents of the archdeaconry of Stafford, but the presence there of families whose roots lay in many different parts of England demonstrates the mobility of at least part of the late medieval population.

Historians who are interested in population mobility have concentrated their attention upon the sixteenth and seventeenth centuries. In a famous pioneering essay, Peter Laslett found that as many as 61.8 per cent of the inhabitants of the Nottinghamshire parish of Clayworth who were recorded in a listing of 1676 were no longer there 12 years later, and that in the Northamptonshire parish of Cogenhoe just over half the population disappeared and were replaced by others between 1618 and 1628. Evidence which has been gathered from all over Tudor and Stuart England since the publication of this essay has supported Laslett's findings. In Elizabethan Buckinghamshire, for example, more than 80 per cent of witnesses who appeared before the church courts had moved at least once in their lives. Between 1580 and 1649, 77 per cent of countrymen in the Kent and Sussex Weald had made similar moves; in early Stuart Suffolk and Norfolk the comparable figure was 82 per cent. At Horringer in Suffolk, only 2 of the 63 family names recorded in the period 1600–34 can still be found in the parish register for 1700–24. These and other examples leave no doubt that moving from one's native parish to set up home elsewhere was a commonplace activity.

Dr R. S. Schofield's analysis of the remarkably detailed enumeration of the Bedfordshire parish of Carsington in 1782 suggests that the old pattern of high mobility in rural areas remained the norm in the Georgian era. The 180 households within Carsington contained a total of 199 families, who lived in four distinct settlements within the parish. Farming was the mainstay of the rural economy and half the heads of households were labourers. The enumeration indicates that children began to leave home from the age of 9 or 10 onwards, but especially after the age of 14. Entering farm or domestic service

A List of the Inhabitants of Sandford taken in Dec.r 1790 — compleat to Dec.r 25.th By Children are meant those belonging to & living with the Head of the Family unmarried, otherwise they are reckoned Inmates, if married.

was the normal expectation, though some of the girls did not leave home until they married. The movement of the younger members of the population out of the parish continued, and was possibly accelerated, upon marriage.

Studies such as these have made it clear that much of the turnover of names in the listings that survive is explained by the movement of young people, some of whom returned in later life upon inheriting the parental home. Unless he was trained to follow his father's trade, a teenage boy could expect to live away from the place where he was reared, either as a servant or as an apprentice. An apprentice would stay with the same master during his term (provided his master stayed alive), but a farm servant often moved to another position upon the expiration of his yearly contract. This took place in the spring in pastoral areas and in the autumn in arable districts. Likewise, girls would expect to leave home to work for a few years as domestic servants until they married.

Dr Ann Kussmaul has shown how farm servants frequently moved from one farm to another, within a limited circuit not too far from home, when their yearly contracts expired. Once he was married, however, a farming man normally remained settled within his particular neighbourhood. Though the institution of farm service was of great antiquity, the peak period was in the decades after the Restoration of Charles II, when they were

A LIST OF THE INHABITANTS OF SANDFORD, DEVON (1790)

Complete listings of the inhabitants of particular places are rare before the 1841 census. Those that survive in local and national record offices are noted in J. Gibson and M. Medlycott, *Local Census Listings, 1522–1930* (Federation of Family History Societies, 1992). The Sandford list names the head of each household and his wife, their unmarried children, servants and apprentices, and married 'Inmates'. It shows how the nuclear family was the norm in pre-industrial England.

kept in large numbers. The laws of settlement, especially those passed in the
1690s, controlled the movement of servants through the hiring fairs and
helped to make it localized. In Hertfordshire, for example, farm servants
moved on average only 3 or 4 miles. Much greater distances were covered by
seasonal migrants who were employed to gather the harvest. This development did not affect the ancient patterns of mobility and stability, however,
for once the harvest was safely in the labourers returned home.

On the whole, apprentices moved within the same restricted circles as the
farm and domestic servants, though exceptions can be found where boys
moved long distances. Dr John Patten's study of the sixteenth- and seventeenth-century apprenticeship registers of Norwich, Great Yarmouth, and
Ipswich points to the heavily localized character of most apprenticeship
mobility, especially in the late Stuart period, and to migration patterns that
were related to the differing economies of individual towns and their hin-

terlands. Upon securing their freedom, the former apprentices tended to settle in the district where they had learned their trade. As most of them had not moved far, they did not thereby add significantly to the stock of local surnames, but sometimes an immigrant established a new name in this way. In time, some of these names became those of families that remained rooted in the same place for several generations.

We do not have records as informative as apprenticeship registers to cover the average adult life span, but it seems likely that unless they were among the young hopefuls who flocked to London, most migrants did not travel very far. In Tudor and Stuart England mobility was usually limited to a 20- or 25-mile radius (often less), to a district that was bounded by the nearest market towns. This was the area that people spoke of as their 'country', the neighbourhood larger than the parish to which they felt that they belonged. The term was still commonly used in Victorian times; for instance, when the Revd Francis Kilvert described the Hay Flower Show of 1870 in his diary, he wrote, 'The whole country was there.' We still speak of the Black Country and we think in terms of local societies as well as geographical districts when we think of the Wolds or the Potteries, and of human groups as well as ancient administrative units when referring to Hallamshire or the Forest of Dean. Urbanization and the modern ease of transport has obscured, if not obliterated, the boundaries between many of these local societies; nevertheless, in many counties these divisions are still real. Once, the whole of England was divided into overlapping 'countries' which were mostly anonymous but none the less powerful in providing local people with a sense of attachment. When an elusive ancestor cannot be located, the first step for the family historian is therefore to consult the records of the parishes adjacent to the one where the surname last appears.

Marriage partners were normally found within the 'country' to which a parish belonged. In the Shropshire parish of Myddle, for instance, between 1541 and 1701 nearly everyone found a husband or wife within a radius of 10 miles of his or her dwelling and most partners came from within the area centred upon the market towns of Shrewsbury, Ellesmere, and Wem. Only the gentry sought their marriage partners from further afield, and even they did not search much further. Studies of other sources confirm that most migrants did not move very far. Professor Peter Clark's analysis of over 7,000 deponents at diocesan courts in 11 English counties during the period 1660–1730 shows that 77 per cent of rural males and 79 per cent of rural females had either never moved or had moved only within the county in which they were born. Dr B. A. Holderness has traced the movements of 2,268 individuals living in the Plain of York between 1777 and 1822 and has shown that only 18 per cent migrated more than 10 miles. Even those who ventured further did not usually travel long distances, for more than 4 in every 5 of them stayed within Yorkshire. In present-day England, where people are obviously far more mobile than in any time in the past, the *Observer* newspaper has nevertheless reported (on 5 April 1987) that

'The median distance moved by someone buying a house is less than four miles.'

Although the parish was the basic unit to which rural people owed allegiance, they were conscious of belonging to a wider local society. Dr Keith Wrightson has written that the core of the social area of people from the Essex parish of Terling was the district within 10 miles of the village, but that it frequently extended much further. Roger Lowe, who kept a diary during his apprenticeship at Ashton-in-Makerfield, Lancashire, during the 1660s, wrote mostly about his life in that parish, but both he and his friends had

THE NECESSITOUS POOR: CAPEL, SURREY (1776)

This 'Register of the poor of the Lower-End part of the Parish of Capell Who Receive Relief And Assistance' was taken on 3 February 1776 and records 'the Occation that Brought them Under that Necessity'. It names sixty-seven individuals.

regular contacts in the neighbouring towns and villages of south Lancashire. Even today, people can have a strong sense of belonging to a particular place, while at the same time being conscious of living in a wider neighbourhood. Family historians therefore need to have a strong grasp of the identity of the local societies of which their ancestors formed part.

Though movement was generally restricted to the 'country' where a person was born, a minority of migrants travelled well beyond these limits. Professor Peter Clark has distinguished two types of migration during the reigns of Elizabeth and the early Stuarts: the 'subsistence' migration of vagrants and the 'betterment' migration of the sort that we have been describing. Poor vagrants often travelled long distances in search of the necessities of life. Many of them left the mountainous regions in the north and the west in favour of the southern lowlands, often walking well over a hundred miles to London or to other southern towns. Those who left home to better themselves did not normally travel as far as did the desperately poor.

During the sixteenth and early seventeenth centuries the numbers of poor people rose considerably as job opportunities failed to match the rapid growth of the national population. The hungry poor were forced to go on tramp in search of work and food. Few sources shed light on the movements of these vagrants. They seem to have been mostly young, single men, some of whom were absorbed in the wood pasture and fenland areas where land was still available, or in the towns and villages where industry was expanding; others moved in stages to test their luck elsewhere. Dr Paul Slack has suggested that the experience of a town was an important factor in turning a man into a long-distance vagrant. Immigration was an everyday phenomenon in the suburbs, and although it is incorrect to speak of a 'subculture' of pauper vagabonds, many vagrants assumed the life-style of the long-distance vagrant after living for a time amongst others who had little hope of bettering themselves. London was the ultimate goal, for wages were higher there and frequent epidemics kept up the demand for immigrant labour.

After the Civil War, long-distance 'subsistence' migration declined dramatically; by 1700 the desperately poor were no longer leaving the highland parts of England in the large numbers familiar to earlier generations. In the lowlands, too, the geographical range of migrants was much more restricted. In Kent, for example, settlement certificates that were granted between 1691 and 1740 reveal that well over half the poor immigrants into Maidstone had journeyed no more than 10 miles and that only 15 per cent had travelled more than 40 miles. The stern application of the Act of Settlement of 1662 inhibited movement, but more positive developments also played their part. Better farming methods, the spread of rural industries, and the growth of industrial towns meant more employment opportunities and a rising standard of living. Most importantly of all, the national population ceased growing, indeed it fell during the second half of the seventeenth century and was slow to recover in the first decades of the eighteenth century.

London was the great exception to the short-distance rule of mobility, for it attracted immigrants from all parts of the country. Samuel Pepys recorded in his diary for 10 May 1669 a conversation with

A stranger, a country gentleman . . . and he pleased with my discourse accidentally about the decay of gentlemen's families in the country, telling us that the old rule was that a family might remain 50 miles from London 100 year, 100 mile off from London 200 years, and so, farther or nearer London, more or less years.

The city grew at an astonishing rate during the Elizabethan and Stuart period. Beier and Finlay estimate that London's population was about 120,000 in 1550; 200,000 in 1600; 375,000 in 1650; and 490,000 in 1700. A century later, it had risen to about 900,000. The rate of growth in the sixteenth and seventeenth centuries was far higher than that of the nation as a whole. In 1550 only about 4 per cent of the national population were Londoners; by 1700 nearly 10 per cent of the nation lived in the capital. During the eighteenth century, some provincial towns grew rapidly and the national population increase matched that of London. In earlier times, the capital had siphoned off much of the natural increase of population throughout the land.

Immigration was vital to London's growth, for the numbers who died in London exceeded the numbers of those who were born there. Five major outbreaks of plague occurred—in 1563, 1593, 1603, 1625, and 1665—and other diseases continually claimed victims. Careful counts of the baptism and

LONDON AT THE BEGINNING OF ELIZABETH I'S REIGN

This detail from a large map of the City of London as it appeared in the 1550s shows that most of the city was still contained within its medieval walls. Moor Field remained a green space where laundresses worked and cows grazed beyond the ancient limits. Roads from the north entered the city via Aldersgate and Cripplegate.

burial registers of London's numerous parishes suggest that in every year between 1604 and 1659 about 3,500 more people died in the capital than were born there. During this time, almost half of the nation's surplus of births over burials were absorbed by migration to London. It has been estimated that between 1650 and 1750 a minimum number of 8,000 migrants a year were needed to boost London's population to the levels outlined above. Londoners were an extraordinary mixture of people from all over the land and from many parts of continental Europe. Only a minority had been born there, yet it was a youthful society, for most of the migrants were in their late teens and early twenties. Many did not stay, but returned to their native 'countries' or moved on elsewhere; others were short-term visitors. Direct experience of London life was widespread in Stuart England. It is thought that perhaps 1 in 8 English people had visited or lived in the capital at some stage in their lives during the two generations between 1580 and 1650, and that the figure increased to 1 in 6 during the following hundred years. Some walked there, others came by carrier's cart. John Taylor's *Carriers' Cosmographie*, published in 1637, shows that by that time, and probably long before, all parts of the land were connected to the capital by weekly carrying services.

The migrants were predominantly single men and women. They came from every sort of social background, attracted by business opportunities or high wages, or a vague hope that the streets of London were indeed paved with gold. Large numbers came from all over England to serve an apprenticeship, though eventually better opportunities in other towns drew lads elsewhere. Dr Peter Earle estimates that by 1660–1730 nearly 2 out of every 3 apprentices came from either London itself or from the eastern and south-eastern counties. Even so, almost every county in England still provided lads, and others came from Scotland, Wales, and overseas. London remained attractive to the ambitious boy seeking his fortune.

Early Emigration

The ultimate step for a migrant was to move beyond the shores of England in the search for a new life overseas. Over the centuries, more people have emigrated from England than have arrived as immigrants. In the early modern period a steady trickle set up home on the European mainland; some families from East Anglia, for example, were attracted by the Low Countries. During the reign of James I, however, the principal attraction for the emigrant was northern Ireland. The government actively encouraged settlement by providing land in those parts of west Ulster which had been troublesome during the reign of Elizabeth. Earlier attempts to found plantations had all failed, but this time the policy was successful. Emigration to Ireland was eventually on a larger scale than was sought by the initial objectives. The counties of Antrim and Down, which lay outside the area of

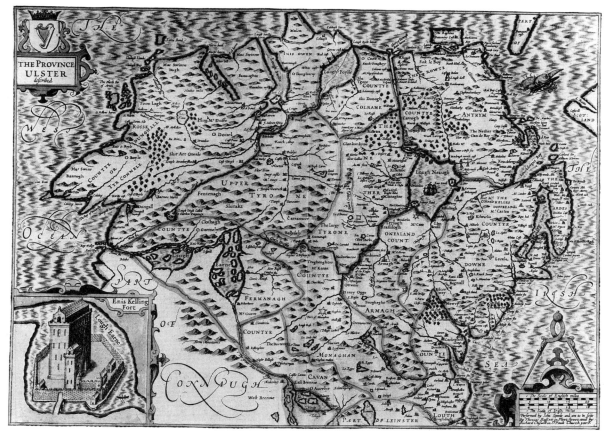

the official scheme, each attracted more settlers than any of the other counties further west. Nor did the movement of Scottish and English families come to an end in 1641, when the native Irish rebelled; indeed, the peak rates of immigration were probably not reached until the second half of the seventeenth century.

Two muster rolls of adult British males, for 1618 and 1631, which survive in the Public Record Office, suggest that the initial response to the government's encouragement was slow. However, by 1659 Scottish and English settlers accounted for 37 per cent of the 70,800 householders in Ulster. Half a century after the plantations were first established, the British and the Irish were clearly segregated at townland level. Scottish and English surnames which were recorded in the poll tax and hearth tax returns of the 1660s show the persistence of immigrant settlers in the original localities, but a high rate of turnover of individual families. In Tyrone 70 per cent of the British settlers were described in the surveys as undertenants with leases of less than 60 acres or as landless cottagers. This broad base of Scottish and English labour was the principal reason for the success of the Plantation policy. Of all the British names on the Tyrone poll tax lists, 32 per cent were recorded as yeomen or farmers, and 68 per cent as labourers and servants. A similar

SPEED'S MAP OF ULSTER
(c.1610)
John Speed's map of the Province of Ulster was made in about 1610 for his atlas of 1612. Although the representation of relief is primitive, the map is useful in naming counties and settlements at the time of the plantations.

73

social structure is observable amongst Irish settlements, where 72 per cent of householders were labourers. This is a much higher proportion than in England at that time.

In no county did the immigrants form a majority of the population, but they outnumbered the Irish in the newly established towns and villages; in the countryside they were thinly scattered among the indigenous population. The English settlers came mostly from western parts of the country, particularly from Devon, Warwickshire, and Staffordshire, Flint, Cheshire, and Lancashire. Some estimates suggest that they were outnumbered by Scottish emigrants by 5 to 1. The Scots came from Galloway, Ayrshire, Renfrew, and Lanark, from the Borders and from near Edinburgh, but not from the Highlands. These Scotsmen did not have far to travel and had few adjustments to make in their new life. Some of their countrymen had already settled in Ulster long before the Plantation policy was launched. These early settlers shared the same Gaelic heritage as the Irish, including a common language and a similar natural environment. The introduction of the English language and the Protestant religion, as well as new forms of settlement and landholding, were important innovations of lasting consequence, but the cultural gap between the planter and the native Irish was not as great as is often supposed. The divisions deepened later.

From the 1630s onwards the new colonies in North America and the West Indies became the most favoured destinations for emigrants. About 20 per cent of present-day Americans trace their ancestry to England and 16 per cent to Ireland, though of course the bulk of these ancestors crossed the Atlantic much later than the seventeenth century. We have no firm figures, but the best estimates suggest that about 540,000 people left England between 1630 and 1700, of whom roughly 380,000 went to the New World. About 69,000 of these Britons sailed across the Atlantic in the 1630s; approximately 21,000 settled in New England and most of the rest went to the Chesapeake and the Caribbean. By the end of the seventeenth century New England had attracted only 39,000 British migrants; much larger numbers went further south, perhaps 116,000 to the Chesapeake and southern mainland colonies and 222,500 to the Caribbean.

The Elizabethan attempts at colonization in the New World had failed. Permanent settlement dates from 1607 with the arrival in Chesapeake Bay of three ships belonging to the Virginia Company of London and the foundation of Jamestown. The colony nearly ended in disaster, for at the end of the first two years only 38 of the 105 people who had landed were still alive. The first 15 years saw a desperate struggle for survival. The Indian crop, tobacco, was the eventual salvation of the colony. Production rose from 400,000 lb. in 1630 to 15 million lb. by the 1660s; then, after a period of slower growth in the 1670s and 1680s, followed by 25 years of stagnation, output rose to 28 million lb. per annum. The phenomenal growth of the tobacco industry in Virginia and Maryland created and maintained a demand for cheap labour, which was met at first mainly by young men and women who came from central and southern parts of Britain. Large numbers went over as indentured servants, who worked for a fixed term on a plantation in order to pay for their passage and board. Between 70 and 85 per cent of the immigrants to the Chesapeake during the seventeenth century arrived as indentured servants, and many more entered the country this way during the following century. During the early eighteenth century, when fewer immigrants arrived, a much higher proportion than before were skilled workers.

The names of 75 per cent of the seventeenth-century settlers in the Chesapeake are known from the records of the Land Office at Richmond, Virginia. Only a small proportion of these immigrants have been traced to their

NOVA BRITANNIA.

OFFRING MOST

Excellent fruites by Planting in
VIRGINIA.

Exciting all such as be well affected
to further the same.

LONDON
Printed for SAMVEL MACHAM, and are to be sold at
his Shop in Pauls Church-yard, at the
Signe of the Bul-head.
1609.

CROSSING THE ATLANTIC
Would-be emigrants to Virginia were encouraged by publications such as this. The small size of the ship depicted on the title page no doubt deterred others.

origins in England, however. Little is known about the way society developed in the Chesapeake during the seventeenth century because the historical records are fragmentary, but it is clear that it was not until the turn of the century that the majority of the white inhabitants along the tobacco coast were native. Great mortalities and extensive out-migration limited the rate of expansion. Nevertheless, the white population grew to about 8,000 in 1640, to 25,000 in 1660, and to about 100,000 in 1700.

The few surviving sources in England that shed light on the servants who formed such a high proportion of the early emigrants to the New World include some indenture records of 1682–92 for London, lists of servants who left from Liverpool, and miscellaneous lists from the 1630s. The most important record, however, is a register (now in the Bristol Archives Office) of over 10,000 indentured servants who sailed from Bristol between 1654 and 1679. The information that was recorded in the early years of registration procedure is very full. Dr David Souden has shown that of the 5,138 indentured servants who emigrated between 1654 and 1662, the bulk signed agreements that lasted for four years. Most servants, both male and female, were aged 18–22. They came from a broad social mix, though most were in low-status occupations; they were certainly not the 'rogues and vagabonds' who were denounced by contemporaries. Souden sees emigration at this time as an extension of the patterns of internal migration; those who left from Bristol were mostly from the port's wide hinterland in south-west England, though some long-distant movement is also observable.

Others were sent to the New World against their will. It has been estimated that more than 30,000 convicts were transported from England to America and the West Indies between 1615 and 1775. P. W. Coldham's *The Complete Book of Emigrants in Bondage, 1614– 1775* is the essential work of reference. Up to 1718 the majority of those deported were sent to the West Indian sugar plantations, but thereafter Maryland and Virginia were the almost invariable destinations until the War of Independence brought this practice to an end.

The Spaniards and the Portuguese were the first to bring Negro slaves from the Guinea coast of Africa across the Atlantic, but their example was soon followed by others. Nearly 3 million Negroes were brought to the Americas during the course of the seventeenth century, 7 million during the eighteenth. The first Negroes in the Chesapeake were treated as indentured servants, but in 1670 slavery was recognized by Virginia law. At that time, the Negro population of Virginia was less than 1,000, but by 1700 it had risen to 16,390. When the 13 states rebelled against English rule in 1776, nearly half of Virginia's people were black slaves.

Less is known about those settlers who opted for the West Indies, where sugar plantations were organized on similar lines to the tobacco plantations of the Chesapeake. Before the large-scale adoption of Negro slavery, the work-force consisted of young indentured servants who worked for a number of years in return for their passage, their keep, and a sum of money upon gaining their freedom. Demand for labour was kept high by the expansion of the sugar industry and by the high levels of mortality. The parallels with the Chesapeake colonies are clear, but the genealogy of the settlers in the West Indies has attracted far less attention.

The Spaniards were the first to colonize the West Indies, but during the seventeenth century they were challenged by the French, English, and Dutch. The first permanent English settlement was that at St Kitts, founded in 1624 by Thomas Warner and 40 or 50 companions. Competing groups of investors then began to establish other plantations. By 1640 the population of Barbados stood at over 30,000, while that of St Kitts and Nevis had topped 20,000. The white population in the West Indies had reached its peak, however, and was to decline rapidly thereafter. During the second half of the seventeenth century, when sugar became the only crop of importance, the racial composition and social structure of the islands was transformed. Barbados had a few hundred black African slaves in 1640; five years later the population of the colony consisted of over 6,000 blacks and about 40,000 whites (both bond and free); 20 years later the number of Africans was the same, but the European population had declined dramatically to 12,000. In the Leeward Islands the same development began a decade or so later, but the changes were quicker and more complete. Many of the white settlers in Barbados moved to Jamaica, where systematic settlement began in 1664. From the beginning, the estates of the sugar-planters in Jamaica were large; few were under 150 acres and some stretched for over 5,000 acres. In 1673 the population of Jamaica consisted of 7,700 whites and 9,500 blacks, but whereas the white population remained stable, the number of Negro slaves rose to 74,000 during the next 50 years. By the early eighteenth century black African slaves formed the great majority of the population of the West Indies.

In contrast to our limited knowledge of the early settlers in the southern colonies, the story of the foundation of Plymouth is well known and the origins of the New England settlers have been traced in detail. In 1608 a group of people from Nottinghamshire, Lincolnshire, and Yorkshire sailed to Holland and settled in Leiden in order to worship as they pleased. The successful foundation of the Virginia colony eventually persuaded them and others to cross the Atlantic. In 1620 the *Mayflower* sailed with 149 people on board, the core of whom were 40 Separatists from Leiden. They missed Virginia by 200 miles and named their new settlement after their port of final embarkation in England. Later settlers turned the colony into a Puritan stronghold. In 1630 John Winthrop of Groton Manor in Suffolk, who was to become the first Governor of the Massachusetts Bay Colony, sailed with four ships and over 500 people. The names of many of these early settlers in New England, and sometimes their places of origin, are given in C. E. Banks and E. E. Brownell's, *Topographical Dictionary of 2885 English Emigrants to New England, 1620–1650*. In 1632, for example, several of the families on board the ship *Lyon*, which sailed from London to Boston, came from particular parishes in Essex and settled in Roxbury and Cambridge, Massachusetts.

David Cressy has made the point that the thousands who sailed to New England in the 1630s, forming what Americans know as 'the Great Migration', represented less than half of 1 per cent of the population of England. Important as the history of New England is from an American perspective, the departure of these people mattered little in the home country and mostly went unnoticed. By the beginning of the English Civil War in 1642 approximately 21,000 men, women, and children had sailed for New England. Unfortunately for the historian, at neither side of the Atlantic did local officials fully record this migration. The passenger lists and customs records are incomplete and problematical. Several passenger lists survive in the Public Record Office for the ports of London, Sandwich, Southampton, Weymouth, Great Yarmouth, and Ipswich, and at their best they record the name, age, place of origin, occupation, and family relationship of each passenger at the point of embarkation; too often, however, they only give names.

Dr Cressy has estimated that it cost about £5 to transport a single person across the Atlantic, £25 or thereabouts to move a family, and £100 or more to establish respectable yeoman status in the New World. Unlike the Chesapeake colonies, New England was not built on bondage, but a considerable number of free migrants must have arrived with obligations or debts. The majority of emigrants travelled in family groups. They were not very different in their occupations and their social standing from the majority of the English population, though they contained fewer gentry at the top of the social scale and fewer labourers and poor people at the bottom. Half of them were ordinary workers, artisans with moderate to low social status. In order to succeed in America they had to learn to be farmers and to turn their hands to whatever work was available. Many of the young came over as servants, though not on the same scale as those who ventured further south; the proportion of servants in New England was probably about the same as in old England, that is, about 25 per cent. The free planters, who paid their own passage and who earned an independent living in New England, often brought servants with them as members of their households. Other servants earned their passage by agreeing to serve the company, or a particular master, at a specific task for three or four years, sometimes more.

The immigrant population of New England in 1630 stood at about 1,800, including the Plymouth settlers, the Massachusetts Bay colonists at Salem and Boston, and others scattered further north. By 1640 the population had grown to 13,500. Migration continued throughout the second half of the seventeenth century, though at a slower rate. The total British American population at the end of the century was about 257,000, of whom just over one-third lived in New England. By that time, Dutch, German, and Swedish settlers had also arrived in significant numbers.

David Cressy has argued that although religion was a powerful motive, especially in the minds of the leaders and preachers, it was not the principal reason why emigrants settled in New England. Secular and circumstantial motives often came to the fore. The vast majority of English people in the seventeenth century remained indifferent to colonial America and most of those who emigrated to the New World settled in colonies to the south. Moreover, hundreds of the emigrants to New England in the 1630s eventually returned home. One consequence of this back-migration was the presence in English towns and villages of numerous people who had direct experience of the New World. Others kept up a correspondence with their kin across the Atlantic. The claims of association through extended kinship networks were an essential source of practical help to the emigrant. The evidence of surviving letters shows that even distant relatives were prepared to help a newcomer to find a home and work.

Having crossed the ocean, the journeying was not yet over for many of the new settlers. The patterns of mobility that were common in seventeenth- and eighteenth-century England were repeated in the New World, though, of course, the distances that were travelled were usually far greater. Some moved to better themselves, others because of the shortage of work. Although there were no towns to attract immigrants, a mobile population responded to the ways in which the colonial economy developed. Recent research has revised the view that the New England colonies were the epitome of residential stability and has pointed to considerable variations in the levels of mobility and to important regional differences. J. P. R. Horn has identified the first signs of a significant volume of out-migration from

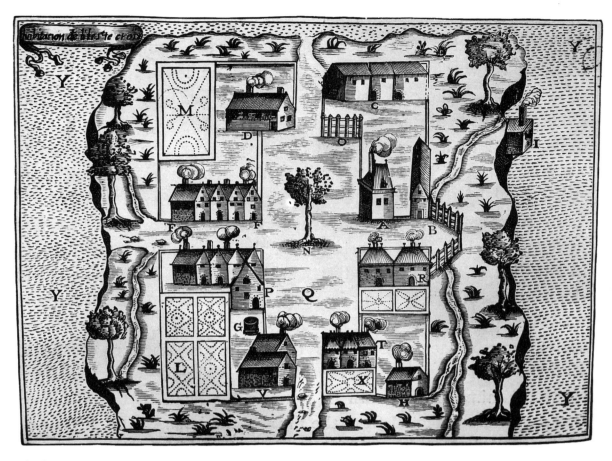

Virginia to Maryland as early as the middle decades of the seventeenth century. Some of the migrants from the Chesapeake went to North Carolina, but most moved to Pennsylvania, where the population rose from about 700 people in 1680 to 18,000 by 1700. A substantial British presence had by then been established along the Atlantic seaboard. By 1733 the British colonies—Virginia, Massachusetts, New Hampshire, New York, Connecticut, Maryland, Rhode Island, Delaware, Pennsylvania, North Carolina, New Jersey, South Carolina, and Georgia—numbered 13.

Meanwhile, the French had become well established in Canada. The Newfoundland cod fishery and the St Lawrence fur trade had attracted early settlers, so that the population of the colony of New France approached 3,000 by 1660. In the decade after 1666 more than 4,000 immigrants were sent to New France at the expense of the Crown. By the middle of the eighteenth century, just before Britain's military victory over the French, Canada's population had reached 60,000. The number of British immigrants increased after the American Revolution and rose substantially after the Napoleonic Wars, when Quebec was the cheapest New World destination because of the number and kind of ships employed in the timber trade.

THE FRENCH IN CANADA (1604)

The French explorer Samuel de Champlain, whose *Voyages* was published in 1613, is a major source of information about the earliest French activities in Canada. Ile Ste Croix was the first settlement in Acadia, whose name conjured up images of rustic contentment according to classical ideals.

By 1815 nearly 600 ships per annum called at Quebec alone. By that time, emigration to the New World was on a scale undreamed of by earlier generations.

Residential Stability

While some people roamed the land or emigrated overseas in search of a better life, many others remained loyal to the neighbourhood in which they were born. We have noted in Chapter 2 how each of the English counties still has its distinctive set of surnames. Local studies of both rural and urban communities in the sixteenth and seventeenth centuries have often stressed the importance of a stable core of families that remained in or near the same place for generation after generation. The populous open-field parish of Wigston, Leicestershire, had its long-established families of Boulters, Freers, Smiths, Vanns, Wards, Johnsons, Langtons, Holmeses, Noones, and Abbotts, while 80 miles to the west, the pastoral farmers of the Shropshire parish of Myddle included such long-term residents as the Lloyds, Gittings, Goughs, Braynes, Groomes, Tylers, Juxes, and Formstons. Most of these families were the owners or occupiers of small or medium-sized farms. They had neither the resources nor the ambition to move to a larger holding, but they earned a sufficient living to survive. The families that moved on tended to be either the rich or the very poor.

The surnames of these core groups of stable families are the ones that appear time and time again in parish registers. In sixteenth- and seventeenth-century Myddle, 4 out of every 5 entries in the parish register noted the names of a stable group of small farmers and craftsmen, some of whose families had been there for five, six, or seven generations. As the families that failed in the male line often passed on their property through a daughter, continuity in a direct line is even more common than a study of surnames would suggest. Some of the richer farming families were also long resident in the parish of Myddle. The poor cottagers were the ones who were most likely to move on, though even some of this group stayed for two or three generations.

Such was the long-term stability of the small farmers of Myddle that it was the holdings that did not remain in the hands of the same family that were the exception. Many of the farming and craft families that held land in Myddle at the beginning of the eighteenth century had been there since at least the reign of Henry VIII. A John Lloyd is named in the lay subsidy rolls of 1524 and 1544, and in the manorial rolls of 1528–42, and six generations of his direct descendants continued to live in a freehold tenement near the north door of the church in Myddle throughout the sixteenth and seventeenth centuries. A William Formston of Marton, who was recorded in the manorial court rolls for 1529, was the ancestor of the various branches of the

Formston family which held three different leasehold tenements in the parish in the Elizabethan period; the family remained in Myddle until well into the nineteenth century. The Braynes were descended from a William Brayne, who contributed to the lay subsidy that was collected in 1544 and who was subsequently described as a husbandman. The senior line failed with the fifth William Brayne, but a junior branch continued the name for at least another two generations in the same parish. They are just a few of the farming families that were resident in Myddle over a long period of time.

The Lloyds, Formstons, and Braynes—and many others like them— were members of larger family groups, or dynasties, that were resident in various parts of the 'country' around Myddle. The hearth tax returns of 1672 note 146 householders in Shropshire with the common surname Lloyd, 11 named Brayne, and 8 named Formston. The Braynes and the Formstons were among those families whose surnames had been derived locally and who were still largely confined to their county of origin. Shropshire was similar to other counties at this time in having relatively small numbers of house-holders who bore distinctive surnames that were unknown or very rare in other parts of England. Many of the householders who shared the same un-usual surname may have had a common ancestor. These distinctive names in Shropshire included some that were derived from local place-names, such as Blakeway (24), from a farm near Much Wenlock, Millychopp or Mellychopp (27), from Millichope, Corfield (34), Noneley (8), and possibly Chidlow (7), Kynaston (16), and Rowley (31). Baugh or Bough (12) and Fewtrell (12) are two other characteristic Shropshire surnames, whose derivations are uncertain.

The 146 Lloyds were high on the list of those numerous families which possessed surnames that are commonly thought of as being Welsh in origin, but which may equally have arisen on the English side of the border. Though the 202 Shropshire householders who still had ap forms of surnames were undoubtedly from Wales, many of the people with surnames such as Edwards or Williams may have been descended from families who had al-ways lived in Shropshire or another of the Welsh border counties. The most frequent surnames in Shropshire in 1672 were of this type: Jones (377), Davies (368), Evans (219), Williams (175), Pryce or Preece (160), Edwards (153), Lloyd (146), Morris (143), Thomas (117), Griffiths (110), Phillips (107), Powell(s)(107), Roberts (107), Hughes (103), Owen(s)(97), Richards (87), Lewis (84), Rogers (81), Reynolds (71), Gough (70), Gittins (62), Howell(s)(55), Bowen (51), Vaughan (47), Maddox (45), Beddowes (42), Meredith (39), Prichard (39), and Pugh (39). Amongst the names of un-doubted English origin, only Smith (170), Browne (110), Taylor (103), Farmer (47), and Corbett (40) ranked with these common names.

The hearth tax return of 1672 for Shropshire lists 17,737 householders, but only 16,380 names in the list are legible. The pattern of migration into the county suggested by these names is most striking. Very few of the locative

YEOMEN'S HOUSES

Henry Best's House, Elmswell, East Riding of Yorkshire (above)
In the Middle Ages the manor of Elmswell was held by St Mary's Abbey, York. It was bought in 1597 by Henry Best, a London scrivener, who sold it to his brother James. It passed to James's eldest son Paul, who in 1618 sold it to his brother Henry, the author of a famous detailed account of farming practices. Henry Best was a yeoman farmer whose main interest was in sheep.

The house retains much of its seventeenth-century character, though it was altered both internally and externally in the late eighteenth and early nineteenth centuries. The property remained in the possession of the Bests for another 200 years, though they moved away during the early eighteenth century. They sold it in 1844.

Bishops' House, Sheffield (below)
The Blythe family lived at Norton Lees, now part of modern Sheffield, from the reign of Edward III. John de Blithe held land at 'Le Lyes' in 1376. Benjamin Blythe sold the property nearly 400 years later in 1753. Several memorials of the family are in Norton Church.

Their timber-framed house dates from *c.*1500, with the parlour range (to the left) remodelled about fifty years later. The Blythes were yeomen farmers who were middlemen in the scythe trade, selling scythes all over Yorkshire and north-eastern England, and in Scotland. The name Bishops' House was attached to the building in Victorian times in memory of the two brothers who were bishops in Henry VII's reign.

surnames from the north of England that were found in other Midland counties had appeared by that time in Shropshire. The common surnames listed above, which had originated either in Wales or in the Welsh border counties, accounted for 1 in every 4.8 householders; if we add the less common names of a similar origin, the proportion would be about 1 in 4. The people who bore these names could not all be related to each other, yet the distribution patterns of even the popular surnames suggest that families had moved only in a restricted area. Indeed, the experience of the Lloyds, Goughs, and Gittings of Myddle shows that some of these families remained loyal not only to the wider district of the Welsh borders; they put down roots in a particular parish which remained their base for several generations.

The residential stability of a great part of the English population in the early modern era is evident when the histories of individual families are examined in detail. The work of demographic historians who have emphasized the extent of geographical mobility has not taken sufficient account of this underlying structural continuity. It is true that in the Nottinghamshire parish of Clayworth no less than 61.8 per cent of the people who were recorded in a listing of 1676 were not there 12 years later, but a closer examination of these and earlier listings shows that the turnover of families, as distinct from individuals, was not exceptional. The people who moved out of the parish were the young farm lads and domestic servants, who left upon the expiration of their yearly contracts. The established farming families stayed put. A comparison of the listing of 1688 and the protestation return of 1642 shows that 2 out of every 5 surnames that were present in Clayworth in 1688 had been there for nearly half a century. Some families had lived in the parish over a much longer period of time.

The sharp contrast between a stable core of families and a mobile, temporary population is made clear by Jos Kingston's analysis of the 1,319 entries in the burial register of the Derbyshire parish of Norton between 1560 and 1653. Nearly half the entries were accounted for by 27 families of farmers and scythe-makers. The remaining entries noted 258 different surnames, 125 of which appeared only once and 45 only twice. This sort of pattern is repeated in rural parishes in every part of England.

The scythe-makers of Norton were a prosperous group of craftsmen-farmers, whose investment in premises and craft skills was passed on to their children. Some of these families were still making scythes in Norton when a local directory was published in 1787. Millers, maltsters, tanners, dyers, and a host of other craftsmen were equally likely to stay put, whether they practised their trades in the towns or in the countryside. Tradesmen and specialized occupational groups in certain quarters of the major towns and cities could be equally tenacious in their choice of homes. Dr Mary Prior's study of Fisher Row, Oxford, has revealed how 'a very tight-knit community of boat-people who were united both by occupation and kinship' formed a stable group on the riverside, while a transient body of carters, drovers, and seasonal workers were continually moving in and out. It was these stable groups that formed the core of the local communities of England.

Even in London, the stability of certain families—at least in the better-off quarters of the city—was greater than one might expect. Dr Jeremy Boulton has shown that in Southwark during the early seventeenth century the overall levels of residential persistence compare favourably with those found in the countryside. His evidence is taken from parish records, including a series of Easter books that list all the householders. After one year 79 per cent of his sample from St Saviour's parish were living in the same dwelling and after 10 years 24 per cent were still there. Those who moved often remained within the parish; others who disappeared from view may not have travelled very far beyond the parish boundary. Families moved to larger houses when they could afford to, and back to smaller houses in old age, as they tend to do today.

The old saying that it was 'better to wed over the midden [or mixen] than over the moor' was current in Scotland and the north of England by the seventeenth century. Thomas Fuller quoted it in his account of Cheshire in 1662 and glossed it by remarking that 'The gentry in Cheshire find it more profitable to match within their County, than to bring a Bride out of other Shires.' His observation rings even more true of families further down the social scale. Wherever marriage patterns have been studied from the evidence of parish registers the conclusion has been that partners were overwhelmingly chosen from within a radius of 20 miles or so.

The families which remained loyal to the neighbourhoods where they originated were the ones which transmitted the local culture from one generation to the next. Incomers, or their children, adapted their behaviour to the accepted customs of their new settlement. In particular, they learned to speak like the natives. Even today, an informed listener can often place an accent within a relatively small area, corresponding to the old notion of a 'country'. These persistent differences in local speech can be explained only by the residential continuity of a core group of families who set the norms to which immigrants eventually conformed. Local speech patterns confirm the evidence of the marked concentration of certain surnames in pointing unerringly to the long-term stability of certain families in the midst of all the coming and going of others.

AFTER 1800

From the second half of the eighteenth century onwards the national population grew at an unprecedented rate. At the beginning of the nineteenth century the population of England and Wales stood at about 9 millions. By the First World War it had quadrupled to 36 millions. Some of the Victorian towns and cities grew at even quicker rates and many an industrial village was transformed. Entirely new communities were founded alongside mines, quarries, and iron works. People left the countryside in droves in search of work at these places or in the hope of a better life overseas. The railways and the steamship made long-distance migration an attractive option. Quick, cheap transport offered everyone the opportunity to be far more mobile than earlier generations. Yet clearly many were content with their lot. The residential stability of certain families is as marked a feature of Victorian England as it had been in Tudor and Stuart times.

Mobility

The Registrar-General, in his report on the 1871 census, commented that

The improved roads, the facilities offered under the railway system, the wonderful development of the mercantile marine, the habit of travelling about and the increasing knowledge of workmen have all tended to facilitate the flow of people from spots where they are not wanted to fields where their labour is in demand. The establishment of a manufacture or the opening of a new mine rallies men to it, not only from the vicinity but from remote parts of the kingdom.

In a famous pioneering article in 1885, E. G. Ravenstein identified five types of migrants: those who moved only from one part of a town or rural parish to another; those who 'journeyed but a little distance'; those who migrated by stages, until on census night they were far from their place of birth; those who moved long distances; and temporary migrants. He concluded that most migration was of the first two categories, of local or short-distance movement. The 1881 census data revealed that 'of every one hundred migrants enumerated in England and Wales as many as 53.7 had gone no further than a border county'. The older patterns of mobility, by which the majority moved around their 'country' but rarely ventured outside, still remained the norm.

One group who were prepared to travel long distances were the coalminers. The opening-up of the nation's coalfields on an undreamed-of scale offered opportunities for men to obtain work in places far from their original homes. At the beginning of the nineteenth century only about 50,000 men were employed in Britain's mines; by the eve of the First World War the work-force numbered over 1 million. Who were the people who moved to the new pit villages that sprang up alongside the mines, sometimes in places where there had been little or no settlement before?

Brinley Thomas, writing in 1930 before the census enumerators' returns were made available for study, observed that most migrants into the Glamorganshire coalfield between 1861 and 1911 were local in origin or were farm labourers from Wiltshire, Somerset, Devon, Herefordshire, and the Cirencester district of Gloucestershire, who were attracted by higher wages.

He noted the large number of single young men amongst the immigrants and the fact that married miners often left their families to look after their smallholdings in the Welsh countryside, returning to them for a few weeks every summer. Different patterns have been noted elsewhere. Michael Sill's study of Hetton-le-Hole, a Durham coalfield village with a population of 641 in 1851 (618 of whom were immigrants), has revealed that most of the miners had moved with their families, not as young, single men, and that they moved frequently from colliery to colliery; 95 per cent of the migrants were born in County Durham or the neighbouring counties of Northumberland, Cumberland, Westmorland, Yorkshire, and Lancashire.

Andrew Walker's work on the south Yorkshire coalfield parish of Darfield points to more complicated patterns. Between 1861 and 1881, when this part of the coalfield was being developed, most immigrants travelled only short distances, principally from other parts of the West Riding. Long-distance migrants came in surges, whenever a new colliery was opened. During the decades of slower population growth further immigration was much more local in scale; growth was achieved mainly through the considerable natural increase of the indigenous population. The West Midland counties of Staffordshire, Shropshire, Warwickshire, and Worcestershire formed by far the most common area from which long-distance immigrants were drawn. The mid-Victorian exhaustion of Black Country seams and the drainage problems which hampered further expansion there caused many miners to

SOUTH WALES COAL MINERS

A group of Welsh miners in Clyne Valley pose with their safety lamps after completing a shift in 1913. At that time, the South Wales coalfield employed 250,000 men.

try their luck elsewhere. Over 75 per cent of the West Midlands miners who moved to Darfield village, Low Valley, and Snape Hill came with their young families. However, the men who worked alongside them, who came from other areas, were often single; the Irish miners in Darfield were nearly always single men. The immigrants tended to cluster together, sometimes in the same row of terraced houses. Once they had settled, the miners and their families tended to stay put. Most did not even move short distances to other settlements within the same parish. The new pit villages thus quickly gained a strong sense of community. Migration did not lead to a severe dislocation of family life. Even the single men who were recorded as lodgers on census night were often living with someone they knew before they moved to Darfield. About 1 in 3 lodgers shared a common birthplace with another member of the household.

Martin White's study of immigrants into Victorian Scunthorpe shows the same large degree of familial migration in search of employment at the new iron works. Many of these immigrants also came from the Black Country. The fact that both the coal industry and the iron trade offered few opportunities for female employment may have made it easier for whole families to decide to move. Here again, the main exception to the general rule that men moved with their families was the body of single Irish men.

Movement into industrial towns that were sited away from the coalfield followed similar patterns. Professor Michael Anderson's detailed analysis of Preston has shown that in 1851 no less than 80 per cent of the town's migrant population had been born within 30 miles of their new homes. He showed that kinship links were not destroyed by the creation of industrial societies; instead, those societies actually fostered such links. Migrants retained their connections with their home base, and family members clustered together in their new locations. In 1851, 23 per cent of the households in Preston contained lodgers; 1 in 5 of the lodgers who were not born in Preston or in Ireland had been born in the same community as a co-residing member of the nuclear or extended family of the household head.

The Irish had emigrated to England, Scotland, and Wales in large numbers long before the famine years of the 1840s. The 1841 census returns for England and Wales numbered 289,404 Irish-born residents in England and Wales and that for Scotland listed 126,321. Ten years later the totals had soared to 519,959 and 207,367, respectively. In England and Wales the peak was reached in 1861 when 601,634 were recorded, but in Scotland the peak was not reached until 20 years later, when 218,745 were counted. These figures underestimate the size of the Irish population because they do not include those children who were born to Irish parents who had already moved to England, Scotland, or Wales. We need, therefore, to inflate the estimates that only 3 per cent of the population of England and Wales in 1861 were Irish and that in Scotland the Irish never accounted for more than 7 per cent. The Irish immigrants and their children may eventually have reached 1 million.

No. of House-holder's Schedule	Name of Street, Place, or Road, and Name or No. of House	Name and Surname of each Person who abode in the house, on the Night of the 30th March, 1851	Relation to Head of Family	Condition	Age of		Rank, Profession, or Occupation	Where Born	Whether Blind, or Deaf-and-Dumb
					Males	Females			
36	Gt. Howard St.	Marg.t Donohugh	Wife	M		30		Ireland	
"	" "	William Rogers	Lodger	Un	16		Labourer	Do	
"	" "	Barthlow Donough	Do	Un	6		Scholar	Do	
37	Trafalgar Place Gt. Howard St.	Pat.k Cummings	Head	Mr	37	-	Dock Labourer	Ireland	
"		Cth Do	Wife	M		37		Do	
"	" "	James Do	Son	Un	14		Scholar	Do	
"	" "	Pat.k Do	Dr.	Un	12		Do	Do	
"	" "	James McDonough	Lodger	M	35		House Joiner	Do	
"	" "	Ann Do	Do	M		26		Do	
"	" "	Mary Do	Do	Un		1		Lancashire Lpool	
38	Do Do	Hugh Hurley	Head	M	40		Dock Labourer	Do	
"	" "	Marg.t Do	Wife	Married		34		Do	
"	" "	Eleanor Do	Dr.	Un		8	Scholar	Lancashire Lpool	
"	" "	James Do	Son	Un	6		do	Do Do	
"	" "	Mary Do	Dr.			3	Do	Do Do	
"	" "	George Do	Son			4 years		Do Do	
"	" "	Eleanor Do	Visitor	Widow		60	Annuitant	Ireland	
"	" "	Tho.s Winn	Lodger	M	44		Shoemaker	Do	

Total of Houses: 1 2 U B   Total of Persons: 4/10 38

The migrant often followed a well-worn route from his particular part of Ireland. Ulstermen favoured Scotland, people from Munster went to London, and a significant number of those who ended up in Bradford started either from Queen's County or from Mayo and Sligo. London was the most favoured destination, but even there those who were born in Ireland amounted to only 4.6 per cent of the population in 1851. In only three Registrar-General's districts—St Giles-in-the-Fields, St Olave, Southwark, and Whitechapel—did the numbers of Irish-born people exceed a tenth of the population. The proportions were much higher in the northern industrial cities. Liverpool's proximity made it an obvious choice for the Irish emigrant. By 1851, 22 per cent of Liverpool's population were Irish-born. In Glasgow the Irish accounted for 18 per cent of the population, and in Manchester they accounted for 13 per cent. Slightly higher proportions were recorded in a few smaller Lancashire towns such as Wigan, but in many of the largest places the Irish formed only a small minority. In Bristol in 1851 and in Sheffield 10 years later the Irish numbered less than 3.5 per cent of the population. The impact of Irish immigration was therefore highly selective.

The Irish peasants who settled in the industrial slums were confronted with the suspicion, and often downright hostility, of the native population. Alan O'Day has commented on how the Irish tended to cluster in certain districts of the towns that they settled in and on how within each Irish cluster there were smaller groupings based on the county of origin in Ireland. Those whose fortunes improved gradually moved to new homes on the fringes of the Irish settlements. The great majority had to remain in poor, sometimes squalid, accommodation, for most workers were unskilled. In 1881 it was said that 82 per cent of the Irish-born immigrants were day-labourers. The 1891 census report noted that in Liverpool the Irish were 'engaged in the rougher kinds of unskilled labour, the proportions of artisans and of dealers of all kinds and grades being very small'. Historians have confirmed that Irish advancement was very slow.

The Irish came in dwindling numbers after the 1860s, but throughout the nineteenth century they remained the largest group of immigrants. The Germans who came to live in London, Manchester, and Bradford formed a distinctive and relatively prosperous group, many of whom were involved in finance, but they never formed more than 0.1 per cent of the population. In the late nineteenth century London also attracted small communities of Italians and Chinese and between 1881 and 1914 provided homes for much larger numbers of Jewish and other refugees from parts of the Russian empire, notably Poland and Lithuania. The 1911 census recorded 82,844 Russian Poles, who formed 0.3 per cent of the population of England and Wales. They settled mainly in Stepney and adjacent parts of the East End of London, but distinctive communities were also created in the Leylands area of Leeds and the Redbank district of Manchester. Later refugees, such as the Poles, Ukrainians, and Hungarians, were not as selective, but the large numbers of immigrants who came from the former colonies in the Caribbean,

India, Pakistan, and elsewhere between the 1950s and 1970s have settled in as concentrated a manner as did the Irish and the Russian Jews in the nineteenth century, so that whole areas of London, Birmingham, Leicester, Bradford, and many other industrial towns are now almost exclusively occupied by first- or second-generation immigrants from the Commonwealth.

The immigrants were not the only people on the move in the nineteenth century. For example, although the majority of people in north Staffordshire were born locally, the coalfield attracted immigrants from Lancashire, Flintshire, and Denbighshire. The east Warwickshire coalfield provided employment for men from Leicestershire and Northamptonshire as well as from other parts of Warwickshire. Migrants to Birmingham and the Black Country came mostly from other parts of Staffordshire, Warwickshire, and Worcestershire, but some travelled from Lancashire, Yorkshire, East Anglia, Wales, and London. Short-distance migration was the norm in the East Midlands, too, but here again the great centres of commerce and industry attracted people from much further afield. The distances that immigrants travelled increased as the economy expanded and as transport improved. In Nottingham in 1861 half of those who had not been born in the town had been born in the county; by 1891 this proportion had been reduced to 20 per cent. In Leicester 45 per cent of the inhabitants in 1851 were migrants; by 1911 newcomers comprised 62 per cent of the population; most of them came from the surrounding villages. So too did most of the migrants who had moved into Lincoln by the mid-nineteenth century; other small groups of 20 or so came from the neighbouring market towns of Boston, Gainsborough, Louth, Horncastle, and Sleaford. Of the 17,536 people who lived in the city in 1851, 47 per cent were born outside its boundaries; 22 per cent came from other counties, mainly Nottinghamshire and Yorkshire. Meanwhile, far more people were moving out of Lincolnshire in search of employment elsewhere.

The mass movement of country-folk to the towns and industrial districts gathered pace during the reign of Victoria. While the national population soared to new heights, that of many rural areas declined significantly. Only three English counties (Cornwall, Huntingdon, and Rutland) and three Welsh counties (Cardigan, Montgomery, and Radnor) recorded absolute decreases between 1841 and 1911, but in many other counties the extent of rural depopulation is hidden in such figures because of the growth of neighbouring towns. In Norfolk, for instance, the population of Norwich, Yarmouth, and King's Lynn grew by 20.6 per cent, while that of the rest of the county fell by 2 per cent. Professor Alan Armstrong has shown how the statistics relating to registration districts, rather than counties, reveal a persistent, considerable drain away from the countryside. The net outflow was most marked in the south as a whole during the decades 1851–61 and 1871–81, and in the north during 1881–91. This movement does not coincide neatly with the ebb and flow of agricultural prosperity, but it represents a substan-

tial absolute decline in the agricultural labour force. By 1911 this had fallen by 23 per cent from its mid-nineteenth-century peak. The 'Ag. Labs.' of the census returns and parish registers formed 21.5 per cent of the total occupied labour force in 1851, but only 8.5 per cent 60 years later.

One of the best-known verses in A. E. Housman's *The Shropshire Lad* reads:

> Clunton and Clunbury,
> Clungunford and Clun,
> Are the quietest places
> Under the sun.

These places were particularly quiet at the time that Housman was writing because their population had fallen dramatically in the late nineteenth century. The effects on the countryside of the drift to the towns is nowhere more evident than in the beautiful, under-populated Welsh borders. In the Clun registration district the population dropped by 23 per cent in a single decade. Similar figures could be quoted from all parts of Britain that relied purely on farming or whose industries had collapsed. Thus, in Swaledale, where the lead-fields became exhausted, the population declined by nearly 50 per cent between 1871 and 1891. The young were the most likely to leave.

OLD GANG SMELT MILL, NEAR REETH, YORKSHIRE
The ruins of this smelting mill in Swaledale provide a powerful visual reminder of the lead industry, which fell into decay during the reign of Victoria. Emigration was on such a scale that the population of Swaledale declined by nearly 50 per cent between 1871 and 1891.

The rector of Welborne, Norfolk, commented in the late 1890s that of the 56 names on the school register in 1881 only 2 remained in the village. Young girls were particularly prone to depart, for the demand for domestic servants remained buoyant. On the eve of the First World War domestic service was still by far the largest single occupational category. Ravenstein had noted in the 1880s that short-distance migrants were more commonly women than men. The majority of urban immigrants were female.

We have as yet little idea of whether migrants tended to move just once or by stages. The birthplaces of children recorded in census returns offer some clues. The railways were clearly important, not just for their ability to move people quickly and cheaply, but for stirring imaginations. They also hastened the decline of many rural crafts and small industries by increasing the competitive power of the towns. Rural craftsmen joined the farm labourers and the domestic servants who left the countryside in the Victorian era. Whereas the drift of the national population had anciently been in a southern or south-eastern direction, it was now reversed towards the coalfields of northern England, Scotland, the north Midlands, and south Wales. The exhaustion or severe contraction of these coalfields in recent times has meant that the old pattern has been re-established as people once again head for the south-east.

A steady trickle of emigrants heading south had long been a familiar feature of the social history of north-west England. In the nineteenth century the pressure to move out of the area increased as Cumberland and Westmorland shared the national experience of a huge rise in population, but at the same time coastal industries attracted immigrants from other parts of the United Kingdom. The patterns of mobility became more complicated than before. Over 5,000 agricultural labourers and female servants left the Cumbrian countryside during the three decades after 1851, and this outflow was sustained during the remainder of the Victorian and the Edwardian period. The younger sons of farmers and rural craftsmen joined the labourers and servants in this mass exit. By 1891 well over 100,000 Cumbrian-born people were living in other parts of England or Wales; they corresponded to almost a third of the total population of Cumbria at that time.

Dr John Marshall has shown that those who moved from the fells were at first cautious in their movements. They tended to go for the nearest town or industrial district, where they probably knew other migrants and where the speech was reassuringly familiar. Many moved reluctantly; even though wages were higher in the coalfield, lead-miners moved only when they were forced to by unemployment. The Cumbrian parish officials who supplied information to the Poor Law Commissioners of 1832 did not regard their local labourers as especially migration-prone. Dr Marshall concludes that migration in the region must not be considered in purely economic terms. The habit took time to grow, and psychological as well as economic pressures played a role.

Following the initial move to a place that was not far from home, the

Cumbrian migrant sometimes decided to try his luck in an industrial town in a neighbouring county, often settling there alongside his fellow Cumbrians. By far the greatest attraction was Liverpool. At the time of the 1891 census, 5,801 Liverpudlians were recorded as having been born in Cumberland or Westmorland. The experience of most Cumbrian migrants paralleled that of English people elsewhere. They tended to move only short distances at any one time, except when the opening of a railway or the sinking of a pit created new opportunities. On the whole, migration took the form of a slow, steady drift.

Meanwhile, outsiders were attracted to the industrial areas on the Cumbrian coast, especially in the boom decades of the 1870s and 1880s. Thus, nearly 60 per cent of the inhabitants of the ore-mining settlement on Cleator Moor in 1861 were Irish. In 1883 about a third of the population of Dronfield, Derbyshire, moved from their town upon the closure of the steel works of Wilson Cammell; most of them followed the firm to its new site at Workington, where the town's population rose from 14,000 in 1881 to 25,200 in 1891. In the words of a local newspaper, 'Never before had an almost complete community been transplanted into West Cumberland.'

The Cumbrian population remained overwhelmingly local in origin, however. Dr Marshall has written:

It is abundantly clear, from an analysis of common regional surnames . . . that native Cumbrians took full advantage of opportunities on their doorsteps. In

A LAKELAND SCENE (1832) This engraving after Henry Gastineau's painting of *The Vale of Keswick and Crosthwaite Church from Applethwaite* shows a peaceful rural scene before the railways had opened up the Lake District to the traveller.

Maryport, Dixons, Messengers and Nicholsons were well established in trade; in Cockermouth, Bells, Bowmans and Huddarts; in Workington, Armstrongs, Coulthards, Fishers, Kitchins and Mossops. Every one of these names goes far back into Cumbrian history, and nearly every one can be found in abundance in the present-day regional telephone directory.

As we shall see, in all parts of the country some of the old local families remained attached to their roots in this way while others tried to improve their fortunes by migrating. The migrants increasingly tried their luck overseas.

Emigration

The number of people who emigrated from Europe to the United States of America and the colonies during the course of the nineteenth century will never be known with certainty. Emigration was voluntary; some countries did not count their migrants in the early decades; and even when data were collected the gathering was done on different bases. The British government, for instance, simply recorded the departures of passengers according to ship. It is now thought that the old estimate of 60 million emigrants from Europe is too high. Nevertheless, it seems likely that during the course of the nineteenth century about 10 million people left the British Isles, never to return. The population of Ireland in 1900 was half that of what it had been 50 years earlier. By contrast, the population of the United States of America rose from about 4 million in 1790 to 23 million in 1850. Emigrants went from every European country and included people from every occupation and social class.

Before this unprecedented mass movement, about three-quarters of the residents of colonial America were descended from earlier British settlers. The English were scattered throughout the 13 states; the Welsh were concentrated in Pennsylvania; some of the Scots and the families from Ulster had ventured beyond the Appalachians. Charlotte Erickson has estimated that in 1790 about 60 per cent of the white population of the USA were of English and Welsh stock, 8 per cent were Scottish, 6 per cent were Scots-Irish, and less than 4 per cent were southern Irish. After a century and a half of settlement and a war of independence, most of these families no longer thought of themselves as British. The restoration of peace in Europe in 1815 allowed the unprecedented immigration of numerous Germans, Irish, and Scandinavians. Later in the century, Italians, Slavs, Jews, and Orientals swelled the immigrant tide. These newcomers caught the attention of the American Press, but this same era also witnessed an even larger influx of migrants from Great Britain.

In the late 1820s trade depression forced thousands of skilled artisans to flee abroad. A constant stream of industrial workers followed in their footsteps during the rest of the century. Many of those who had worked in industry were attracted by the prospect of cheap land. One settler commented, 'It is very rare that I come across an Englishman who follows farming that followed the same occupation in England; they are generally from the manufacturing districts.' Letters from emigrants to their families back in England constantly refer to the opportunities of obtaining cheap land and livestock and to the availability of game, as well as to the attractions of constant employment and easy social relations. More than half of the English people who had settled in the USA by 1850 were to be found in predominantly rural states. The 1841 census for England and Wales, which was taken at a time of great hardship in many of the industrial districts, placed the West Riding of Yorkshire and Lancashire at the head of the counties whence people emigrated. Charlotte Erickson has noted, however, that the majority of emigrants came from a few agricultural counties in the south and south-west and on the north-west coast. She concludes that perhaps we should not be so sure that the industrial worker was pre-eminent among English migrants.

During the first part of the nineteenth century emigrants crossed the Atlantic in wooden ships which left from many small ports in the spring, so as to arrive as the ice was breaking in the St Lawrence. Steamships began to take passengers in the 1840s, but the huge numbers of Irish people who hoped to escape from the potato famine were transported in the old fashion. Some of the worst tragedies on the Atlantic crossing occurred during this time when every ship that was available was pressed into service. It was not until the late 1860s that virtually all emigrants to the USA and Canada came by steamship. The great majority travelled steerage, with hundreds of

ON BOARD AN EMIGRANT SHIP (1871)

Passengers on a transatlantic ship near the end of their journey, as depicted by M. W. Ridley in *Land Ho!*.

people crammed together below decks. About two-thirds of the emigrants embarked at Liverpool, where British people were joined by others who had already travelled long distances from many different parts of continental Europe. Poverty and persecution drove many to the New World; others went in the hope of bettering themselves. In the first half of the nineteenth century the typical emigrants were young couples with children; males and females went in similar numbers. During the later nineteenth century, however, many more single males travelled alone.

By the mid-Victorian period large numbers of specialist workers were being attracted to the mills and mines of America. The American textile industries were heavily reliant on the experience of skilled operatives from Britain. The mills that were erected about Fall River in the 1860s and 1870s and in New Bedford in the 1880s drew many workers from Lancashire to southern Massachusetts. Some of them were the children of Irish people who had settled in Lancashire towns earlier in the century. The American woollen and worsted industries were equally dependent upon West Riding workers, and the silk industry in Paterson attracted about 15,000 Macclesfielders between 1870 and 1893, as well as many Frenchmen.

A NEW ENGLAND TEXTILE MILL (1870)

Emigrants from the Lancashire and Yorkshire textile towns did not find their working conditions very different once they arrived in America. This pen-and-ink sketch shows the weaving room in the Northampton Mills.

Coal- and ore-miners came from many depressed parts of England, notably Cornwall, potters came from Staffordshire, and metalworkers moved from Birmingham and Sheffield.

Overseas emigration to the colonies, but not to America, received some encouragement from central government and local authorities. Even before the Poor Law Amendment Act of 1834 magistrates regarded emigration as a cure for the problem of a 'surplus population' in southern England. The authorities responsible for the New Poor Law were ready to help those who wished to emigrate; between 1836 and 1846 about 14,000 English and Welsh people received assistance from Poor Law guardians in order to emigrate to the colonies, especially Canada. Another source of funding was the Colonial Commission of Land and Emigration, which was set up in 1842 to administer funds raised by the sales of Crown lands in the colonies so as to aid the emigration of successful applicants. By 1869 the commissioners had assisted well over 300,000 UK (including Irish) citizens to emigrate, chiefly to Australia. Professor Alan Armstrong has concluded that while such sources of assistance were probably crucial in the case of agricultural labourers, the bulk of British emigration was financed privately and was often independent. A large majority of those who emigrated went not to the colonies but to America. During the first 30 years of Victoria's reign the USA received some 3.5 million migrants from the United Kingdom, whereas Australia and New Zealand received 1 million and Canada took 0.75 million.

As the agricultural depression began to bite in the 1870s, rural areas lost far more people than before by overseas emigration. Farm labourers, shepherds, gardeners, and carters were prominent amongst those who left the countryside at this time. The new agricultural trade unions promoted emigration on the grounds that a smaller work-force would benefit from higher wages. Yet the movement of such people was not a massive one. Charlotte Erickson has used American passenger lists of 1885–8 to show that almost 4 out of every 5 men landing in New York gave a principal town as their place of last residence. (Of course, many of these men may have lived in a town for a relatively brief period after moving from the countryside.)

By the late 1870s some colonies had begun to phase out their various assistance programmes. Even so, the number of emigrants from England and Wales continued to rise sharply, reaching over 600,000 in 1881–90 against about 160,000 in 1871–80. The number of emigrants born in 34 rural counties rose in absolute terms by just over a third, but fell as a proportion of all emigrants. During the 1880s, the peak decade for emigration, about two-thirds of British emigrants were from the cities and industrial districts; only one-sixth were farm labourers. Alan Armstrong has concluded that despite a well-marked preference for country-men on the part of receiving countries, it seems probable that the majority of the labourers who left the land were destined to fill the places of townsmen who at most times showed a greater propensity to emigrate.

The total number of British immigrants living in the USA has been esti-

EMIGRANTS FROM
LIVERPOOL (1903)
This engraving from the
front page of the *Sphere, an
Illustrated Newspaper for the
Home*, dated 16 May 1903,
depicts some of the 1,200
passengers who left
Liverpool on the *Ionian* in
search of a new life in
Canada.

mated at about 600,000 in 1850 and at over 2 million in 1890. By 1870 the
Irish (mainly Catholics from southern and western Ireland) comprised 33
per cent of the foreign-born population of the USA. The English, Scots, and
Welsh together constituted another 14 per cent. It has been claimed that during the next half-century more English, Scots, and Welsh people settled in
America than during the whole previous 250 years. The figures cannot be established with certainty, but something in the order of 2.5 to 3 million English migrants settled in the USA between 1870 and 1920, together with well
over half a million Scots, and fewer than 100,000 Welsh. They were soon to
be heavily outnumbered by immigrants from other parts of Europe. Many
of these settlers eventually decided to return, however. It had never been
their intention to stay for ever. As many as 1 in 4 of those who emigrated

to America from Europe in the early twentieth century did not settle there permanently.

The United States of America remained the favourite destination of British emigrants throughout the nineteenth century. Until 1852 Canada was the second most popular choice, but in that year gold was discovered in Australia; it was 15 years before Canada regained its ascendancy. At the time of the 1881 Canadian census, 33 per cent of the English- and Gaelic-speaking population were Irish by ancestry, 30 per cent were English, 25 per cent were Scottish (mainly uprooted Highlanders), but less than 0.5 per cent were Welsh. By the early twentieth century the USA was no longer the favoured destination of those who emigrated from Britain. By 1905 more Englishmen were going to Canada instead and by 1907 more Scots were going there also. This was partly because the supply of cheap land in the USA was becoming exhausted, partly because the opportunities for skilled work were no longer as great as they had once been. Unlike the Irish and the emigrants from continental Europe, the British sought more remunerative employment than rough work in the ports and industrial cities. After the First World War the number of Britons emigrating to the USA declined considerably.

The use of the penalty of transportation overseas fell into disuse after the American War of Independence, but was revived in 1788 upon the founding of a penal colony in Australia. The first fleet of ships that left Portsmouth for Botany Bay carried 1,493 passengers, including 586 male and 192 female convicts. The names of the convicts are listed in a book edited by P. G. Fidlon and R. J. Ryan, entitled *The First Fleeters*. The rest comprised officials and large numbers of Royal Navy and merchant seamen and their families. During the long voyage to a safe anchorage in Sydney Cove 45 people died and 7 children were born. Many thousands of convicts subsequently followed in their wake. New South Wales received convicts until 1840, Van Diemen's Land (renamed Tasmania in 1856) and Norfolk Island until 1853, and Western Australia until 1868. It has been estimated that between 1788 and 1868 approximately 162,000 men and women (together with some children) were transported from Britain to the other side of the world and that for the first 50 years of the new colony's history about 40 per cent of the total population were convicts.

Meanwhile, government land grants and other concessions were designed to attract 'free settlers' to Australia. By the 1830s determined efforts were being made to attract non-convict workers by offering passages as cheap as those across the Atlantic. The word was spread back home amongst the friends and neighbours of the emigrant. A passage in the diary of the Revd F. E. Witts of Upper Slaughter, Gloucestershire, illustrates the sort of network of preference and information that must have been common:

26 February 1838: Wrote to the Secretary of State for the Colonies on behalf of the Smith family of Eyford to enquire about emigration to New South Wales. The enquiry was suggested in a letter from Sam Smith who emigrated about a year ago,

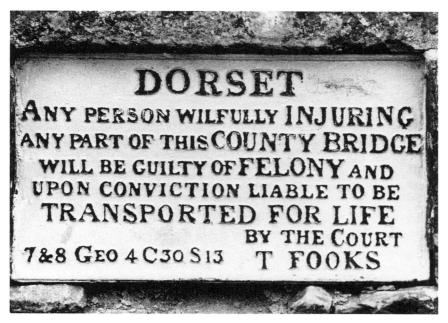

DORSET
ANY PERSON WILFULLY INJURING
ANY PART OF THIS COUNTY BRIDGE
WILL BE GUILTY OF FELONY AND
UPON CONVICTION LIABLE TO BE
TRANSPORTED FOR LIFE
BY THE COURT
7 & 8 GEO 4 C 30 S 13   T FOOKS

TRANSPORTATION:

A Dorset Warning
A number of Dorset bridges have a notice such as this, dating from 1827, warning that the penalty for damaging the bridge could be transportation to Australia. In 1835 the penalty was reduced to £2. One of these plaques has been presented to the Mitchel Library in Sydney.

A Convict Ship
The engraving shows convicts being transported to Australia under armed guard.

accepting an invitation from a Colonist from the neighbourhood of Cheltenham, named Arkell, now advanced in life, who has acquired a valuable property in land, stock, etc., and wished for a young Gloucestershire farmer to come out to assist him in cultivating his property in the interior of Bathurst county. Sam Smith has been cordially received and is now engaged to marry the daughter of Arkell. He considers himself on the high road to prosperity, and wishes members of his own family to follow his example, and desires them to send out to him four married labourers with families whom Arkell will engage and also a carpenter.

Official statistics record only 485 migrants to Australia and New Zealand in 1825, but then a rapid rise to a peak of 32,625 in 1841. Between 1825 and 1851 a total of 222,955 British people emigrated voluntarily to Australia and New Zealand, compared with 834,306 to Canada, 1,750,682 to the USA, and 44,056 to all other places, a grand total of 2,901,999. Australia's fortunes were built on sheep-farming and the lure of gold. In 1851 its population stood at 437,665, by 1858 it had reached 1 million, by 1877 it had topped 2 million, and by 1889 it had passed 3 million. Of those 612,531 Australians who in 1861 were recorded as having been born in the United Kingdom, 56.3 per cent came from England and Wales, 15.48 per cent from Scotland and 28.19 per cent from Ireland; the proportions remained roughly the same for the rest of the century.

The recent bicentenary celebrations have created a great deal of new interest in family history in Australia; families that once kept quiet about their convict ancestors now rejoice in being descended from the first white settlers. The types of record of this mass migration that are available at the Public Record Office at Kew are described in the information leaflet *Australian Convicts: Sources in the Public Record Office* and are illustrated in David T. Hawkings' book *Bound for Australia*. Many details of the convicts and free settlers have been listed by the Archives Authority of New South Wales. It is often easier to find information about convict ancestors than about those who were free settlers. The records that may be consulted in the Archives Office of New South Wales provide the date and place of the trial, which leads to information about the age and place of birth of the convict. The records of absolute or conditional pardons give the place and year of birth, the name of the ship in which the convict arrived, the name of the master of the ship, the year of arrival, the occupation of the convict, the place and date of his conviction, his sentence, a physical description, and the date of the pardon. Tickets of leave and certificates of freedom for convicts contain similar information. The same archives office contains indents (records) of convict ships, 1788–1842, and lists of convicts, 1788–1820.

The records of assisted immigration are very informative during the periods for which they survive. They give the age, education, and occupation of the migrant, his birthplace or place of residence prior to embarkation, his father's full name, occupation, and place of residence, his mother's name and maiden surname, together with her father's occupation and often the maiden surname of her mother. In 1835 the government launched a bounty scheme whereby the immigrant's passage was paid if he or she had testimonials of good character. These testimonials usually have baptismal certificates attached to them. The registration of births, marriages, and deaths in the various states of Australia began between 1841 and 1856, but the census returns that are such a useful source of information in Britain and elsewhere have been destroyed in Australia. The exception is the New South Wales census of 1828, which has been published by the Library of Australian History and which lists the name, age, year of birth, and religious affiliation of every person in the colony, together with the name of the ship and the year of arrival, occupation, place of residence, amount of land and stock, and, where the individual was a convict, his sentence. In New Zealand, the registration of European births and deaths began in 1848; marriages are registered from 1854 onwards. Prior to these dates vital events were recorded in the parish registers.

The other principal destination for the British emigrant in the nineteenth century was South Africa. Here, the relatively small numbers of British settlers make genealogical research comparatively easy until numbers began to grow in the later nineteenth century. The Dutch East India Company had been responsible for the earliest white settlements in the seventeenth and eighteenth centuries. By 1740 the Cape colony consisted of some 4,000 free burghers and their families, who were of Dutch, German, Walloon, and Huguenot descent, and 1,500 Company servants and soldiers with

MAP OF SOUTH AFRICA (1802)

This map was published by A. Arrowsmith in London and dedicated to 'The Committee and Members of the British Association for discovering the interior parts of Africa'. Settlement was still confined to the coastal parts south of the Great Karroo and the lands of the 'Wild Hottentots'.

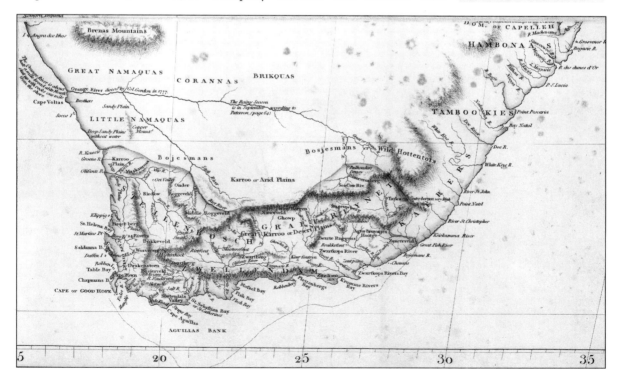

their families. By the beginning of the nineteenth century the colony contained some 16,000 Europeans, 17,000 slaves, and an unknown number of Hottentots and Bushmen. Military success in 1795 encouraged British settlement, but even by the 1820s the 8,000 British emigrants were heavily outnumbered by the 43,000 Dutch. It has been estimated that by the middle years of the nineteenth century the combined white population was about a quarter of the black. The Great Trek northwards, which began in 1836 and which attracted about 14,000 Dutch people in the first 10 years, led to the creation of the new Dutch states of Natal, Orange Free State, and Transvaal. The trekkers set off in small, neighbourhood groups of 20 or 30 families to join other groups beyond the frontiers of the original colony. These states were not reunited with the Cape until the creation of the Union of South Africa in 1910.

Stability

The unprecedented scale of migration during the course of the nineteenth century to the new industrial districts or to new worlds overseas arrests our attention and is of great importance to the family historian, but it is not the

ROBIN HOOD'S BAY
This photograph by the Whitby photographer Frank Meadow Sutcliffe (1853–1941) shows Robin Hood's Bay from the beach at East Scar. A crowd of people on an outing in their 'Sunday best' have just arrived.

whole story of these times. Despite the tremendous growth of the national population and the development of rapid forms of transport, the underlying pattern of the residential stability of core groups of families can still be observed in every part of the country during the modern period. The persistence of farming and craft families within a restricted area was as remarkable a feature of the Victorian countryside as it had been in the past, and in the towns, too, the continuity of certain families over long periods of time is remarkable.

In his study of the remote community of Robin Hood's Bay, Alan Storm has shown that 13 surnames which were present in the village in 1540 were held by no fewer than 130 people there in 1841; 2 of these distinctive surnames were shared by no less than 90 people. Within the wider unit of the parish of Fylingdales, 27 surnames which were once connected with Robin Hood's Bay, or were still found there, can be traced from 1540 to 1841, when they were borne by 193 persons. Altogether, some 41.6 per cent of the enumerated population of this Yorkshire village in 1841 bore surnames that had entered the parish by 1650.

Professor John Beckett and Trevor Foulds, having analysed the 1851 and 1861 census returns for the open-field village of Laxton, Nottinghamshire, have concluded that the mid-nineteenth-century patterns of mobility and stability there were similar to those in earlier times. The high turnover of individuals was matched by the long-term stability of the farming families. Though half the population of the village in 1861 had not been there 10 years earlier, as many as 75 of the 99 properties remained occupied by the same families. During the 1850s only 1 in 7 farms had changed hands and only 1 in 4 cottages. Even those people who had moved into the village were nearly all from the surrounding 'country'.

In Westmorland, Dr John Marshall has demonstrated that at the time of the 1851 census the overwhelming majority of country people in sample areas of the county were either born in their own parishes or had originated only a few miles away from their residence on census night. Much of the movement of the minority was related to the nature of their occupations or activities, as farm servants, reapers, drovers, tailors, carriers, carters, navvies, mariners, or pedlars. As in earlier times, the people who moved did not travel very far. Even by 1861, the total number of people living in Furness who were born in Cumberland or Westmorland did not exceed 12 per cent of the total population there.

The national census returns of 1851 revealed that 13,691,914 of the 17,165,656 persons who had been born in England and Wales— that is 80 per cent—were living in the registration county of their birth. It may be objected that this figure includes young children, who would naturally not have moved far, but as the percentage of children who were under the age of 14 formed only 36 per cent of the total population at that time, it is clear that the overwhelming majority of adults must still have been living in the counties where they were born.

In the succeeding decades more people were prepared to move much further distances than earlier generations normally did. Professor Charles Phythian-Adams has drawn attention to the general reduction in the proportion of native inhabitants within each county between 1841 and 1861. In 1841 as many as 37 of the 40 shires could claim that over three-quarters of their enumerated populations were natives. In 1861 the number had dropped to 25. Even in 1861, however, the proportion of locally born inhabitants was still over 65 per cent in 37 of the 40 shires, ranging from Cornwall with 91.94 per cent to Durham with 67.58 per cent. Moreover, those counties which were becoming urbanized and industrialized still contained large rural populations which were essentially native.

A considerable degree of regional variation is evident even in 1841. In the south-west, the proportions of native inhabitants ranged from Cornwall (94.85 per cent) through Devon (90.4 per cent), Dorset (89.1 per cent) and Wiltshire (88.3 per cent) to Somerset (86.7 per cent). In East Anglia the proportions varied from Norfolk (93.2 per cent) and Suffolk (91.3 per cent) to Essex (86.3 per cent). These very high figures demonstrate that county boundaries, though invisible, were effective barriers to migration. The population of Cornwall was not integrated with that of Devon, Dorset people were not the same as those in Somerset, and a Norfolk person was different from one from Suffolk, even though physical limitations on mobility were absent. Although Bedfordshire was one of the most accessible English counties, here too the great majority of the mid-nineteenth-century population had local origins. Even in the 53 parishes which border on other counties the average proportion of Bedfordshire natives was 78.8 per cent. The distinctive local surnames that were so evident in the hearth tax return of 1671 were still common within the county two centuries later.

The mapping of blood groups in various parts of Britain today confirms the tenacity of people's loyalties to their native 'countries'. Such evidence points, for instance, to a genetic divide within modern Northumberland between a group of people on Tyneside and another on the western hills. It also confirms the importance of the original border between Herefordshire and Wales. The different populations on either side of these boundaries apparently rarely intermarried.

Farming families continued to be prominent amongst those who remained attached to a particular 'country'. In 1853 William Dickinson described the farmers of 150 to 400 acres in Cumbria as a relatively stable and homogeneous group:

A large number of these are the descendants of farmers from generation to generation, some of whom are tilling the same farms, along with additions, which their grandfathers, and even great-grandfathers, held in tenancy under the same race of owners. Others are yeomen, cultivating the patrimonial estates in whole or in part.

The intensely local nature of the outlook and connection of farming dynasties in Victorian Kent has been demonstrated by Professor Alan Everitt.

Many rural families bore the surnames that had been adopted by their ancestors in the Middle Ages and which were still peculiar to their county. Most people in the Kentish countryside lived all their lives within 20 miles or so of their birthplaces and they took as their brides women from a similar restricted area. By the reign of Victoria a vast local cousinage of farmers and craftsmen had been created, with numerous branches in the small, scattered settlements and market towns.

In south-west Wales the continuity of the native families in an area which attracted few immigrants was even more pronounced. Dr David Jenkins has shown that 54 per cent of the residents of the south Cardiganshire parish of Troedyraur in 1861 had been born there. A further 27 per cent had been born in adjoining parishes and another 9 per cent came from neighbouring (but not adjoining) parishes. No less than 90 per cent of the population had therefore been born in the 'country' of which Troedyraur formed part. Within this 'country', and indeed within this parish, people had often moved from farm to farm. Nevertheless, each family was closely associated with the farm that it occupied, even if they stayed for only a short period. Dr Jenkins comments that it was common practice to refer to a man by his Christian name and by the name of his farm, so that a man who moved several times to a different farm was known variously by his Christian name and the name of one of several farms, among them that which he had occupied 60 years earlier. If someone left the locality to work elsewhere and returned to the district of his birth many years later to spend his retirement, he was sometimes known by the name of the house in which he had lived before migrating. The naming-practices of this remote Welsh community in the nineteenth and twentieth century shed some light on the origin of surnames in other parts of Britain at a much earlier period.

Farming and trading dynasties can be recognized in all the various 'countries' of Victorian and Edwardian Britain. Nevertheless, more people were on the move than ever before. The railways hastened the process by which people poured into the industrial towns from the countryside. Sociologists once spoke of *anomie*, the sense of utter loneliness and depression that overcame those who moved into the alien world of the Victorian city, but it is likely that the experience of most rural migrants was nothing like that. Many of them moved into a world already inhabited by relations and friends. Professor Michael Anderson has shown that in the Victorian industrial towns and cities family links and community bonds might have been strenghtened rather than weakened as migrants came in from the countryside. In Sheffield the break with the distant past was far from complete. Much of the industrial expansion in the town meant more of the same—more cutlers' workshops organized on traditional lines as small, family firms. They are disappearing now, but many Sheffielders can trace their ancestry back through successive generations of metalworkers. The Peace family have been making files in the town from the early eighteenth century, the Nowells have been making cutlery since the seventeenth century. The Gallimores can be traced back through six generations of metalworkers to Thomas Gallimore, an immigrant button-maker from Staffordshire, who was married in Sheffield in 1737. Many more examples could be given.

In the seventeenth and eighteenth centuries newcomers to Sheffield had not travelled very far. Nearly three-quarters of the boys who were apprenticed to the cutlery trades came from within 15 miles, while only 4 per cent migrated more than 40 miles. In the Victorian era, a lot of people came from much further afield, from Staffordshire or Lincolnshire, and other counties. Nevertheless, the bulk of the migrants came from a much more restricted area, from no further north than Leeds or Wakefield and from not much further south than Chesterfield. Some members of the Sheffield and District Family History Society have found that all their eight great-grandparents were born in Sheffield and that several of their great-great-grandparents were also born there. Present-day Sheffielders are frequently able to trace their ancestors by means of the Sheffield parish register back into the seventeenth or eighteenth century and sometimes into even earlier times. The various branches of these families come from all parts of the city, thus helping to give Sheffielders a real sense of community even in the closing decade of the twentieth century. Even in an urban setting some families have been

A THIRD CLASS CARRIAGE IN A PARLIAMENTARY TRAIN
This engraving of 1858 by William M'Connell shows how the masses could travel quickly and cheaply, if not very comfortably, once 'railway mania' had connected nearly all the towns in Britain.

remarkably tenacious in their attachment to a locality over a very long period of time.

Let us return one more time to the remarkable persistence of certain surnames in and around the localities where they originated. One final example will suffice. The Dungworths came from a Pennine farm (which has since become a hamlet) on the moors near Sheffield. In 1672 7 Dungworth households were taxed on their hearths; 4 of them lived in their original township, 1 lived in an adjoining township in the same moorland parish, and 2 had moved 6 or 7 miles to work as cutlers at the other side of Sheffield. At the beginning of Victoria's reign the Dungworths were still confined to the same area. All of the 37 Dungworths whose births were registered between 1 July 1837 and 30 June 1842 were born in the two adjoining districts of Sheffield and Ecclesall. Even today, despite the mobility of recent generations, 50 per cent of the Dungworths who subscribe to the telephone service are listed in the Sheffield directory.

CHAPTER FOUR

Family and Society

BEFORE 1800

W E HAVE no firm statistics on the size of the national population before the first official census of 1801. This recorded 8.9 million people in England and Wales, a figure which is usually adjusted to 9.2 million to allow for under-recording. The population at that time was rising sharply. Certain industrial towns and villages had been growing throughout the eighteenth century, but in most places growth had not begun until the 1740s. In earlier centuries the national population had been far smaller.

Estimates based on Domesday Book suggest that in the late eleventh century between 1.5 and 2.25 million people lived in England. During the twelfth and thirteenth centuries the population expanded considerably; historians have recently revised previous estimates to suggest that by 1300 it had reached at least 4 millions and may have been much higher. This was the period when the many new farmsteads that were carved from the moors, woods, and fens gave rise to hereditary surnames. Throughout England the majority of people lived in small family farms, many of them on the margin of subsistence with resources that were inadequate to cope with the crises that came in the fourteenth century in the form of harvest failures, livestock disasters, and virulent epidemics. In 1348–50 the Black Death reduced the national population by at least a third and possibly by a half. Other major epidemics occurred in 1361–2 and 1375; plague remained endemic until the seventeenth century. We have few records on which to base an estimate of the national population in the late Middle Ages, but by 1500 the country may have had only half the number of people that it had supported in 1300.

The work of the Cambridge Group for the Study of Population and Social Structure has provided a firm understanding of national population trends during the early modern era. The earliest surviving parish registers, which consistently record a greater number of baptisms than burials, suggest that demographic recovery was underway by the 1530s and 1540s. All over Western Europe the trend for the next hundred years was towards moderately fast growth. E. A. Wrigley and R. S. Schofield have demonstrated that between 1540 and 1640 England's population rose from about 2.75 millions to roughly 5 millions, surpassing its medieval level. This period of growth was followed by 60 years of stagnation; indeed, during the period 1656–86 the national total declined slightly. Soon, however, it was to soar to unprecedented heights. Since the 1740s it has never stopped rising.

The population of medieval and early modern England was overwhelmingly rural. In 1700 about 75 per cent of English people lived in the countryside, in villages, hamlets, and scattered farmsteads. Amongst those who lived in places that were thought of as urban were many who belonged to communities with no more than 1,000–2,000 people, often less. London was in a different league to other places, for it already had over half a million inhabitants. The next largest city was Norwich, with about 30,000 people, followed by Bristol with 20,000, and Exeter, York, and Newcastle with even fewer. The places that were to become the great Victorian industrial cities were beginning to grow but they were still smaller than these ancient centres. Two and a half centuries ago, England was still a thinly populated country.

The Nuclear Family, Servants, and Apprentices

For as far back in time as records go, English families have taken the form that is familiar to us in the twentieth century. Historians have long since discarded older notions of extended families with close kinship ties living under the same roof. A census drawn up at Coventry in 1523—the earliest that has been analysed in detail—shows that of the 1,302 households in the city, only 3 contained members of more than two generations and that only 1 per cent of all households contained adult relatives of any sort. Coventry was at that time one of England's greatest cities; other evidence points to a similar familial structure in the countryside. A decade after the Coventry census, a list was made of about 51,000 people in the archdeaconry of Stafford. Only about 10 per cent of the family groups recorded in the list included relatives of the head of the family who were not spouses or children. Most of these relatives were the parents of the head, some of whom were dead when the list was made. Only two entries go back to an earlier generation. This evidence from the West Midlands suggests that the nuclear household was the norm by the end of the Middle Ages. Perhaps it had always been usual in England. The taxation returns of the fourteenth century indicate that the nuclear family was firmly established as the basic social institution by the time that surnames were becoming hereditary.

In the early modern period the evidence leaves no doubt that most English households were based on nuclear families. An analysis of 61 censuses or population lists from different parts of the country has revealed a consistent picture from the late sixteenth century to the early nineteenth century. Over 70 per cent of the households recorded in these lists were based on families of two generations only. Less than 6 per cent of households contained three generations extending to grandparents. It was very rare for a household to contain two married couples. The elementary family of parents and children was the basic unit of English society.

The size and composition of households in medieval and early modern England was always liable to be affected by sudden death. Miranda Chaytor has shown that some of the households of the parish of Ryton, County Durham, consisted of 'hybrid' families of parents, stepchildren, and foster-children as well as the offspring of the current marriage. In such cases, where the structure of the household was constantly changing, the 'family' was

LATE MEDIEVAL
COVENTRY
These timber-framed
houses in the northern part
of the city survived into the
nineteenth century, when
this drawing was made.
They stood just inside
Cook Street Gate.

very different from the simple conjugal unit. We need to be aware of how flexible and adaptable the English family could be. Nevertheless, only a small proportion of households shared the experiences of the few 'hybrid' families that were living in Ryton over a period of some 20 years at the turn of the sixteenth and seventeenth centuries. Dr Keith Wrightson contrasts the broad homogeneity of structure shared by families throughout England with the considerable regional heterogeneity found in France or Germany. Although the English pattern was not a rigid one, the usual residential unit was the simple nuclear-family household.

The size of a household varied considerably according to the stage that had been reached in the family life-cycle and according to the social status of the head. The population lists that survive for various communities before the first national census in 1801 show that people at the top of the social scale tended to have the largest families and that people at the bottom had the smallest. Professor Charles Phythian-Adams found that at Coventry in 1523 the building-workers, who formed the poorest section of society, had average-sized households of only 3 or 4 people, whereas the merchants had a mean number of 7.4 persons per household. Historical demographers have come to accept an average of about 4.75 people per household throughout the late medieval and early modern periods, though particular communities might range far from the norm. Like any average, this figure masks a range of sizes for individual households, ranging from the solitary widow upwards, but it is useful in helping us to focus on the fact that extended families did not live under the same roof at any recorded stage of English history.

The larger size of the wealthier households was achieved through the presence of greater numbers of living-in servants. At every level of society, children expected to leave their parental home at the age of puberty to become servants or apprentices, and only the poorest families did not take in the children of other families. This represents a fundamental difference between early modern society and the present. Listings of the population of individual parishes in the sixteenth, seventeenth, and eighteenth centuries show that, at any one time, a large proportion of households contained living-in servants, the great majority of whom were not related to the other members of that household.

The term 'servant' conjures up images of Victorian and Edwardian country houses, with girls and women working at domestic chores and men serving as butlers, grooms, or gardeners. In the medieval and early modern periods, however, the word had a much wider application. The upper servants of a great household were drawn from the ranks of the gentry; in the world of commerce the word might be used to describe any employee; in the countryside a servant could have been an apprentice, a domestic servant or a farm-worker. The term was mostly used, however, to describe young, unmarried people who lived with their employers on terms specified in an annual hiring contract.

Children expected to leave home in their early teens to live and work with another family. Dr Ann Kussmaul has estimated that in the early modern period about 60 per cent of the population aged 15–24 were employed as servants, including apprentices. In 63 listings of the inhabitants of parishes scattered throughout England between 1574 and 1821, servants amounted to 13.4 per cent of the population. The institution of service was admirably suited to the requirements of an age when most work was performed at home. Employers seeking adolescents at times when their own children were not yet old enough, or had left to set up home themselves, found a ready supply of labour amongst the children who could not be offered work in their own homes. Service was particularly appropriate in rural areas which were characterized by small- and medium-sized farms, but it was equally efficient in solving the labour problems of craftsmen and traders in the towns.

The terms by which a boy or girl entered the service of a master or mistress were different from those of formal apprenticeship. When a boy was apprenticed, the terms were set out in a written contract, the agreed period was a lengthy one (commonly seven years), and the boy's parents paid the master for lodging, board, and training. When a country lad entered farm service, it was by verbal contract for shorter periods (usually a year), and the masters not only provided board and lodging but an agreed wage, according to rates set by the JPs. Dr Kussmaul estimates that between one-third and one-half of hired agricultural labour in the early modern period was supplied by servants. They formed a distinctive group, who were clearly separate from the day-labourers. Farm servants were teenage boys and unmarried men, who lived on the farm and commonly moved on at the end of their year, whereas labourers were married men who lived elsewhere (often in tied cottages) and who were paid by the job. The distinction between a farm servant and an agricultural labourer is one that a family historian needs to bear in mind in later periods, for example, when looking at census returns or nineteenth-century parish registers.

Few records relating to farm service survive for the early modern period. Even our accounts of the annual hiring fairs are from later times. The age at which children left home to enter service or an apprenticeship was not fixed, but on average was about 14. Most youngsters did not travel very far at first, but as they grew older and more experienced they ventured further afield, within the bounds of their 'country'. The death of a member of their family, or the acquisition of a larger farm by a father, sometimes meant that a lad would return home for a while, but most were content to sample life on a number of farms before they married. Some never married and remained servants all their lives. The majority remained in farming in adult life, but some left agriculture when they reached the age of 21 and moved to the towns.

The frequency with which farm servants moved from one farm to another distinguished their life-style from that of their contemporaries who

were bound as apprentices. Their mobility formed a sharp contrast with the behaviour of most adults. Annual contracts between farmers and servants were agreed at hiring fairs, which were held at customary times. In the arable parts of southern and eastern England hiring fairs were held at Michaelmas; in the north Martinmas was the favoured time. By then, the harvest had been gathered and the autumn ploughing completed. In pastoral areas, such as much of western England or the fens of Lincolnshire, May Day was the conventional date of hiring, for at that time of year livestock were turned out to grass. A study of Poor Law settlement examinations has revealed that over 90 per cent of hirings took place at Michaelmas, Martinmas, or May Day. It has also shown that most servants did not renew their agreements at the end of the year, but preferred to find a new master nearby. Most lads moved less than 10 miles at a time.

Dr Kussmaul has described how the incidence of farm service declined from a high point in the fifteenth century to a trough in the mid-seventeenth century. This can be attributed to the effect of population growth, which created a large body of poor adults seeking labouring work. Once the population ceased to rise, the demand for servants rose again, reaching a new peak by the mid-eighteenth century. The labour surplus disappeared as population stagnation coincided with increased migration to London and new employment opportunities became available in rural crafts. This situa-

'THE REAPERS' (1783)
This oil painting by George Stubbs depicts a popular subject of the period. The farmer on horseback watches the reaping of his wheat . A man cuts the crop with a sickle, a girl makes bonds of straw for the man who is binding sheaves, and another puts the sheaves in stooks.

tion did not last long. As we shall see, by the last quarter of the eighteenth century farmers in southern England were abandoning the age-old custom according to which their young farm servants lived in the farmhouse as one of the family. In some other areas, however, the custom survived well into the twentieth century.

Apprentices moved only once as teenagers, unless their master died, but their initial journey was frequently longer than those made by farm servants. Even so, the majority of apprentice lads did not venture beyond the 'country' in which they had been reared. Nearly three-quarters of the boys who were apprenticed to Hallamshire cutlers between 1624 and 1799 came from within 15 miles of the town centre, while only 4 per cent migrated more than 40 miles. Once they were free, the opportunities to practise their craft usually restricted their movements. Nor did moving once a year encourage farm servants to carry on moving after they were married. On the contrary, their mobility usually came to an end when they left service.

London of course was a magnet for apprentices from all over England. In the sixteenth century it was still possible for men of humble background to find London masters for their sons, but by the second half of the seventeenth century the cost of a London training had risen sharply. Dr Peter Earle has written that by then 'most apprentices, or at least those likely to end up as

COVENT GARDEN IN THE 1720S
Covent Garden Piazza and Market were laid out to the north of the Strand in the 1630s on the Earl of Bedford's estate. The 1754 edition of John Stow's *Survey of London* noted that the area was 'well inhabited by a mixture of nobility, gentry and wealthy tradesmen . . . scarce admitting of any poor, not being pestered with mean courts and alleys.' This scene was painted by Joseph Van Aken in about 1726–30.

independent businessmen, were the sons of yeomen or gentlemen if they were countrymen, while increasing numbers were the sons of urban professional or commercial people or of such "middling" members of rural society as innkeepers, clothiers, millers and the like'. Apprentice lads were a large, though not a homogeneous, group in London society, particularly in the City, where they formed 10 per cent of the population.

Dr Earle has found that very few boys were apprenticed to masters of the same surname or that of their mother's family. He concludes that most apprentices seem to have found masters with whom neither they nor their parents had any prior relationship of any sort. A master was sometimes found by a professional intermediary, such as a scrivener, or by advertisement, but most were contacted by 'friends', who might have been relatives or godparents, or perhaps business or social associates of the apprentice's father. Most provincial families had at least one 'friend' in the capital city.

A similar situation prevailed in the provinces. Fewer than 4 per cent of a sample of 500 Norwich apprentices during the sixteenth and seventeenth centuries bore the same surname as their masters. The likelihood of obtaining a place with a relative was partly dependent on social status. Peter Laslett has calculated that in a sample of communities from the sixteenth to the early nineteenth centuries, 27.6 per cent of gentry households contained resident kin, compared with only 17 per cent of yeomen households and 7.9 per cent of the households of the poor. Even at the gentry level, however, servants cannot be seen as part of an extended family with ties of blood.

Marriages, Births, and Deaths

Another myth that has been firmly laid to rest by social historians is that English people used to marry when they were very young. Shakespeare's Romeo and Juliet cannot be taken as representative of the early modern era, though of course aristocratic families often arranged the marriages of their children at a very young age. The evidence is inconclusive for the medieval period, but the study of parish registers has left no doubt that since the sixteenth century at least England has shared the north-west European pattern of a late age at marriage and a large number of individuals who never married at all. Brides and grooms were normally in their mid-twenties. At least 1 in 6 people never married; sometimes the proportion was as high as 1 in 4.

So well established was this pattern by the beginnings of parish registration, that it is unlikely that medieval experience was much different. Evidence from Halesowen, Warwickshire, points to an earlier age at marriage in the fourteenth century, but it is not clear how typical this community was. In early modern England, marriage was delayed until a young person had spent several years in service or as an apprentice. Young servants were as common a feature of thirteenth- and fourteenth-century England as they were in the Tudor and Stuart era. Indeed, the proportion of households in

Rutland that contained servants in 1377 was higher than in later times. It is likely that a late age at marriage was normal long before the period for which we have firm evidence.

It is of course possible to find many examples of marriages at much earlier ages than the norm. Young couples in Stratford-upon-Avon in Shakespeare's day, for example, did not wait as long as most. Nevertheless, the broad pattern is clear. Only a very small proportion of the population of Elizabethan England married before the age of 20. This has obvious implications for the size of families. Delayed marriages and the high proportion of people who never married at all ensured that the population of early modern England did not rise dramatically. Greater employment opportunities in the eighteenth century lowered the age at marriage, thus increasing the chances of larger families. Demographers now agree that this factor, rather than declining death-rates, was the major reason why England's population began to grow at an unprecedented rate during the course of the Industrial Revolution.

Marriage was normally delayed until a couple had the means to set up home on their own. In many cases they were not free to marry until an apprenticeship had been served. Most young people had to rely upon the savings they had made during a period of service or paid employment. Parents helped their children to establish a home if they could. Boys might be given part of the family holding or set up in business; girls were given a 'marriage portion', the size of which might determine whom they were able to choose as a partner. In rural Shropshire in the seventeenth century, marriage portions for girls from farming families ranged from £30 to £100. In some cases, the inheritance of property upon the death of a parent provided the economic opportunity for marriage. The timing of marriage was clearly influenced by economic considerations. During the later sixteenth century, for instance, the incidence of marriage declined sharply as real wages fell in value.

The children and wards of substantial landowners often had their marriages arranged, with little reference to their wishes. Further down the social scale, when parents tried to influence their offspring's choice of marriage partner, they were not always successful. Richard Gough of Myddle noted that Mary Amis married 'without her father's consent, which soe displeased him that hee gave his lands to Martha, the younger daughter, and married her to Edward Jenks'. Michael Brayne married Susan Lloyd, 'which soe displeased her father that, allthough hee had but that onely child, yet he gave her nothing'. Anne Baker married 'more to please her father than herselfe', but she was exceptional. The great majority of people were free to marry whom they chose. In any case, half or more of young adults in the early modern period had lost one parent or both by the time that they got married.

The children of the middle and lower ranks of society frequently met their future partners while they were servants or apprentices, away from parental supervision. They appear to have had considerable freedom to meet whom they wished, in the streets or country lanes, in the market-place, shops, or alehouses. Cases brought before the church courts show that all ranks of society aspired to romantic love and that they commonly experienced passionate attachments. Richard Gough thought that an ideal marriage had been achieved by Richard Hatchett when he married a Shropshire woman: 'Hee had a great fortune with her; butt that which is worth all, shee is a loveing wife, a discreet woman, and an excellent housewife.'

During the Middle Ages the Church had forbidden marriage during Advent, Lent, and Rogationtide. Parish registers make it clear that Lent remained a prohibited season through to the nineteenth century and that Advent remained an unpopular time for marriage until the later seventeenth century. Practical considerations also affected the seasonal marriage pattern. August was the month when the harvest was gathered and people were too busy to get married or to attend weddings. The peak periods were those when servants were released from their annual contracts, i.e. the spring in pastoral areas and the autumn in arable farming districts.

Ecclesiastical law stated that a couple should marry at the church that served the parish in which one or both partners were resident, after the calling of banns or by a special licence obtained from the diocesan consistory court. Until the reforms of Lord Hardwicke's Marriage Act (1753) clandestine marriages, which avoided the usual procedure, were valid if performed by clergymen who were outside episcopal jurisdiction. The Church had a long battle to make people accept that solemnization of a marriage should precede its full consummation. Popular opinion insisted that pledges of mutual acceptance and fidelity were valid matrimonial contracts, even before a marriage service in church. In Shakespeare's *Measure for Measure*, Claudio defends himself against a charge of fornication by pleading:

> I got possession of Julietta's bed.
> You know the lady—she is fast my wife,
> Save that we do the denunciation lack
> Of outward order.

This is part of the explanation of why so many brides were pregnant by the time of their wedding in church.

Contrary to popular belief, illegitimacy rates were not high during the early modern period. They were consistently much lower than those reached in the early years of the nineteenth century. A series of bad harvests sometimes thwarted marriage plans and caused a temporary rise in illegitimacies, but even in the 1590s and the first decade of the seventeenth century, when illegitimacy rates were at their highest, they accounted for only 3 per cent of baptisms. These rates were unequalled before the 1750s.

The relatively late age at which women married, together with the everpresent threat of early death, meant that few couples had offspring as numerous as those in a mid-Victorian family. As we have seen, the average household size in the early modern period was 4.75, i.e. two adults and two

From an Original Picture in the Possession of the Family, painted 1647.
Sir Thomas Remmington of Lund, in the East-Riding of the County of York, Kn.t
Dame Hannah his Wife, Daughter of Sir William Gee of Bishop Burton Kn.t & their Issue.

or three children. Numerous examples of large families can of course be found, but the average household size was kept small by the vulnerability of young children to infectious diseases, especially in their first year. The evidence of burial registers suggests that 15 per cent of children died within a year of being born and that about a quarter of all children failed to reach the age of 10.

Many men and women who reached the age of 30 could expect to live for another 30 years, though far more people died in their thirties, forties, and fifties than in old age. About 6 or 7 per cent of those who survived childhood to become adults lived beyond the age of 80. The likelihood of death striking at any time meant that only a minority of people lived long enough to become grandparents and that a high proportion of the adult population was widowed. A study of 70 communities in different parts of England between the late sixteenth and early nineteenth centuries shows that on average 20 per cent of householders were widowed. Many others who had lost their first partner had remarried. Widows greatly outnumbered widowers; the householders of Coventry in 1523 included nearly nine times as many widows as widowers. Elderly widows who could no longer cope for themselves feature extensively in the Poor Law records of the early modern period.

THE REMINGTON FAMILY (1647)

This engraving from an original painting by J. Halfpenny shows the fifteen living and the five dead members of the unusually large family of Sir Thomas and Dame Hannah Remington of Lund in the East Riding of Yorkshire. Sir Thomas (1611–81) was knighted at Dublin Castle in 1633, two years after his marriage to Hannah Gee of Beverley.

SIR THOMAS ACTON AT
THE DEATHBED OF HIS
WIFE (1635–6)
John Souch's oil-painting
depicts the bedchamber in
which Acton's wife died in
childbirth on 2 June 1635.
She is shown not only as a
corpse but (in the bottom
corner) as she was when
alive, with her husband and
eldest son. The artist thus
depicts the survival of the
soul after the death of the
body.

The oldest people in the Tudor and Stuart period reached the same age as the oldest inhabitants of the modern world but they formed a far smaller group than the senior citizens of today. The population of the early modern period was overwhelmingly youthful in its composition; about 40 per cent were dependent children. The age-structure of Elizabethan and Stuart society was thus radically different from that of the late twentieth century.

Kinship and Inheritance

Social historians have proved that the ties of kinship amongst medieval and early modern English families were not as strong as was formerly thought. Anthropological studies of primitive societies in other parts of the world have little to teach us in this respect. As far back in time as the documents allow us to see, kinship ties in England have been rather weak. Only on the northern border, where kinship groups known as 'the surnames' protected their members as late as the reign of Elizabeth, has there been anything similar to the Scottish clan system. John Armstrong, a young recusant questioned in 1613 prior to his entry into the English College in Rome, claimed that 600 kinsmen of his name and blood lived within 60 miles of his home in Northumberland. Here, and in Cumberland, however, these groups were

AN DNI 1567.   ÆTATIS SVÆ 69.

*Rogers Comptroller
to Queen Elizabeth*

SIR EDWARD ROGERS
This portrait by an un-
known artist was painted in
1567 when Sir Edward
Rogers was in his 69th year.
He died soon afterwards. A
Devonshire man and an ar-
dent Protestant, he had
risen in the court circle to
become the Comptroller of
Queen Elizabeth's House-
hold. He is shown here with
his staff of office. One gets a
strong impression of the authority which age could be-
stow on such a man.

already an anachronism that withered after the union of the English and
Scottish crowns.

Historians have reached different conclusions on how valuable the ad-
mittedly weak kinship bonds might have been, for the evidence is ambiva-
lent and differs according to social group and from region to region. Family
historians need to be aware of the ways in which kin might have been of mutual assistance in times of need, such as borrowing money, securing work, or
finding a new home, and they need to have some understanding of who
might benefit from a will or who, for example, might act as a witness to a
marriage.

Twentieth-century sociologists distinguish among a person's kindred,
firstly the ones he recognizes, and then more specially the 'effective' kin with

whom he has social contacts. An even narrower circle is formed from within these groups by the 'intimate' kin with whom he has a close and lasting relationship. The nature of these groups is determined, as in the past, not by any clear set of rules but by individual preferences and circumstances.

English people in the past did not recognize their kin according to firm conventions or rules. Whether or not a person thought of his kin as a narrow circle or as a wide group of relations was a matter of individual circumstance and preference. The terms 'kinsman' and 'cousin' were used without any attempt at precision. The width of the kinship circle depended on the inclinations of the person who wished to recognize such a group and on his social status. In the early modern period, many aristocratic and gentry families were prepared to acknowledge a wide range of kin, including those from lower social groups. Amongst the upper and middle ranks of society, mourning clothes and rings were customarily provided for large numbers of the relatives of the deceased, and male kinsfolk often served as pallbearers. However, there can be no doubt that many people were little concerned with their kin, beyond those of the immediate family circle. The Essex diarist the Revd Ralph Josselin mentioned no ancestors further back than his grandparents, nor any relatives beyond first cousins. Other contemporary diaries and autobiographies suggest that Josselin was typical of many people of middle rank in this respect. The study of large numbers of wills by social historians reinforces this impression. Below the ranks of the gentry, people rarely left bequests to large numbers of kin.

In his study of *The English Family, 1450–1700*, Dr Ralph Houlbrooke has observed,

There was no well-defined group of kinsmen larger than the elementary family to which most individuals owed loyalty. Men's strongest personal obligations, legal, customary and moral, were to spouse and children. They generally recognised, for example, their moral obligation to leave the bulk of their property to their wives and offspring, to whom it would descend by the laws and customs of inheritance if they made no dispositions of their own.

Analyses of wills from all over the country indicate that the widows and children of testators were the ones who were most often chosen as executors. Brothers and brothers-in-law were sometimes called upon to serve in this way, or to act as overseers, but other kin were not normally asked to undertake these roles. It seems that close kinship links were often maintained with grandparents, uncles, aunts, nephews, nieces, and in-laws, but not often with other kin beyond this rather restricted circle.

The nature of the evidence is unsatisfactory, however; we are left with the uneasy feeling that the absence of bequests in wills merely reflects the lack of wherewithal to provide gifts for large numbers of relatives. Kinship networks may have provided necessary help in ways that are not documented. Thus, kin often eased the paths of those young hopefuls who migrated to the cities or overseas. Nearly a third of those female migrants to London who

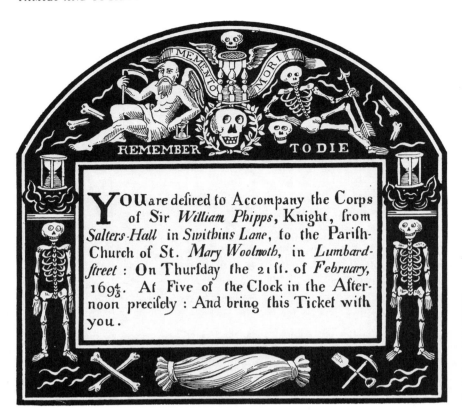

MEMENTO MORI

REMEMBER · TO DIE

YOU are defired to Accompany the Corps of Sir *William Phipps*, Knight, from *Salters-Hall* in *Swithins Lane*, to the Parifh-Church of St. *Mary Woolnoth*, in *Lumbard-ftreet* : On Thurfday the 21ft. of *February*, 169⅘. At Five of the Clock in the Afternoon precifely : And bring this Ticket with you.

A Seventeenth-Century Invitation to a Funeral
This *memento mori* and invitation to a London funeral in 1695 shows how the reality of death was confronted.

married there by licence between 1598 and 1619 had relatives other than parents living in the capital; nearly a fifth of this sample lived with these relatives. Two and a half centuries later, the web of connection through kin and neighbours helped people from the countryside to settle and obtain work in the new industrial towns.

Family letters show that a much wider range of kin than the immediate family were approached when assistance was required. At all levels of society, kinsmen acted as contacts who could be called upon to find places and secure favours, to give advice, or to act as securities for loans. The 'close family network' that Dr Margaret Spufford found amongst some seventeenth-century Cambridgeshire yeomen and the extensive family networks revealed by Dr Mary Prior in her study of the boat people of Fisher Row, Oxford, show how valuable the kinship network could be. Amongst the middling and lower ranks of society, kinship networks were probably widest and strongest in those parts of the country where the population was most stable. As we have already seen when considering the slow spread of surnames, many families were remarkably persistent in their attachment to certain localities. Kinship may thus have been more important in Lancashire or Shropshire, for example, than it was in Essex. In the Essex village of Terling in 1671, less than half of the 122 householders had relatives among the other householders, while most of those related to another householder had only one such connection. In the contemporary Shropshire parish of Myddle, however, the residential persistence of the yeomen and the husbandmen strengthened the bonds that tied families together in a community. We must be prepared for much regional variation, in this as in so many other matters.

Sixteenth- and seventeenth-century gentry families were deeply interested in their ancestry and their kinship connections. Their correspondence and personal memoranda, together with the genealogies that they so painstakingly constructed, indicate a broad knowledge of kin that went much further than their immediate family. Sentiment played a part, but the knowledge was also of practical value, for in the absence of a descendant, property passed to a collateral relation. Moreover, it paid to know who one's ancestors were in an age when claims at law were pursued unscrupulously.

Dr Houlbrooke has noted how, in nearly every autobiography which includes some survey of the author's ancestry, paternal kindred occupy more space than do maternal ones. The shared surname perhaps made it natural to think along these lines. On the other hand, early genealogists proudly recorded famous ancestors on the maternal side of the family, and it is clear that connections on the mother's side were often as important, emotionally or materially, as were those on the father's side, sometimes more so.

Extended kinship networks formed the basis of county society for the gentry families of early modern England; marriage partners were normally sought within the county's bounds. Professor Anthony Fletcher has argued that 'kinship was the dominant principle' of social and political life in seventeenth-century Sussex. The same was true of Kent, where the term 'Kentish cousin' was applied to very remote relatives who were nevertheless accepted as kin. In south-western England, a contemporary saying had it that 'All Cornish gentlemen are cousins'. And where kinship did not exist in a literal sense, it could be created artificially by choosing friends to act as godparents.

Kinship links were also valued by the merchant and business community in the early modern period. Further down the social scale, it is less easy to see the practical use of such contacts. Contradictory evidence may be quoted. The diary of Nicholas Assheton of Downham, Lancashire, reveals that 30 per cent of the people whom he recorded meeting in 1617–18 were kinsfolk and that 40 per cent of the people mentioned in the diary were kin. He supported his kin in times of trouble and his social life was much concerned with family gatherings.

Assheton was a member of a leading county family. Adam Eyre was a Yorkshire yeoman who often visited his immediate relatives, who lived close by, but most of his social life during the period 1647–9 was shared with friends and neighbours to whom he was not related. When practical help was needed, it was given to or accepted from these neighbours more than from kinsmen other than his father-in-law and his cousin Joseph. Dr Houlbrooke concludes from these and other examples that kinship was a reserve that could be drawn upon, but that it was not of overriding importance. 'Neighbourliness' rather than 'kinship' was a notion much favoured by sixteenth- and seventeenth-century people.

Neighbours were often approached to help with the formalities of transferring property from parents to children. In most parts of England it has been the custom for property to pass from one generation to another through the eldest son. Over time, the fortunes of an elder branch of a family have therefore differed greatly from those of junior branches. People descended from a wealthy family in a junior line often ended up after only a few generations in very humble circumstances. If the senior line failed, however, the fortunes of a junior branch of a family were sometimes restored at a stroke as they came into their inheritance. Victorian novels are full of such dramatic reversals of fortune.

In practice, inheritance customs often softened the stark contrasts in expectations between the elder and younger members of a family. In the first place, certain parts of the country did not use the primogeniture system, but insisted on a form of partible inheritance whereby all children received a share of their parent's estate. In Kent, for example, a type of partible inheritance known as gavelkind brought all sons equal shares of the patrimony. Secondly, even where primogeniture was the official system, parents commonly provided for all their children. In rural districts, the eldest son would inherit the family farm, but parents would try to ensure that younger sons received other property and that daughters were provided with a marriage portion. Parents felt a sense of obligation towards their younger children and, in return, expected to be looked after in their old age. Provision for younger children naturally depended on the ability of parents to provide and the strength of their affection for their offspring. Men were generally reluctant to bequeath to their eldest son an estate that was smaller than the one that they themselves had inherited, but anything they had on top of that might be given to younger children.

Part of the parental estate was commonly passed on to children long before the death of the father. Nearly half the resources flowing from Ralph Josselin to his surviving children in the shape of land, goods, and payments for education, apprenticeship and marriage portions, had already been transferred before he made his will. It was normal practice to settle land or money on children upon their marriage. Often, the family farm was given to a son when the father became too old to work it himself. Arrangements would then be made for the son who inherited to look after his parents in their retirement. Wills tell only part of the story of inheritance. Indeed, Dr Margaret Spufford has argued that will-making was necessary mainly to men who had not lived long enough for their children to have inherited in this less formal manner.

Whenever an estate was transferred from father to son the widowed mother had to be provided for. Wills commonly specified the accommodation, furniture, and income that were to be enjoyed by the widow. Local custom determined the size of the bequest. A common provision was that a widow was entitled to a third of her deceased husband's estate, but in some places she was allowed a half, two-thirds, or even the whole. On some manors her widow's rights might last for her lifetime, on others she had to relinquish her property when her eldest son came of age. The customs of some manors insisted that the widow lost her rights on remarriage, but more commonly her property passed to her new husband during her lifetime. The decline of customary tenures led to a withering away of these customs, though they survived for most of the seventeenth century in western England and it was not until 1692 that the widow's third was abolished in the province of York. Among the wealthier families it had become common in the later Middle Ages to agree upon marriage to a 'jointure', by which property was held jointly by the husband and wife, and after death by the widow. Amongst the rest of society men tried to provide for their widows as best they could. Widows were commonly appointed executrices and guardians of the children and they often continued to run their husband's business.

In her study of the merchants of medieval London Sylvia Thrupp noted that many of the families that died out in the male line survived through daughters. She concluded that

These London women, remaining for the most part attached to city property and city ways and marrying within their class, must have contributed immeasurably to the stability of its culture. When sons failed to grow up, their places were often filled by nephews or cousins or by the children of friends in the provinces who were taken in tutelage as apprentices. Country immigrants therefore did not necessarily represent so much alien raw material to be assimilated only through the process of education offered in apprenticeship but often fitted in a most welcome and intimate way into some family situation.

These words ring true for provincial England as well as the metropolis and for later periods of time as well as the Middle Ages.

Social Mobility

In his monumental book *South Yorkshire: The History and Topography of the Deanery of Doncaster* (1828) the Revd Joseph Hunter printed a list of the local gentry whose claims to arms were upheld by the heralds in their visitation of 1584. He was struck by 'the fact of how few of these families still remain' 250 years later. His observation could have been applied with equal truth to other parts of the country and to aristocratic families as well as to the gentry. The composition of the richest and most powerful families in the land has constantly been renewed. The aristocratic families of Victorian England were rarely descended from medieval barons or Norman knights. Today, only a dozen or so gentry families still own the lands from which their medieval ancestor took his name.

The great landed families that have retained their estates over the centuries are exceptional. Failure in the male line and the strict rules of primogeniture meant that many peerages became extinct. In 1838 it was estimated that only 22 per cent of the 359 contemporary peers belonged to families that had held a title a century and a half earlier at the revolution of 1688. Very few could trace a noble pedigree that stretched back into the Middle Ages. Only 17 peers (5 per cent of the total) had been ennobled before the accession of the House of Tudor. The lesser nobility had no greater claims to antiquity. Only 295 (24 per cent) of the 1,226 baronetcies created between 1611 and 1800 survived in 1928; nearly 22 per cent of all baronetcies had failed in the first generation.

This fluidity of membership has persuaded many genealogists that the English aristocracy was a uniquely open society. They have contrasted the supposedly closed castes of the Continent unfavourably with the lack of formal constraints to upward social mobility to the very top in England. But, as Professor John Beckett has shown, these claims do not stand up to close examination. Although it was possible for newcomers to enter the ranks of the lower gentry, admission to a hereditable title was dependent upon the ownership of a suitably sized landed estate. Entry into the highest ranks was always very difficult. A man might rise quickly if he was a trusted servant of the Crown, but for most families progression was slow and often frustrating. Before a person could be considered for membership of the aristocracy, he had to establish his pedigree. The early county histories are full of the pedigrees of the local landed families, for demonstrating one's descent was a matter of great practical concern. Daniel Defoe thought that only the third generation of a new family would be acceptable to the established members of landed society.

The key difference with the Continent, where all of a nobleman's sons enjoyed noble status, was that in England a title descended only in the eldest male line. The rules of primogeniture established the order of progression through a younger brother, nephew, great-nephew or uncle, and finally a cousin. Even so, families continued to fail in the male line and new creations were necessary to maintain the numbers of peers and baronets. Where families produced a surplus of sons, the younger branches gradually—and sometimes quickly—descended the social scale. After the development of strict family settlement in 1660, younger sons received a cash payment and had to seek a career in the Church, the law, or the armed forces. In turn, their sons often had to accept something less.

The Norman Conquest was the last time that the membership of England's landowning élite was replaced at a stroke. William's commanders became his barons and his fighters became his knights. The baronial families of England remained predominantly Norman by male descent until the end of the fourteenth century. The other major transference of landed property occurred late in the reign of Henry VIII, when the monasteries were dissolved. Most of the existing élite availed themselves of the opportunity to add to their estates, but lesser families were able to acquire a major stake for the first time. The Cavendishes, Russells, and Thynnes, for example, rose in this way.

The Tudor monarchs were reluctant to create new peers, but their successors, James I, Charles I, and Charles II, felt no such constraints. Financial worries caused James to create the order of baronetcy in 1611 and to raise 46 commoners to the English peerage. In the first four years of his reign Charles I added another 26. Between 1603 and 1629 the number of peers was thereby doubled. Charles II raised many more to the peerage upon his Restoration and created several dukes (five of them his bastard sons). After the 1688 revolution the initiative for creating peers passed to the sovereign's ministers, who rewarded men for political service. The period 1780–1830 and the later Victorian decades saw further large increases. In 1658 the English peerage was estimated at 119, by 1900 the number had risen to over 520.

The 3,000 or so landowners who formed the governing élite in the early fourteenth century had all been considered noble, whether they were earls, barons, knights, or esquires, and each bore a coat of arms. The distinction between the titled peerage and the untitled gentry developed gradually during the fifteenth century. The unauthorized use of the terms esquire and gentry had become so common by 1530 that the heralds began a series of visitations, county by county, to test all claims. The heralds were unable to enforce their orders, however, and the practice of holding occasional visitations was abandoned in 1688. Many a seventeenth-century 'gentleman' had no legal claim to such an address but was nevertheless considered by his neighbours to have acquired such status, even though some were prosperous townsmen with little or no land. This vagueness of definition at the lowest level of nobility was in sharp contrast to continental practice. It also frustrates the historian who attempts to count the numbers of families involved.

In the 1630s the heralds accepted the claims of 1,172 Londoners to be gentlemen, but the claims of many more men would have been accepted by their friends and neighbours. Dr Peter Earle has calculated that 91 per cent of these London gentry were younger sons of gentlemen who lived in the country. An intricate web of relationships therefore connected the gentle families of metropolitan and rural England. Moving to London or to one of the provincial cities to enter the world of commerce or one of the professions was the accepted way for a younger son of a country gentleman to earn a living. Many of the City merchants who had risen to unofficial gentry status were immigrants or the sons of immigrants. Having made their money they often purchased a country seat and retired from business. Sylvia Thrupp concluded that in the Middle Ages merchant families with a long tradition of urban life never formed more than a small core:

The percentage of the members of the greater companies who represented a third generation of successful trade in London can never have been very large. In the story of such long-lived and wealthy families as clung to the city the curve of fortune was usually downward . . . Family ties with relatives in remote provincial towns and villages remained surprisingly close.

In the Tudor and Stuart period successful City merchants commonly founded a school or an almshouse in their native place as their personal memorial.

'We in England', wrote the Essex parson William Harrison in 1577, 'divide our people commonlie into foure sorts.' The first degree was that of gentleman, including the peerage, knights, esquires, and 'they that are simplie called gentlemen'. Second in rank came the freemen of the cities and third the rural yeomen. Harrison's 'fourth and last sort of people' were 'the day-labourers, poor husbandmen . . . copy-holders, and all artificers as tailors,

JOHN ROYSE'S SCHOOL, ABINGDON, OXFORDSHIRE (FORMERLY BERKSHIRE)
Many a London merchant remembered his place of birth when he made his will. In the sixteenth and seventeenth centuries provincial schools and almshouses were often founded in this way. Characteristically, they display the founder's name and coat of arms. This Free Grammar School was founded in 1563.

shoe-makers, carpenters, brickmakers, masons, etc.' This 'last sort' formed by far the largest section of society. Many families remained in this group for centuries, but its membership was constantly changing as people moved up or down the social scale.

In considering the great majority of the rural population it is best to think in terms of broad social groups rather than the distinctions formulated by lawyers. A countryman's status depended more upon the amount of land that he held than his form of tenure. The yeomen were the most substantial of the working farmers, the husbandmen were the smallholders who formed the backbone of most farming communities, and the cottagers had to supplement their incomes by day-labouring. Hard work or good fortune enabled families to move up the rural social scale. Idleness, extravagance, drunkenness, a series of bad harvests, or other misfortunes could send a family tumbling the other way. Members of each of these groups often earned part of their living from a craft. To have a dual occupation was the normal way of life in many parts of rural England. In such districts the divisions between the various social groups were even more blurred than usual. A man who was described in local records by the name of a craft might have been a humble cottager or a smallholder or sometimes a yeoman. Urban craftsmen were equally varied in their wealth and standing in the community.

The way in which a person held land did not necessarily affect his status. Farmers were sometimes said to be yeomen even though they were not freeholders, while many an owner-occupier rented extra fields. In the Middle Ages the arrangements by which people held land other than by freehold varied from manor to manor, according to local custom. The most common system was copyhold, under which tenants paid a large entry fine at the beginning of their tenancy and then low annual rents. Customary tenures remained widespread in the early modern period, especially for smaller properties, but they were gradually replaced by leases. The sixteenth century had been a time of high inflation, which benefited those with sound customary tenures that guaranteed fixed annual rents and certain entry fines, but in many parts of the country landlords were able to prove that entry fines and rents were 'arbitrary' and they were thus able to raise their revenues considerably. In eastern parts of England leasehold tenure commonly took the form of 21-year leases, whereas the western counties tended to favour leases for three lives, but there was much variation in practice. Yearly tenancies held at rack-rents, which were negotiable, were common in the Midlands for all rented farms and elsewhere for small properties, especially those which were sublet. Families often held land by a variety of tenures; it was only in times of serious dispute that the method of holding had any importance. As we have seen, very many farming and craft families stayed in the same locality, often on the same property, for generation after generation. They moved neither up nor down on the social scale.

A SEVENTEENTH-CENTURY WIDOW
Simon Du Bois's portrait of Lady Jones, the widow of Sir William Jones, was painted in 1682, the year of her husband's death. Sir William's distinguished legal career had culminated in his appointment as Attorney-General. Lady Jones, who was now widowed a second time, died in 1700.

WILLIAM CAVENDISH, 1ST EARL OF DEVONSHIRE

William, the second son and principal heir of Sir William Cavendish and Bess of Hardwick, is shown here in 1576 in his 25th year. He was created Earl of Devonshire in 1618. The family had no possessions in Devonshire, but the title was vacant and that of Earl of Derby was held by the Stanley family who were based in the hundred of West Derby, near Liverpool. The fourth Earl was given the title of 1st Duke of Devonshire as a reward for his part in the 'Glorious Revolution' of 1688. He built the present house at Chatsworth around Sir William and Bess's sixteenth-century home. Andrew Cavendish, the eleventh Duke, is descended from the first Earl.

SIR HUGH MYDDLETON (1628)

Sir Hugh Myddleton, the London goldsmith and overseas trader, was born in Denbigh in c.1560. He was made a baronet in 1622. He is best known as the 'Projector of the New River', a ten-foot-wide canal that was opened in 1613 and which brought a much-needed supply of water to London from Hertfordshire. He died three years after this portrait was painted.

Some of the farming families that had survived the Black Death and later outbreaks of plague had been able to increase the size of their holdings and thus to climb a rung or two of the social ladder. Many of the minor gentry families of the seventeenth century had risen from this sort of background. The drastic fall in the national population had also enabled humble cottagers to fill vacant holdings and to demand higher wages. The easing of population pressure was beneficial for the survivors. Once the population recovered to its old levels, however, the number of people with little or no land rose again. Queen Elizabeth's government was preoccupied with the problem of the poor who had neither land nor regular work. Rootless vagrants who haunted alehouses and slept rough were a constant problem in the towns and a summer concern in the countryside. All over England the number of men who were dependent on the wages that they earned increased until by the later seventeenth century they formed about half the population. The Elizabethan and Stuart era saw some spectacular examples of upward social mobility, but far more people—especially younger children—slipped downwards into the poorest class of all.

AFTER 1800

In 1801 the population of England and Wales stood at 9.2 millions. During the next hundred years it soared to levels undreamed of in earlier times. This prolonged period of growth had begun in the 1740s; the fastest rate of increase occurred during the second decade of the nineteenth century. By 1851 the national population had almost doubled to 17.9 millions and by 1911 it had doubled again to 36.1 millions. During the last two decades of the nineteenth century birth-rates began to decline, but the increased expectation of life ensured that the total population kept rising. It has continued to rise at a slower rate throughout the twentieth century.

The 1851 census marked a historic turning-point in the demographic history of the country. For the first time, more people were classified as living in urban than in rural places. Although the census definition of urban as a place with more than 2,000 people might now seem low, this is how contemporaries judged it. The trend is clear. By 1881, 2 out of every 3 people were defined as urban and by 1911, 4 out of every 5. At the beginning of the nineteenth century only London had more than 100,000 inhabitants. By 1831 Manchester, Glasgow, Liverpool, Edinburgh, Birmingham, Leeds, and Bristol had grown to this size; together with London they housed one-sixth of the national population. Another one-quarter lived in the 90 per cent of British towns that had less than 20,000 inhabitants. By 1901 nearly 40 towns had over 100,000 inhabitants and well over a third of the national population lived in them. Fifty years later, over half the British population lived in places that had over 100,000 people.

A few examples from Yorkshire illustrate the huge rise of the urban population during the course of the nineteenth century. In the borough of Leeds the population rose from 53,162 in 1801 to 428,572 a hundred years later. In the parish (later the borough) of Sheffield it rose from 45,755 to 380,793, and in the parish of Bradford it increased from 29,794 to 290,297. Most of the towns that grew into large Victorian cities had long histories going back to the Middle Ages, but a few new towns were created from almost nothing. Middlesbrough had only 239 inhabitants in 1801, but by the end of the century it had 90,936.

During the course of the nineteenth century, London grew into the biggest and most complex city in the world. Starting with 865,000 inhabitants in 1801, it contained 4.5 million people a hundred years later, that is, more than one-sixth of the population of England. In Lancashire, by the middle of the nineteenth century, half the population were accommodated in the 14 towns which had more than 10,000 inhabitants each. The age of steam-powered cotton factories had made Lancashire the most urbanized county in Britain. In Birmingham and the towns of the Black Country population growth was sustained by a radically different economic structure based on numerous small workshops of a traditional type. The deep division between master and workers that was so evident in Lancashire was absent here. Many of the workers were skilled and relatively well paid. Family networks remained important in the transmission of skills, the provision of credit, and the support that was needed in times of hardship. The Victorian industrial districts were, therefore, hugely varied in their economic and social structure, as well as in their physical appearance and their human composition.

COTTON MILLS AT MANCHESTER (1835)
The population of Manchester rose by 45 per cent between 1821 and 1831 to 142,000. Here, more than anywhere else in Britain, industrialization was associated with the factory system. The period of the spectacular growth of the Lancashire cotton industry lasted from 1770 to 1840. Cotton was Britain's leading export between 1803 and 1938.

CRADLEY HEATH
CHAINMAKERS (*c.*1910)
Chainmaking was a new
Black Country trade of the
early nineteenth century.
Chains were made in a few
large workshops such as this
and in about 300 small
workshops in Cradley and
two or three other places.
Industrialization in this part
of Britain was not depen-
dent on the factory system.
The men rented space and
worked their own hours in
the time-honoured manner.

It used to be thought that the phenomenal growth of such places must
have created a potentially explosive situation with great numbers of rootless
people living in misery. The poorest immigrants certainly did live in appalling conditions, as the literature of the time testifies. The majority of
working people, however, were reasonably accommodated close to old
friends and relatives. A familiar feature of many a Victorian town was that it
contained small districts which were largely populated by people who had
come from the same place. Although nearly every large town in 1851 had
more immigrants than natives, most immigrants had not travelled very far
and they had naturally sought out their old acquaintances. The young girls
who had come to work as domestic servants were exceptional in being scattered throughout the better-off areas. As Michael Anderson has argued, the
Industrial Revolution strengthened rather than weakened the ties of
kinship.

The nineteenth-century growth of population must not be viewed
merely in an urban context, however. In south Lancashire, the Black Country, and the West Riding of Yorkshire industrial villages sprawled over the
countryside at an equally astonishing rate. The Yorkshire parish of Birstall,
for instance, had no recognizable urban centre at the beginning of the nineteenth century, but the population of its collection of villages grew from
14,657 in 1801 to 67,424 a hundred years later. The numbers employed in the
traditional handicrafts continued to expand during the first half of the nineteenth century. Elsewhere, the sinking of a coal pit, the opening of a quarry,
or the establishment of an iron works attracted a work-force to places which
had previously had only a tiny number of people. Many old villages were
dwarfed by the new ones that sprung up alongside them. Yet, at the same

time, in many parts of rural England the population declined as young people left home in search of work in the industrial districts, or increasingly overseas. Some rural settlements contained fewer inhabitants in the mid-Victorian era than they had in the early Middle Ages. Nineteenth-century Britain was therefore a far more varied country than it had ever been before.

Marriages, Births, and Deaths

In *The Population History of England, 1541–1871: A Reconstruction,* Wrigley and Schofield have calculated that only about one-third of the national population growth that occurred between 1750 and 1871 can be accounted for by a reduced death-rate. Two-thirds of the growth was the result of rising fertility from earlier marriages. The age at which women married fell slowly—the mean age was still about 25 by the middle of the nineteenth century and teenage marriages accounted for only 2 or 3 per cent of the total—but until the 1870s marriages were also becoming more frequent. Many more children were therefore born. A gradual shift back to an older age at marriage started in the late 1870s, so that by 1901 the mean average was 26. Meanwhile, the proportion of women who never married also rose again. This reversal to older patterns of behaviour coincided with increased knowledge of contraception techniques. From 1878 onwards both the crude birth-rate and the fertility rate have declined, but the rising expectancy of life has sustained the growth in population.

Increased population levels ensured that the total number of marriages in a year continued to rise. In the whole of Britain about 180,000 couples a year were married in the 1850s; by the 1870s the number had risen to 226,000 per annum and by the 1890s to 250,000 a year. Those people who never married formed a small but nevertheless significant proportion of the total population. In England and Wales about 11 per cent of males were unmarried at the age of 45 early in Victoria's reign. This figure declined to about 9 per cent in the 1870s and 1880s, then rose back to 11 per cent by 1901. The number of females in England and Wales who were unmarried at the age of 45 amounted to about 12 per cent in the 1840s, 11 per cent in the 1870s and 1880s, and almost 14 per cent by 1901 (when about 20 per cent of Scottish women of this age had never married).

The upper class and the middle classes rarely chose marriage partners who were not their social equals, though the daughters of lower middle-class parents sometimes married beneath themselves and working-class girls who had been introduced into middle-class homes through domestic service sometimes married into a higher social class. Little research has been done on who married whom amongst the working classes. At present our conclusions must rest on the evidence collected in three studies of marriage licences, i.e. 11,000 for the contrasting towns of Northampton, Oldham, and South Shields during the period 1846–56, over 8,000 for Deptford, Greenwich, and Woolwich during the two periods 1851–3 and 1873–5, and about 2,000 for Edinburgh during 1865–9 and 1895–7. This research shows that amongst the 75 per cent or so of the population who belonged to the working classes, the great majority of marriages were made within occupational subgroups. The old tradition whereby an artisan or a manual worker married into a family from a similar craft background remained strong. The largest single category of wives came from the same occupational background as their husbands.

In the first quarter of the nineteenth century the average aristocratic family had 5 children. Fifty years later this average had fallen to 4 and by 1911 it had dropped to 2.5. By then, middle-class family sizes had fallen to about 2.8 children. Professor Michael Thompson has suggested that the small size of Edwardian middle-class families had less to do with aping social superiors than with the costs of an ambitious life-style that included servants and the education of children in public schools. He has also shown that family size varied not only between the social classes but between occupational groups. In marriages contracted before 1861 the largest families were those of miners, agricultural labourers, masons, and boiler-makers, with an average of

'AGRICULTURAL LABOURERS AT HOME' (1872)

H. K. Johnson's engraving is composed of a series of images, each accurately observed. The Great Agricultural Depression had not yet hit the corn-growing regions of Britain.

about 8 children; the smallest were those of spinners (about 6) and weavers (6.86) in the woollen and worsted industry. But mine-owners and colliery managers, as well as the miners, had an average of 8 children; so too did the butchers and master builders. These averages mask a range from childless couples to those with 12 children or more. The patterns of behaviour were varied and complex. Professor Thompson concludes that an average of 8 children born alive was probably the normal tally for early Victorian families regardless of social class or occupation.

By 1911 the general decline in family size was evident amongst all groups. Amongst the working class, the miners still had the largest average number of children (4.33) and the textile workers still had the smallest (3.19). Between them, in ascending order, were the skilled workers, the semi-skilled, the unskilled, and the agricultural labourers. Those who had large numbers of children were therefore mainly engaged in manual labour, but these averages conceal many variations.

In the early Victorian period, when population growth was at its quickest, the illegitimacy rate reached 7 per cent, more than double the highest figure that it had reached in the Tudor and Stuart period. It then declined gradually from 7 per cent to 4 per cent by the end of the century. Of course, the greater size of the population meant that the actual number of illegitimate births was much higher than before. Their recording is therefore more readily observable in nineteenth-century parish registers than in earlier ones.

'PAYING ONE'S RESPECTS'
In James Hayllar's painting, *The Old Master* (1883), the widow sits by the coffin as friends and neighbours pay their last respects.

Falling death-rates from the later eighteenth century onwards helped to sustain the increase in the national population. By 1800 the mortality rate had fallen below 25 per thousand and by 1820 it had dropped to 20 per thousand. Despite a temporary rise, it dropped again to 17.2 per thousand by 1900. These averages hide considerable local variations, however. The rate was much higher in the burgeoning industrial towns and cities and it rose sharply when cholera reached epidemic proportions.

Infant mortality rates fell in the middle of the eighteenth century, but diphtheria and other diseases prevented another significant fall until about 1900. Improved diet, better housing and sanitation, and medical discoveries allowed the general expectation of life to rise steadily. By 1881 men could expect to live an average 43.7 years, women 47.2. By 1938 these ages had risen again to 61.8 for men and 65.8 for women. They have continued to rise since.

The Landed Aristocracy and the Gentry

In 1755 Dr Johnson had defined a gentleman as 'a man of birth: a man of extraction, though not noble'. Many agreed with him that the gentry were not to be counted amongst the aristocracy. In *The Imperial Dictionary* (1850) John Ogilvie described the gentry as 'the classes of people between the nobility and the vulgar'. Yet others continued to insist on the older notion of the nobility of the gentry. The preface to the fourth edition of Burke's *Landed Gentry* (1862) claimed that 'the well-born English gentleman was in fact a nobleman' even if he had no title.

AN UPPER-CLASS GATHERING (1894)
Louisa, Duchess of Abercorn, is shown with 103 of her descendants in the garden of Montagu House, London.

John Burke's first directory of 1833 did not include the word 'gentry'. It purported to record the pedigrees of those commoners who possessed considerable estates but who did not claim hereditary honours. Its original title was *A Genealogical and Heraldic History of the Commoners of Great Britain and Ireland, Enjoying Territorial Possessions or High Official Rank; but Uninvested with Heritable Honours*. The word 'gentry' did not replace 'commoners' until the 1840s, by which time families which had acquired land through fortunes made in industry or trade were being included. Until the outbreak of the First World War the editors continued to insist that the ownership of a substantial landed estate was a necessary condition of entry. In 1914, however, they conceded that men 'who had never owned land, but have won their way to distinction and position in the service of the King and in other ways' could be included.

The strength of the desire to have official recognition of one's social status is demonstrated by the number of licences to display a coat of arms that were issued by the heralds. These rose from about 7,000 in 1830 to a peak of 43,000 in 1868. Burke's *Landed Gentry* appeared to offer legitimacy to the pedigrees that it published until Edward A. Freeman, Regius Professor of History at Oxford, dismissed them in 1877 as 'much wild nonsense'. He was particularly scathing about claims that families had come in with the Conqueror or were even older; these claims, he felt, sapped every principle of truth.

The quickest way to a peerage was through service to the State. Otherwise, admission to the upper ranks was a difficult and protracted struggle. Most men who were elevated to the peerage in the first half of the nineteenth century had a landed background. The prejudice against newcomers who had made their money from business was strong. During the second half of the nineteenth century successful businessmen therefore tried to imitate the aristocratic life-style by, for example, sending their sons to public schools. The old barriers against first-generation wealth were gradually broken down as the nineteenth century drew to a close.

New entrants traditionally sought acceptance through marriage into the lower ranks of the aristocracy. Such opportunities were, however, severely restricted as the members of the upper classes felt that their social status was endangered by marrying beneath them. During the eighteenth century the 81 dukes contracted 102 marriages, of which 53 were with the daughters of peers (including 12 with the daughters of other dukes) and 49 with commoners (only 5 of whom lacked a gentle background). Although cases of peers marrying the daughters of a butcher, a boatman, a barber, a blacksmith, a printer, a labourer, and a college servant can be found in the eighteenth and nineteenth centuries and it is well known that other peers occasionally married singers and actresses, such alliances form a very small proportion of the whole. The social status of the entire family could be endangered by the actions of an individual. Younger sons of peers therefore married much less frequently than did the heirs to titles and estates. Financial difficulty was sometimes an overriding consideration, however, and,

A VICTORIAN COUNTRY
HOUSE PARTY
The group has been
arranged carefully by the
photographer to give a sense
of leisure and contentment.
The photograph was taken
about 1889 but, as so often
with photographs of this
period, the people and even
the place have not been
identified.

when the situation was desperate, wealthy City brides were sought to relieve
the situation. Nevertheless, during the eighteenth century, only 3 per cent of
aristocratic men married the daughters of wealthy merchants. Prejudice
against such marriages remained strong in the following century.

Men who had made their money in trade and commerce knew that to become accepted—however gradually—they had to buy a landed estate. A
substantial shift in attitude did not occur until the agricultural depression of
the last quarter of the nineteenth century. Falling agricultural prices meant
that landowners then no longer formed the vast majority of very rich men.
They survived only if they had minerals to exploit or urban ground-rents to
collect. Meanwhile, careers in the Civil Service had been opened up to competitive examination, the practice of purchasing a commission in the Army
had been abolished, and the political power of the aristocracy had waned as
the right to vote was extended to all. Business peers who possessed little or
no land were admitted to the House of Lords. Until the First World War it
was still possible for aristocratic families to maintain a life-style centred
upon a grand country house, but since then the decline of that life-style has
been inexorable.

During the twentieth century the number of peers has grown considerably. Just over 300 men were raised to the peerage between 1830 and 1895, and
more than 600 were ennobled between 1895 and 1957. Most of the modern
peers therefore have titles of no great antiquity. For example, in 1956 only 144
of the 550 baronies pre-dated 1832. Baronetcies and knighthoods have also

been offered on a liberal scale during the twentieth century. Since 1958, however, the usual practice has been to create life peerages rather than hereditary titles. The connection with land has been considerably weakened. During the present century peerages have been given as a reward to retired politicians of ministerial rank and to top Civil Servants. Of the 556 new peers created between 1901 and 1957, only 46 (8 per cent) came from landholding backgrounds, whereas 91 (16 per cent) were industrialists and a further 100 (18 per cent) were professional men. By 1967 43 per cent of the members of the House of Lords derived their income wholly or partly from estate ownership and 46 per cent wholly or partly from business directorships. Less than one-quarter were simply landowners.

Farmers, Servants, and Labourers

The growing divide between an affluent middle class and the working classes was very evident in the countryside. By the late eighteenth century, farmers in the grain-growing regions of southern and eastern England were beginning to question the institution of farm service. Increasing prosperity, especially during the war years, made some farmers (or perhaps their wives) regard their resident farm servants as a social embarrassment. Thus, Arthur Young noted in 1804 that in parts of Norfolk 'a custom is coming in . . . of allowing board wages to farm servants instead of the old way of feeding in the house'. This new practice was not adopted in all parts of England, however. The census returns of 1851 highlight a major division between the south and east, which relied mainly on agricultural labourers, and the north and the west, where the custom of farm service continued to flourish. At that time, in Britain as a whole, 25 per cent of 19-year-old girls and 17 per cent of 19-year-old boys were living-in servants or living-in apprentices.

In southern and eastern parts of Victorian England farming households were fundamentally different from their predecessors in the Tudor and Stuart era. The creation of larger farms in the late eighteenth century altered the structure of English rural society, long before similar developments took place on the Continent. A threefold division between landlords, tenant farmers, and wage-labourers now became the norm in arable areas. By the latter part of Victoria's reign, the 'servant in husbandry' had largely disappeared, except in special districts such as the Yorkshire Wolds, where the institution continued to thrive in the 1920s and 1930s. The majority of people described in late Victorian records as servants were domestic servants, employed to maintain the social status of a family rather than to contribute to the household economy. By this time, the great majority of servants were female; boys in the south and east now worked as day-labourers.

Professor Tony Wrigley has written that the most important change in the composition of the family between Tudor and Victorian times 'was probably the decline in the importance of live-in servants in husbandry'. The con-

VICTORIAN SERVANTS

Men servants at Wepre Hall, Connah's Quay, North Wales, *c*.1900.

Women servants at Wepre Hall, *c*.1890.

temporary decline in the custom according to which apprentices lived with their masters worked to the same end. Once, it had been normal for young unmarried people to live in the households of families of higher social status. The new trend sharpened class divisions, isolating the poor from the rich.

By the middle of the nineteenth century the decline of farm service based on the annual hiring fairs meant that lads in southern and eastern England no longer moved around their 'country' as freely as before. Dr Keith Snell has argued that the relative immobility of farm-workers in the south led to a stronger sense of village 'community' than had existed in the past two centuries. Annual fairs gave way to short-term migratory task gangs (including many women and adolescent children) who gathered the harvest or did other seasonal work. Low wages, tied cottages, and ignorance of other opportunities caused the labouring poor of the south to stay put. The rural population continued to rise until the middle of the century, when the railways and the steamships began to provide means of escape. In the north, by contrast, the proximity of the industrial districts meant that farmers had to pay higher wages than in the south. The northern farm labourers were not reduced to the abject poverty of their southern counterparts. The growing split between 'north and south' had become obvious by the 1770s. By the mid-nineteenth century the division between the poorly paid, 'de-industrialized' south and the high-wage, industrial north was clear to all.

The decline of farm service, the social effects of enclosure, the reduced opportunities for female employment on the farms, and the lowering of male wages consequent upon the national increase of population and competition for jobs severely lessened the ability of young people to save for marriage. The incidence of both premarital pregnancy and illegitimacy rose sharply in the early decades of the nineteenth century. The old saying 'No child, no wife' was widely quoted at this time. More unmarried people lived together than is often supposed and more marriages broke up than is sometimes realized. Divorce was formalized in 1857.

The quality of marital relations was as varied as it is today. By the middle of the nineteenth century the wife of a southern or eastern farm labourer had such little chance of obtaining field work that she was accurately described as 'housewife'. One of her important roles was to manage the household economy. Flora Thompson has described how in rural Oxfordshire in the 1880s the men handed their wages straight over to their wives, who gave them back a shilling for spending-money. With the arrival of each new child the problem of making ends meet became sharper. Dr Snell has concluded that 34 was the age when men were most likely to need assistance from the poor rates. His analysis of Poor Law examinations shows that although uncles or grandparents were frequently mentioned, agricultural families did not normally apply to kin for help unless they were migrating to London or to other large towns and needed a job and accommodation. After the Poor Law Amendment Act of 1834 it became customary for overseers to order sons and daughters to pay part of the cost of relief to the elderly, normally at a rate of one or two shillings a week.

In western and northern parts of Britain small farms worked by the combined labour of the family remained the norm. Dr David Jenkins has shown that in Cardiganshire at the beginning of the twentieth century people associated families with their farms, even though regular movement from one farm to another at various stages in the life-cycle was normal. Marriage was delayed until a farm was secured. When that happened, friends and relatives were invited to a bidding, where they made a contribution towards getting the young couple started. All children received a share of the patrimony, the girls getting a marriage portion in the same way as did their Tudor and Stuart ancestors. As circumstances changed and opportunities arose, families moved to other farms nearby, often to properties which had been vacated by their kin.

Dr Jenkins comments on the strength of the interest in one's society, in one's neighbours and their affairs, their kinship links, family histories, marriages, fortunes, and their movements from one farm to another. Immigration into Cardiganshire was on a very limited scale until after the Second World War. The inhabitants therefore grew up

knowing other people as the fathers, mothers, brothers, and sisters of their school friends and neighbours. In later life they would come to know youngsters as the children and grandchildren, cousins, nephews, and nieces of those with whom they grew up together. That is they grew up with a knowledge of 'who people were' in a locality.

A DORSET COTTAGE (1846)
This interior of a labourer's cottage near Blandford shows rural poverty at its worst. The farm labourers of Dorset and neighbouring counties were the lowest-paid workers in the country. The walls and ceiling have wide fissures and are black with grease and dirt. The cradle is made of rough boards nailed together.

In such small societies people were inevitably concerned in one another's affairs. Dr Jenkins writes that

Talk of relatives and relationships is pervasive, and not only about the speaker's own kinsmen but about other people's as well. Conversations are shot through with references to the relationships of people who are the subject of discussion. There is a general expectation that people will know the main facts about other people's kin connections while their remoter connections are readily the subject of inquiry. But remarkably widespread as the interest in kin is it is also true that knowledge about kin, including one's own, varies from person to person in considerable measure.

A GROUP OF FARMWORKERS
This artificially posed photograph of c.1895, taken at Rattlesden, Suffolk, shows four men sharpening their scythes and two young men gathering the corn into sheaves.

Few local societies were as remote and as exclusive as Cardiganshire, but these attitudes were paralleled in other rural districts where farms were thinly scattered across the countryside. Pastoral farming was not hit as hard as arable farming during the agricultural depression of the late nineteenth century. In the highland parts of Britain an older way of life centred on small family farms was unaffected by the great changes that occurred in the eastern and southern lowlands. Although the proportion of the national workforce that was involved in agriculture fell remorselessly from its high point in the mid-nineteenth century, many families continued in much the same way as had their ancestors. The census returns for England and Wales recorded about a quarter of a million farmers and graziers. The agricultural labour force continued to decline during the rest of the century, but the number of farmers remained steady. They were as stable a group in Victorian times as they had been in the past. Many of them formed part of one or more farming dynasties that had been established for several generations.

'GIPSIES' AND
'BOHEMIENNES'
William Henry Pyne
(1769–1843) was a water-
colour painter of figures
and landscapes. His rural
scenes include groups of
travellers preparing meals.

Accommodation in an Industrial Society

The contrast between an affluent middle class and the rapidly growing
numbers of working-class people was equally evident in the towns. The differences between the two groups were immediately apparent in the style of
housing. Everyone is aware of the appalling slum conditions in which some
of our Victorian ancestors lived. Parliamentary enquiries, numerous official
reports and surveys, contemporary novels, newspapers, and so on leave no
doubt that the poorest sections of society endured a miserable existence.
The problem of bad housing and inadequate sanitation was at its worst in
the 1830s and 1840s, but the evidence of old photographs shows only too
clearly that slum districts remained a disgraceful feature of towns throughout the reign of Victoria and beyond. The rural poor fared little better, par-

A LONDON SLUM
This view of December 1912 was taken near Petticoat Lane in the East End of London.

ticularly in the arable counties of the south and the east, but the urban slums have received more attention, simply because they were the most visible and because of their scale. In the worst cases, families were huddled together in a single room, often a cellar, or they had to share an upper-floor tenement or a backyard dwelling with others.

The knowledge of these very real hardships and indignities has coloured our view of the Victorian industrial cities. It is important to recall that the great majority of the urban working class did not share such a desperate lifestyle. As Michael Thompson has observed, 'The distinction between slum and non-slum was a social as well as a physical distinction, and the corresponding but somewhat wider difference between the disreputable—who might be feckless, bad managers, or big drinkers, and not simply the very poor—and the respectable was the major line of division within the working class.' The respectable working class was composed of not just the skilled artisans; it comprised the majority of employees in the factories, ironworks, coal-mines, etc. and workers in just about every other occupational group.

This basic division was expressed in the types of housing that were available for working-class families during the nineteenth century. The social gradations between the different occupational groups were reflected in the choice of housing and sometimes in the choice of district in which to live. The image that a Victorian city presented to outsiders masked the considerable differences that existed between one quarter and another. The contrast between the middle-class residential districts and the poorest parts was immediately apparent, but subtle signs such as bow windows or carved lintels helped to place an area firmly in the social order, distinguishing it from the rows of plain terraced houses that were rented at cheaper rates.

The one-storey cottage seems to have been the traditional accommodation of the working man until the late eighteenth century, when workers' houses began to be built on an unprecedented scale. It remained the norm for miners and quarry workers during most of the first half of the nineteenth century, but in the towns and industrial villages sufficient examples of two-storey houses survive to demonstrate that by then they had become the usual style for working-class families. During the eighteenth century, builders in the towns could still find spaces, including former gardens and back yards, within the old urban area. The withdrawal of the middle classes to more salubrious areas in the nineteenth century allowed this process to continue for a time. In the countryside, workers' cottages were erected in rows at the edge of villages or in clusters in hamlets, near the place of work.

The employers who provided houses for their workers tended to be those who needed a large labour force. Most were content to leave such ventures to speculative builders or to building clubs. The typical housing estate therefore grew haphazardly, often in groups of four or five buildings in slightly different styles to those of their neighbours. All sorts of people with limited resources put their money into housing as a safe investment. Meanwhile, numerous clubs and friendly societies expanded their activities from providing insurance against ill health, old age, and unemployment to include the building of houses for their members. Thus, the Halifax Permanent Building Society traces its origins back to the Loyal Georgian Society, which was founded at Halifax in 1779.

During the first half of the nineteenth century the typical worker's house was a two-storey dwelling that formed part of a terrace. It consisted of two rooms, sometimes with a small pantry or a cellar. The two- or three-storey blind-back house with a single room on each floor had become a common urban type, particularly in narrow yards. Cheaper accommodation was available in the form of single-room cellar dwellings, which were built beneath a cottage, with the floor level below that of the street, so that the entrance was reached by a descending flight of steps. Poor as this accommodation was, it was often preferred to the accommodation that was available in subdivided houses or tenements, which were created by the horizontal division of a house or block. Working-class widows, the aged poor, and immigrants from Ireland were often forced to accept such accommodation, sometimes having no option but to share overcrowded rooms with other families.

As the old town centres began to be filled, new housing was erected in the fields beyond in a piecemeal, unplanned way. In some towns long, monotonous rows of back-to-backs became the norm. By 1850 Leeds had 360 streets of them. In the textile areas workers' houses were built close to the factories, regardless of the difficulties presented by the lie of the land. On steep slopes, houses sometimes had two storeys above street level and two

A TYNESIDE SLUM
The slum conditions at Dog Leap Stairs, Newcastle, were photographed in 1889.

storeys below at the back. The typical mill-worker's cottage was a two-storey dwelling in a terrace, with a single room on each floor, and no back door. A weaver's cottage contained space for working at a loom in a well-lit upper storey. In the woollen and worsted industry weaving was not mechanized until long after the spinning process, so weavers' cottages continued to be built throughout the first half of the nineteenth century. In the second half of the century some outstanding housing was provided by philanthropic mill-owners, notably Edward Ackroyd and Titus Salt, but most workers still had to rent accommodation from landlords who had no connection with the workplace.

The way that a town grew can be observed from large-scale ordnance survey maps, rate-books, and local directories. During the 1860s most munici-

pal authorities issued bye-laws to regulate building standards. From then onwards working-class housing became more uniform, though with regional variations. In the textile towns of the West Riding improved back-to-backs were the norm; in Tyneside two-storey flats built on top of each other were preferred; in the Midlands and the south terraced housing with small extensions at the rear were usual; and in the Lancashire cotton towns similar terraces without outbuildings were favoured. The depressing gridiron patterns of terraced housing that characterized so many Victorian industrial towns date from this period. By the last quarter of the nineteenth century, when local authorities were actively promoting higher standards and the model housing movement had got underway at Port Sunlight and Bournville, working-class housing was markedly better than it had been at the beginning of Victoria's reign. The back-to-backs, for example, were improved until they contained a basement or cellar, a living-room and a scullery on the ground floor, two bedrooms on the first floor and, usually, a third bedroom in the attic.

Though the overall standard improved gradually, some notorious slums remained. The worst conditions were to be found in Glasgow, where one-quarter of the population in the 1880s lived in one-room apartments in tenement blocks that were four or five storeys high. Groups of these blocks surrounded small courts which opened off a narrow alley, giving access on to the main street. Such places were not typical of the country at large. By the end of the century British workers were, on the whole, better housed than the workers of any other European country.

Subsidized council housing was introduced after the First World War. Until then, most families rented their accommodation from private landlords. One-year leases were common in Scotland, but the normal arrangement in England was that a working-class family would rent a house on a weekly or a monthly tenancy. Landlords were responsible for repairs and maintenance. Despite the lack of security of tenure, many families stayed in the same house for a generation or more. Others were able to move around on a regular basis, for the total number of available houses kept just ahead of the increase in the national population.

Middle-class suburbs appeared on the fringes of all the major towns during the 1830s and 1840s. Houses of many different sizes and styles were built to suit the incomes and tastes of those who could afford a private villa well away from the place of work. Middle-class families were able to move further and further out when rail services were established in the 1850s and 1860s to supplement those of the horse-drawn omnibuses. The 1860s saw the beginning of a period of rapid suburban growth; by the 1880s every large town had its middle-class districts beyond the old urban centre, sited to take advantage of the prevailing wind, which cleared the smoke of the factories in the opposite direction. Greater London grew the quickest of all; between 1881 and 1891 Leyton, Willesden, Tottenham, and West Ham experienced a faster rate of growth than any place in England. By the end of the nineteenth century London's population was increasing by 100,000 people a year.

The Victorian middle classes were not usually owner-occupiers. They normally rented their houses for a short, but fixed, term of years, during which they were responsible for repairs and maintenance. Owning a house did not increase one's social standing in the community. Many different types of people became landlords, for housing was regarded as a reliable form of investment that yielded a regular income. Tradesmen, shopkeepers, small masters, professionals, retired people, and widows were prominent amongst those who owned a few houses for others to rent. Perhaps as few as 10 per cent of all houses were occupied by their owners.

Until the coming of electric trams, the working classes could not afford to distance themselves from the workplace. Indeed, the home remained the place of work in the time-honoured way for certain craftsmen and for women who took in washing or who used their skills with the needle. When the opportunity arose, however, the respectable working classes were just as keen as were those immediately above them in the social scale to find a suitable residential district. Once they had found such a place, they often stayed for the rest of their lives.

A Victorian Villa
Number 5 Troy Road, London, was probably built in the 1880s, for the road was first listed in a street directory in 1886. It stands in the area of Upper Norwood and Crystal Palace in SE19 postal district.

CHAPTER FIVE

A Guide To The Records

Getting Started

THE thousands of people who are actively tracing their family tree are probably outnumbered by those who have thought that one day they would get round to doing just that but who never seem to get started. If the plunge is taken the pursuit of one's ancestors quickly gathers its own momentum. The determined decision to make a beginning is often the most important that the family historian will make. Part of the problem is simply finding the time and the energy, but much of the inertia is due to lack of know-how. The beginner who has never heard of the PRO and the IGI can easily be put off by the insider's jargon and may well be daunted by a microfilm reader, the thought of finding and entering a record office, and the need to understand how to interpret the evidence of unrelated sets of archives. It takes time not to be intimidated and to realize that the principal ingredient of success is common sense. The technicalities of the subject can be learned as one goes along.

Most people have at least some knowledge of their family in the past, even if they cannot go back very far. Before visiting the nearest library or record office it is helpful to assemble this information in a notebook or file. The need to record everything that one has learnt and to make a careful note of the source of that information is a lesson that should be borne constantly in mind. Interviewing one's relatives, especially the older ones before it is too late, is clearly an early task. Very often the information is muddled and sometimes downright misleading. It is common to find a belief that the family has had a romantic past, that they are descended from someone important (perhaps in an illegitimate line), or that vast sums of money wait to be inherited if only a firm link could be proved. But amidst all this dross are usually a few nuggets of priceless information about where a family came from, who was related to whom, what they did for a living, why they moved home, and so on. There is often enough to provide a firm lead in the right direction.

The pooled resources of a family usually supply a varied collection of old

photographs (nearly always unlabelled), newspaper cuttings, birth, marriage, and death certificates, and other mementoes. These help to stimulate interest and are useful props to take when talking to old people whose memories are often stirred by such things. Write everything down, remain sceptical about claims that the family are descended from King Canute, the Duke of Marlborough, Huguenot refugees, Border cattle-rustlers, or all of these people, and follow the leads that promise to point the way back to the unknown. Do not start with some famous person who had the same surname as yours back in the fifteenth century. The golden rule is to work backwards from the known to the unknown. The records of civil registration (outlined below), the census returns of the nineteenth century, and the parish registers are the basic sources for the beginner. It is very common to find that one can quickly get back to the beginning of Victoria's reign. It is then that the real problems begin.

Seeking the help and company of fellow enthusiasts is a natural step to take as one gets started. Adult education departments often provide courses for the beginner and few parts of Britain are now without a local family history society. The national Federation of Family History Societies keeps them all in contact, publishes cheap and useful guides, and has its own magazine, *Family History News and Digest*. Regular programmes of lectures, conferences, and visits offer instruction and a friendly forum of advice. Most societies produce their own journal and many of them publish editions of local records, such as census returns, hearth tax returns, and indexes of parish registers. Making careful surveys of the tombstones in local churchyards—monumental inscriptions, or MIs, for short—is a particularly useful task that is often carried out by society members.

Armed with all the oral information that can be obtained from relatives, the family historian may usefully decide to try to find his ancestors' gravestones. This is another job that should not be delayed because many tombstones are deteriorating badly and others are being removed. In rural areas the graveyard attached to the ancient parish church may still be in use. The oldest tombstones date from the seventeenth century and are found nearest the church, normally to the south, for the north was once regarded as the devil's side where excommunicates, suicides, and unbaptized parishioners were buried. The memorials of the richer inhabitants will be found inside the church. As

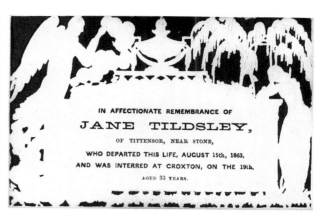

MEMORIAL CARDS
Large numbers of memorial cards survive from the mid-Victorian period onwards. Edged in black and designed in a variety of styles, they often survive amongst a family's mementoes. They provide the family historian with precise information.

churchyards became full and the earlier practice of reusing old graves was prevented by the erection of sturdy tombstones, local authorities had to provide alternative arrangements. The first public cemetery was opened in London at Kensal Green in 1827; soon, other towns and cities followed suit. In 1850 an Act of Parliament authorized the General Board of Health to close old churchyards and establish cemeteries. The records of these cemeteries have sometimes been deposited at the appropriate local record office, but many may still be consulted at the office on the site. They normally record the name, address, age, and occupation of the deceased, the date of death and burial, and the place of the grave. However, this information is filed in chronological order and is not indexed alphabetically, so it helps to have a previous idea of the approximate date of death.

The family historian quickly learns not to take all his evidence at face value. Tombstones may be as inaccurate as any other record, especially if they were erected long after the death of the first person to be named. The recorded age must be regarded with caution. It was common, for instance, to think of someone aged 84 as being in his eighty-fifth year and to note the age as 85. On the other hand, tombstones often convey information, e.g. about a relationship, that the researcher did not know. Write it all down and note the exact position of the tombstone for future reference.

Many of us do not proceed in a systematic way at the beginning, but the sooner the decision is made to organize our material the better. Separate notebooks or files for each branch of the family are obviously desirable, but each individual will develop his own methods to suit his temperament, facilities, and enthusiasm. A computer database helps but is not essential! At all stages of research it will be necessary to construct family trees, however tentative they may be. Do not try to put everybody on the same tree, but use different sheets for each side of the family. Some sheets can be used to include everyone on a particular branch within a particular period, others need to give the barest of outlines so that a clear line of descent can quickly be perceived. It is difficult to give general advice on how to display these trees as the number of children varies so much from one family to another and

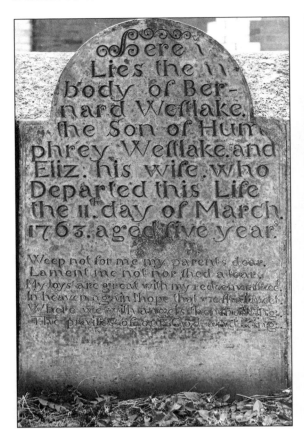

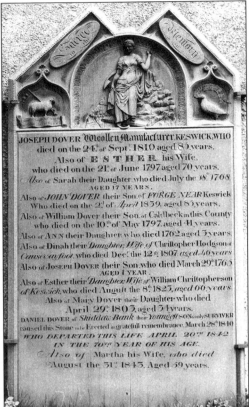

TOMBSTONES

Tombstones were not erected in churchyards until well into the seventeenth century. One of the earliest references to the new practice is from the diary of Samuel Pepys, who on 3 June 1667, 'walked to Stepny and spent my time in the churchyard looking over gravestones' while waiting for company. The earliest tombstones are normally found near the south wall of the church, for the north side was 'the devil's side' where the unbaptized, excommunicated and suicides were buried. The richer families were buried inside the church. An epitaph at Kingsbridge, Devon, in 1795 reads:

> Here lie I at the chapel door
> Here lie I because I'm poor,
> The farther in the more you'll pay,
> Here lie I as warm as they.

The inscriptions attest the spread of literacy. Their styles vary according to region and period, as shown by these two examples from Lostwithiel, Cornwall, and Great Crosthwaite, Cumbria. The Cumbrian example shows how much genealogical information can be stored in this way; the recorded deaths in this one family were spread over eighty years. The last four lines were added after the stone was erected.

Many tombstones are becoming worn and illegible and others are under threat of destruction. Some family history societies have done valuable work in recording inscriptions.

A VICTORIAN FUNERAL
A poignant painting of grief, entitled *Her First Born, Horsham Churchyard*, by Frank Hall in 1877.

from generation to generation. Other people's methods may not be suited to your requirements because no two families are alike. It helps to keep people of the same generation at the same level, with husband and wife side by side, and to use the standard genealogical abbreviations:

b.	born	dau.	daughter
bapt.	baptized	s.	son
d.	died	div.	divorced
d.unm.	died unmarried	unm.	unmarried
d.s.p.*	died without children	=	married
		l	left descendants

* From the Latin *decessit sine prole*.

There is no standard or best way of arranging one's material. One learns from experience and adapts as one goes along. The trees need to be updated regularly, so it does not matter too much if early attempts subsequently look amateurish.

It is now time to make one's first visit to a record office. Its whereabouts can be discovered from a telephone directory or from a local library. In most cases admission is free and professional archivists will offer advice. They are more inclined to help those who have already made some progress and have at least some idea of what they are looking for than to assist those who think that others are going to do all the work for them. Most people will start with parish registers, census returns, and the records of civil registration, so it is with these that this guide will begin.

Civil Registration

The national system of registration of births, marriages, and deaths began on 1 July 1837, the year Queen Victoria came to the throne. The indexes of all these registered events are currently available for consultation at the Family Records Centre, 1 Myddelton Street, London, EC1, which is open on Mondays, Wednesdays, and Fridays, from 9 a.m. to 5 p.m., Tuesdays, from 10 a.m. to 7 p.m., Thursdays, from 9 a.m. to 7 p.m., and Saturdays, from 9.30 a.m. to 5 p.m. Entry is free and no ticket or prior appointment is required.

The indexes are arranged on shelves, with separate sections for births, marriages, and deaths. Their bulk (especially the earliest ones, which have handwritten entries) makes them heavy and cumbersome to use, particularly as there is rarely sufficient space to open them on the crowded tables, but the effort is often hugely rewarded. The records of civil registration must be counted as the most informative of all the family historian's sources, an indispensable record of events over the last 150 years or so.

Each section of the indexes is arranged chronologically up to the present day. The years are divided into quarters, labelled March, June, September, and December, and the surnames in each quarter are grouped alphabetically. The system is easy to understand and to use. If, to take a fictitious example, a search is being made for the birth of Albert Edward Castle, thought to have been born about February 1878, the first index that should be consulted is the one labelled March 1878. If the relevant entry cannot be found, the next step should be to look at the index marked June 1878; births, in particular, may not have been registered straight away. Often, the searcher will have only a rough idea of the date of birth, based perhaps on an age recorded on a gravestone or a death certificate, in which case a number of indexes around the approximate date will have to be consulted.

In each quarterly index the surnames are listed in alphabetical order, then under each surname the forenames are arranged alphabetically. (From September 1911 onwards the mother's maiden name is also noted.) The next column gives the name of the Superintendent Registrar's District where the birth was registered. These district names may cause some difficulty, for registration districts are much larger than parishes or townships; even people with local knowledge may be unaware of their precise boundaries. Location books are available at the front desk at the Family Records Centre, but it is advisable for the family historian to be acquainted with the names of the districts he is likely to be interested in before starting a search of the indexes. Ray Wiggins's booklet *St Catherine's House Districts* (available from the Society of Genealogists, 14 Charterhouse Buildings, London, EC1M 7BA) provides an alphabetical list of the 650 or so original districts, with details of their subdistricts and the adjacent districts, and the Institute of Heraldic and Genealogical Studies, Northgate, Canterbury, has published two smallscale maps that show the approximate positions (but not the precise boundaries) of the registration districts as they were between 1837 and 1851 and between 1852 and 1946.

It is often difficult to be certain that the correct entry has been identified, especially in the early years before the fashion of having a second forename had become widespread. Determining which Mary Turner or William Wright is the ancestor that is being sought will always be problematic. The field of enquiry is narrowed if it is known which registration districts should produce the most likely candidates, but even then one cannot be sure of the identification without confirmatory evidence, perhaps from a census return or a family memory. Most family historians have had the frustrating experience of paying for a certificate which is not the right one.

Once the person who is being sought has been identified (however tentatively), all the details recorded in the index, i.e. surname, forename, registrar's district, volume, and page number, together with the year and quarter recorded on the spine of the index, should be noted for future reference and for filling in an application form for a certificate. The information that has been acquired so far has not cost the searcher anything. A great deal of information can be obtained free; one might be content, for instance, with knowing that the birth of a relative was registered in June 1863, without taking the matter further. With a direct ancestor, however, it is usually desirable to purchase a certificate. Application forms are readily available and, once completed, should be taken to the counter, together with the fee. The certi-

A BIRTH CERTIFICATE
The birth certificate of Lily Townley provides a great deal of genealogical information. She was born on 16 August 1881 at 16 Danby Street, Everton, the daughter of Alfred Edward Townley, a porter, and his wife Mary (née Attwood).

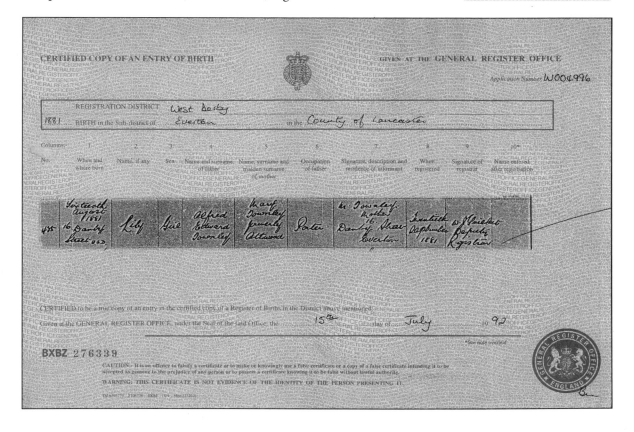

ficate may be collected after four working days; otherwise it will be posted in the envelope that you have been given to address, in about 10 days' time. The cost of a postal request for a certificate is far higher than that of a personal application, even if full details are given on an official application form.

The copy of the certificate that is provided upon payment of the fee is usually freshly made, and as with all copying runs the risk of transcription error. If the original certificate is difficult to read, a photocopy may be issued. Birth certificates provide a great deal of genealogical information. They start by giving the birth date (day, month, and year) and the place of birth (a street name in a town, the name of a village, hamlet, or isolated farmstead in the countryside). This is followed by the name and sex of the individual, the father's forename and surname (or a blank space for an illegitimate child), and the mother's forename, surname, and maiden name. Next comes the occupation of the father, then the name of the informant (who was very often the mother) and her place of residence. During the early decades of civil registration, when illiteracy rates were high, the informant's signature was often in the form of a mark. In any case, the signature is not an original one, but a copy made by the registrar.

The information contained in a birth certificate enables the researcher to go back one stage further. An obvious step is to locate the marriage of the parents by working backwards through the indexes, though this will be a laborious job if the birth certificate relates to the twelfth and final child born to the marriage! Armed with the mother's maiden name, which was recorded on the birth certificate, it is sensible to search the marriage indexes for the rarer of the two surnames and to double-check the finding under the names of both husband and wife.

The indexes of marriages provide a separate record of the surnames and forenames of the bride and bridegroom, the registration district where the ceremony was performed, and the volume and page numbers that need to be copied on to an application form for a certificate. From March 1912 onwards the spouse's surname is recorded alongside that of the bride or groom. The procedure for obtaining a certificate is the same as for births. The marriage certificate gives the name and district of the church, chapel, or register office where the ceremony was performed, and the day, month, and year of the ceremony. At first, relatively few weddings took place in register offices, but the proportion grew steadily and now forms a large majority. The certificates go on to record the full names of both partners, their ages, and their 'condition', as bachelor, spinster, widower, or widow. Before 1870 many marriage certificates do not give ages, but simply note that a person was 'of full age'. This does not imply an age of at least 21, as is sometimes suggested, for many examples can be found where the registrar has taken it to mean the age of consent, which until 1929 might have been even lower than 16. The next columns record the 'rank or profession' of each partner, their residences at the time of marriage, and the full names and ranks or professions of their fathers. Even if a father was dead, he might still be recorded by

CERTIFIED COPY OF AN ENTRY OF MARRIAGE   GIVEN AT THE GENERAL REGISTER OFFICE

Application Number W004996

1891. Marriage solemnized at St Jude's Church in the Parish of East Brixton in the County of Surrey								
No.	When Married.	Name and Surname.	Age.	Condition.	Rank or Profession.	Residence at the time of Marriage.	Father's Name and Surname.	Rank or Profession of Father.
272	May 9th 1891	Samuel Darlington	25	Bachelor	Nurse	58 Shakespeare Road	Joseph Darlington	Mining Engineer
		Ellen Henry	30	Spinster	—	58 Shakespeare Road	James Henry	Tobacconist

Married in the Parish Church according to the Rites and Ceremonies of the Established Church, by after Banns by me, R. Seaman Dean

This Marriage was solemnized between us, { Samuel Darlington / Ellen Henry } in the Presence of us, { Wm S. Henry / William Aldous }

CERTIFIED to be a true copy of an entry in the certified copy of a register of Marriages in the Registration District of Lambeth Given at the General Register Office, under the Seal of the said Office, the 15th day of July 19 92

MX 560434

This certificate is issued in pursuance of section 65 of the Marriage Act 1949. Sub-section 3 of that section provides that any certified copy of an entry purporting to be sealed or stamped with the seal of the General Register Office shall be received as evidence of the marriage to which it relates without any further or other proof of the entry, and no certified copy purporting to have been given in the said Office shall be of any force or effect unless it is sealed or stamped as aforesaid.

CAUTION.—It is an offence to falsify a certificate or to make or knowingly use a false certificate or a copy of a false certificate intending it to be accepted as genuine to the prejudice of any person, or to possess a certificate knowing it to be false without lawful authority.

WARNING: THIS CERTIFICATE IS NOT EVIDENCE OF THE IDENTITY OF THE PERSON PRESENTING IT.

Form A513MX

A MARRIAGE CERTIFICATE Samuel Darlington and Ellen Henry were married at St Jude's Church, Brixton on 9 May 1891. The photographs were both taken in Jersey, where Ellen originated, but on separate occasions. Samuel's was taken by a photographer named Billinghurst, whose business had passed to V. E. Vandycke by the time of Ellen's photograph. Other records show that Ellen's age on the marriage certificate is inaccurate.

his occupation or rank, rather than be described as 'deceased'. Finally, genealogical clues might be obtained from the names of the witnesses, whose signatures follow those of the bride and groom. Here again, the signatures are copies made by the registrar.

The indexes of deaths are arranged in a similar manner to those of births and marriages. From June 1866 they provide an extra piece of genealogical information, namely the age at death. Of course, this has to be treated cautiously, especially with old people, but it may direct an enquiry to a

A Death Certificate

Alfred Edward Townley died in Everton on 22 February 1885, less than four years after the birth of his daughter Lily. His occupation is given as a Cotton Porter; an inquest was held into his death, the Coroner for Liverpool being the 'informant'.

Earlier in his life he was a fireman, and in the photograph he is standing to the right of the fire engine. Supplied by Merryweather to the Borough of Liverpool Fire Brigade in 1865, the engine, Clint, was the first steam fire engine in Liverpool, and one of the first in the country.

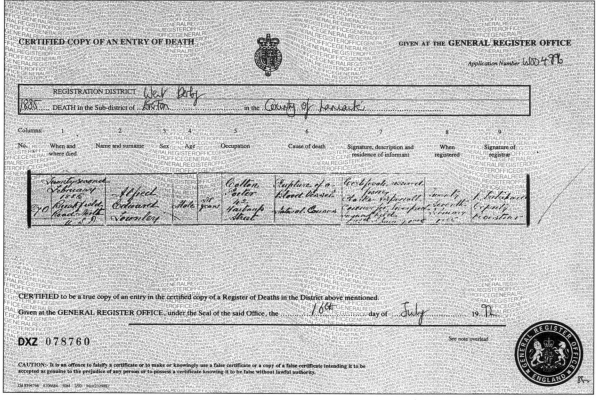

THE NEW REGISTER
HOUSE, EDINBURGH
Exterior and interior views
of the Public Search

baptismal register long before the beginnings of civil registration. The cer-tificates start by noting the date and place of death. They then record the forename(s) and surname of the deceased and his or her sex, age, and occu-.pation. The cause of death is given in the next column, followed by the sig-nature, description, and residence of the informant, who was normally the next of kin or another close relative.

The Family Records Centre also has a section where indexes are shelved under the heading of 'miscellaneous returns'. These indexes record births, marriages, and deaths which occurred overseas. They include records of the armed forces and registers kept by clergymen abroad. They do not, however, form a complete record of Britons who lived overseas. Valuable advice on the whereabouts of such records can be found in Jane Cox and Timothy Padfield's book *Tracing Your Ancestors in the Public Record Office* (chapter 4).

Local Register Offices can sometimes be used to bypass the Family Records Centre, but they do not have the staff or the facilities to deal with many enquiries and indexes are not available for public consultation. A visit to a local register office may reap dividends if fairly precise information about place and date is already known, but sooner or later the search for ancestors is likely to take the family historian beyond the boundaries of a local registration district. A blanket search of all the indexes of civil registration produces a mine of genealogical information. The Society of Genealogists, some public libraries, and Mormon research institutions have microfilms of the indexes at the Family Records Centre, but these are tedious to use and in order to obtain a certificate the researcher still has to visit London or make an expensive application by post.

In Scotland, civil registration started on 1 January 1855. All the records are kept at the General Register Office, New Register House, Edinburgh EH1 3YT, off Princes Street. Scottish certificates are much fuller than the English and Welsh ones, for they give the date of the marriage on a birth certificate, the names of both parents of each couple on marriage certificates, and the names of both parents of the deceased on death certificates. In Ireland, general registration started on 1 January 1864, though the records of Protestant (and some Catholic) marriages go back to 1845. There is, however, no consolidated index; entries from each county are filed together, but it is difficult to trace a family line, especially as the range of surnames is limited. The registration records up to 1922 are held at the Office of the Registrar General, Joyce House, 8–11 Lombard Street, Dublin 2. The records for Eire since 1922 are held in the same place, but those for Northern Ireland are kept at the General Register Office, Oxford House, 49–55 Chichester Street, Belfast BT1 4HL.

From time to time, a search through the indexes will fail to find a name that ought to be there. The most likely explanation for the failure is that the information upon which one is basing the search is not correct in all its details. For example, family memory may insist that an ancestor came from a certain place, whereas the truth of the matter is that he or she lived at that place as a child but was born somewhere entirely different. Another common mistake is to rely on the age recorded on a gravestone of an elderly person. Confusion may also arise if a birth occurred at a hospital, for then the event would have been recorded under the registration district in which the hospital was situated, not in the district where the family lived.

Even if one's prior information about date and place is correct, the entry may remain elusive because of clerical error. The records of civil registration are as prone to mistakes as are any other written sources. The returns of the local registrars were copied into the indexes by another official, who may have misread the original or have made a slip of the pen. In the early decades of registration, when many informants were illiterate, there was no check on what the registrar had written on the certificate. If the informant was not personally known to the registrar, then confusion over the pronunciation and spelling of the name might easily arise. A searcher must therefore try every variant spelling that springs to mind, adding or subtracting the letter H from the beginning of a name, substituting B for P, M for N, etc., varying the first vowel, and so on.

In some parts of England, notably Surrey, Sussex, Middlesex, Essex, and Shropshire, and also in Wales, about 15 per cent of births were not registered between 1837 and 1860. Parents were not penalized for failing to register births until 1875, and many apparently believed that civil registration was unnecessary if the child had been baptized. We also have to face the fact that some people deliberately avoided their legal responsibilities or gave false information. No system of registration has ever been perfect. Nevertheless, the records of civil registration are the family historian's most productive source. The problems are minor compared with the rewards.

Census Returns

The first census for England and Wales, the Isle of Man, and the Channel Islands was taken in 1801, after half a century or so of debate over whether such a measure would infringe the individual liberties of the king's subjects. Since then, a census has been taken every 10 years, with the exception of the war year of 1941. The first four censuses are of little value to the family historian. In 1840, however, responsibility for collecting the data was transferred to the General Register Office; from then onwards the census returns become a prime source of genealogical information. Separate censuses for Ireland and enumerations in the colonies were taken at the same time as those in England and Wales, but Scotland's different legal, constitutional, and administrative system produced a slightly different form of census-taking. In 1861 a separate Registrar-General for Scotland assumed responsibility for the Scottish census; the enumerators' returns are housed in the same place as the records of civil registration. The early census returns for Ireland were lost when the Public Record Office in Dublin was destroyed by fire in 1922.

The enumerators' districts that were drawn up for the 1841 census were retained, as far as possible, up to 1891, in order that comparisons could be made with previous data. They were supposed to be of a standard size and to consist of units, or parts of units, such as parishes and townships, that had a local meaning. The rapid growth of the population in many parts of Britain meant, however, that some districts had eventually to be altered. Alterations are recorded in the printed summaries of the returns, which are available in good reference libraries and in the volumes of the various Victoria County

PLACE	HOUSES		NAMES of each Person who abode therein the preceding Night.	AGE and SEX		PROFESSION, TRADE, EMPLOYMENT, or of INDEPENDENT MEANS.	Where Born	
	Uninhabited or Building	Inhabited		Males	Females		Whether Born in same County	Whether Born in Scotland, Ireland, or Foreign Parts.
Bowers Row			Martha Thomas		40		Y.	
			Ann do		15		Y.	
			David do	14		Tailor ap	Y.	
			David Smith	25		Cotton Spining	N	
			Thomas Hays	25		Cotton Spining	Y.	
do No 3		1	Thomas Phythian	30		Cotton Spining	N	
			Ann do		50		Y.	
			Eliza Berkley		35	Cotton Spining		J
			Maria do		12	Cotton Spining	Y.	
			Emma do		5		Y.	
			Hannah Gale		35	Cotton Spining	N	
do No 4		1	Thomas Hallmark	60		Carpenter J.	Y.	
			Elizabeth do		60		Y.	
			Sarah do		15	Cotton Reeler	Y.	
do No 5		1	Sarah Jewitt		75	Ind. 100	Y.	
do No 6		1	Matthew Baker	30		Printer J	Y.	
			Ellen do		30		Y.	
			Charles do	8			Y.	
			Sarah do		6		Y.	
			Matthew do	4			Y.	
			Thomas do	6 months			Y.	
do No 7		1	James Ingram	50		Cotton Spining	N	
			Rebecca do		50		N	
			James Hall	3			N	
Do No 8		1	John Merry	50		Cotton Spining	N	
TOTAL in Page 9		6	✓	12 6	13 4	✓		

Histories, which give population statistics derived from the nineteenth-century returns.

The 1841 census was a trial run for the Registrar-General's office. Some significant improvements were made in 1851, in the light of this experience. In 1841 the enumerators were asked to record names according to household or to institution (workhouse, prison, etc.), but the relationship of each member to the head of the household was not noted. Precise ages were recorded for children under 15, but anyone older had his or her age rounded down to the nearest five. The family historian needs to be fully aware that, for example, someone recorded as age 30 in the 1841 census return could have been any age between 30 and 34. The column headed 'profession, trade, employment or of independent means' has fewer pitfalls, except that many Victorian people had more than one occupation; numerous craftsmen, for example, still followed an old way of life by combining their craft with a smallholding. The final column is of little practical use to the family historian; the census merely asked whether or not a person was born in the same county as he or she resided, or whether the birthplace was in Scotland, Ireland, or 'foreign parts'. None of the questions was designed with the needs of future family historians in mind; nevertheless, the improvements made from 1851 onwards may be noted with gratitude.

The 1841 census was taken in June but, as some itinerant workers who were sleeping rough were not recorded, it was decided that any future census should be taken in March or April. Moreover, nightworkers who were absent from home on census night but who returned the following morning were to be enumerated with the other members of their household. The household was retained as the basic institution, and from 1851 onwards the relationship of each member to the head was noted. Another improvement was the decision to record exact ages instead of rounding them down to the nearest five. The most important change of all for the genealogist was the decision that from 1851 onwards the exact place of birth should be given. This information frequently points the researcher in the right direction when an attempt is made to go back beyond the period of civil registration to parish and chapel registers.

Because of the secrecy imposed by the 100-years rule, census records are available for consultation only up to 1891. Although they cover only half a century or so—not even the full length of the reign of Victoria—they are none the less a prime source for the family historian, covering much the same period as the early decades of civil registration. They provide snapshots of all the households of Britain at 10-yearly intervals and offer many a clue for further research.

The enumerators' returns for 1841–91 may be consulted on microfilm at the Family Records Centre, 1 Myddelton Street, London, EC1. The indexes (which are arranged by census year in a distinctive colour) are of places, not of surnames. They provide a reference number for an enumerator's district, which enables the researcher to obtain the relevant microfilm, in the hope that his or her ancestor was residing in that particular district on census night. The search may well be a long one.

In recent years, it has become normal practice for county record offices and the reference libraries of large towns and cities to obtain microfilm copies of the enumerators' returns of all the available censuses of the district that they serve. In some cases, local family history societies have made indexes of at least one of these returns. A major project, organized by the Mormon Church with the co-operation of family history societies and individual volunteers throughout the land, is currently indexing the whole of the 1881 census.

It does not take long to look at a return for a rural parish, but tracing an ancestor who was living in London or one of the larger provincial cities can be a very time-consuming task. Towns and cities had to be divided into numerous districts, the boundaries of which sometimes ran down the middle of a street. In many cases, the route taken by an enumerator when he collected the returns can be followed street by street. Even in the towns, however, houses were rarely numbered before the 1850s and often a formal system of numbering was not introduced until much later. The rapid expansion of Victorian towns and the subdivision of properties made the

THE 1851 CENSUS
RETURN FOR BURY ST
EDMUNDS, SUFFOLK

The census taken on 31 March 1851 is much more informative than that taken ten years earlier. Later censuses followed the same format. The inhabitants of this part of Southgate Street were Suffolk born and bred. They earned their living by manual

address system chaotic. In heavily built-up areas it is often difficult to decide what actually constituted a 'house', as distinct from a 'room', and to compare the information obtained from one census with that of another.

These problems are minor ones compared with those posed by the task of deciding whether or not ages are recorded accurately. Even after the practice of rounding ages down to the nearest five had been abandoned, it is best to treat the recorded ages with suspicion. In many cases people do not appear to have aged 10 years by the time of the next census, and these discrepancies are sometimes too great to be explained by the different month in which the census was taken. Most of the discrepancies are of a year or two, but some 4 or 5 per cent are for longer periods. Some people, of course, had only a rough idea of their age, others may have thought of their age as being the one that would be reached next birthday, but some deliberately misled the enumerator. The recorded age does not always lead to a precise year in a baptism register; the searcher who is looking for the baptism of, for example, someone aged 46 in 1851 should therefore consult the baptism registers for the years 1803–7.

The information about the place of birth should be treated with similar caution. Sometimes the nearest town, rather than the actual village or hamlet, is given, especially if a family had moved far from the birthplace by the time of the census return. People may have said that they came from a certain place because that is where they spent most of their childhood or youth, yet they may have been born elsewhere. Generally speaking, the information is more likely to be accurate the younger the person to whom it relates. It is a common experience to find that an ancestor's place of birth was recorded differently in two succeeding census returns. Professor Michael Anderson found that in mid-nineteenth-century Preston, 14 per cent of a sample of 475 persons whom he traced in successive censuses had a discrepancy in their birthplace; some of these discrepancies were unimportant, but some involved considerable distances. Sometimes, parents may have forgotten which child was born where, sometimes they may have deliberately falsified their entry. On other occasions, an enumerator may have recorded the parish where the birth occurred rather than the smaller unit within the parish that was noted earlier. Nevertheless, these problems should not be overstated. In general, the census returns are an invaluable guide to birthplaces, and although they do not set out to record movement between census nights, the birthplaces of successive children often indicate the approximate dates when a family moved home and the routes by which they came to settle in a particular place.

The occupations that are recorded seem, on the whole, to be accurate and to conform with descriptions derived from other sources such as trade and commercial directories. They rarely take account of dual occupations or casual employment, however. In the Victorian period many people worked at different jobs at different times of the year. A man who appears in the returns under the description 'labourer' may have performed a variety of tasks, some of them skilled. The contribution of women and children to the household economy is also understated; many of the 'scholars' may have been casually employed.

The information derived from the census returns can often be linked with that obtained from other sources. It may help, for example, in the search for a death certificate, for if a person appeared in the 1861 census but not in the one taken 10 years later, the civil registration indexes of deaths should be consulted from June 1861 onwards. Microfilms of the census returns are kept on another floor at the Family Records Centre, 1 Myddelton Street, London EC1, so such clues can be followed up immediately. Likewise, the age of the eldest child in an enumerator's return will suggest a starting-date for a search of the marriage indexes, though of course older children may have died or have left home. The ages and birthplaces recorded in the census returns are valuable pointers in the right direction for further genealogical evidence, provided they are treated cautiously and not regarded as concrete evidence that should never be challenged.

Trade and Commercial Directories

A good reference library will normally have a collection of trade and commercial directories stretching back well into the nineteenth century and sometimes into the eighteenth. In London, the earliest was Samuel Lee's list of the City merchants in 1677, but this example was not followed for another half-century. Brown and Kent's London directory of 1734 was revised each year by Kent up to 1771, and then by others until 1826. In the provinces, the people who ran the registry offices of the growing industrial towns took the lead. James Sketchley published an alphabetical list of the names and addresses of the merchants and tradesmen of Birmingham in 1763, and Elizabeth Raffald published similar information for Manchester in 1772. Many of the early compilers of directories came from a printing and publishing background, but firms were often small and ephemeral. The information in the early directories is of limited value to the family historian, but by Victoria's reign much fuller directories were published on a regular basis. These must certainly be consulted.

The two essential works of reference are J. E. Norton's *Guide to the National and Provincial Directories of England and Wales, Excluding London, Published before 1856* and G. Shaw and A. Tipper, *British Directories: A Bibliography and Guide to Directories Published in England and Wales (1850–1950) and Scotland (1773–1950)*. These list the holdings of each major library and indicate where directories may be found.

In the late eighteenth century it was thought worth while to publish directories that covered wide geographical areas. William Bailey's *Northern Directory* appeared in 1781 and continued to be published until 1787. *The*

Directory. SOUTHWOLD, &c. **Suffolk.**

Clavering Robert, farrier, Wangford
Goldsmith John, shopkeeper, East st
Housego Charles, gardener, Wangford
King John, watch & clock maker, Gaol st
Money William, basket maker, Church lane
Palmer Benjmn. auctioneer, Market place
Peirson Robert, game dealer, East st
Preston Edmund, salt manufactr. Southend
Sawyer Charles, cabinet maker and up-
  holsterer, High street
Stannard Robt. sergeant at mace, Back st

Storkey Moses, lapidary and fancy reposi-
  tory, High street
Strange Samuel, sergeant at mace, East st

CUSTOM HOUSE.
Collector—Benjamin Baswood, jun.
Comptroller—Benjamin Sadler Candler.
Harbour Master—Francis Ellis.

CARRIERS.
To HALESWORTH, George Martin, from
  the Red Lion, every Tuesday—& John

Bedingfield and James Newson, from
  their houses, every Wednesday & Sat.
To NORWICH, Beccles & Loddon, Jos.
  Foyster's Van (for passengers & goods),
  from his house, every Tuesday & Fri.
To SAXMUNDHAM, George Martin,
  from the Red Lion, every Friday.
To YARMOUTH, James Newson, from
  his house, every Monday and Thursday
  —& George Martin, from the Red Lion,
  every Tuesday.

STOWMARKET

Is a flourishing and respectable market town in the parish of its name and hundred of Stow, 75 miles N.E. (through Sudbury) from London, 14 E.S.E. from Bury St. Edmunds, and 12 N.N.W. from Ipswich, situated very nearly in the centre of the county, at the junction of the three rivulets which form the river Gipping; two of these streams wash the east side of the town, and the other meets them at the south end of it, near Combs Ford. A great source of the prosperity of Stowmarket is the navigable canal from hence to Ipswich, opened in 1793, and which has been the means of reducing the price of land carriage one half. A very considerable business is done in the corn, coal and timber trades; that in barley, especially, is very extensive; there are several large maltings; hops are cultivated to material advantage in this vicinity, and the market of this town is frequented by numerous farmers, and well attended by purchasers, from a great distance round. Formerly bombasins and stuffs were woven here, which have been succeeded by the manufacture of hempen cloth, sackings, ropes and twine: there is also a considerable tannery in the neighbourhood, iron and brass founderies, and two extensive brick and tile works. Being centrally situated the county meetings are chiefly held in Stowmarket, and three magistrates

meet every alternate Monday: a court baron is also held annually under R. Marriott, Esq. the lord of the manor.

The church, dedicated to St. Peter and St. Mary, is a spacious and beautiful building, with a square tower, and slender spire of elegant and light appearance, one hundred and twenty feet in height. In the church is a monument to Dr. Young, once vicar of this place, and tutor to the immortal Milton. The contiguous parish of Stow-Upland (which has neither church nor chapel), is consolidated with Stowmarket, the living of which is a vicarage, in the gift of Miss Bevan: the present vicar is the Rev. Arthur G. H. Hollingsworth. There are places of worship for baptists, independents and Wesleyan methodists, national and Sunday schools, and several benevolent institutions for the relief of the poor. The principal seat in the neighbourhood is 'Great Finborough hall,' the residence of Lady Hotham, standing in one of the most delightful situations in the county, and surrounded by a beautifully laid out park, comprehending upwards of two hundred acres. The market, which is a large one for corn and cattle of all kinds, is held on Thursday; the fairs are on the 10th of July for toys, and the 12th of August for lambs. At the census taken in 1831, the parish contained 2,672 persons.

POST OFFICE, Market place, John George Hart, *Post Master.*—Letters from LONDON, BURY ST. EDMUNDS and the North arrive every morning at seven, and are despatched every evening at half-past six.—Letters from IPSWICH, ESSEX and NORFOLK arrive every morning at nine, and are despatched every evening at five.

NOBILITY, GENTRY AND CLERGY.
Birch Mrs. —, Tavern st
Crawford Rev. Wm. Haughley park
Daniel Rev. R. Combs
Elliott Mrs. Elizabeth, Ipswich st
Hollingsworth Rev. Arthur G. H. Ipswich st
Hotham Lady, Great Finborough hall
Hunt Mr. James, Stow-upland st
Lockwood Mrs. Elizabth. Ipswich st
Marriott Mrs. —, Thorney hall
Marriott Rev. Henry S. One house
Mills Mrs. Sarah, Tavern st
Robinson Rev. J. B. One house
Rust John Edgar, esq. Abbott's hall
Sheldrake Miss —, Tavern st
Smith Mr. William, Bury st
Symonds Mrs. —, Bury st
Ward Rev. William, Ipswich st
Webb Mr. Holman, Ipswich st
Webb Mrs. Rebecca, Ipswich st

ACADEMIES AND SCHOOLS.
Betts Mary, Bury st
Carter Mary, Ipswich st [road
Elliston Misses (boarding), Ipswich
Isaac James (boarding), Violet hill
Larkham Louisa (boarding and day), Ipswich st
NATIONAL SCHOOL, Church yard—Wm. Anness Sheppard, master; Mary Frewer, mistress
Paul Sarah (boarding), Bury st
Peck Harriet (boarding), Ipswich st
Tydeman George, Stow-upland st

ATTORNEYS.
Archer Edward Peter, Bury st
Gudgeon James, Bury st
Lyas George, Tavern st
Marriott John (and clerk to the magistrates, and clerk to the commissioners of taxes), Stowmarket
Ranson William, Childer house

AUCTIONEERS.
Downing Henry Shuckforth, Crow st
Payne James, Butter market

BAKERS.
Marked thus * are also Confectioners.
*Aldridge John, Stow-upland st
Barnard Edward, Stow-upland st
Blomfield Thomas, Bury st
*Greengrass George, Bury st
Mallett Joshua, Stow-upland st
Mayhew James, Combs
Raffe William, Ipswich st
*Tricker Robert, Ipswich st

BANKERS.
EAST OF ENGLAND BANK, Market place—(draws on the London and Westminster Bank)—Jos. Antrim Lankester, manager
Oakes, Bevan, Moor & Bevan, Market place—(draw on Barclay, Bevan & Co. London)—John George Hart, manager

BASKET MAKERS.
Collins William, Tavern st
Stevens William, Stow-upland st

BLACKSMITHS.
Boon John, Combs
Clarke Jesse, Earl Stonham [st
Colson, Wilding & Co. Stow-upland
Hart John, Stow-upland
Orams Thomas, Ipswich st
Purr John, Bury st
Smyth William, Ipswich st
Taylor William, Stow-upland

BOOKSELLERS & STATIONRS
Mann John, Market place
Woolby Thos. Brackett (& printer), Market place

BOOT AND SHOE MAKERS.
Barritt Edward, Stow-upland st
Codd William, Ipswich st
Diaper George, Tavern st
Gyford Samuel, Bury st [ket
Lawrence Jos. Hewes, Butter mar-

Orams Thomas, Crow st
Palmer Robert, Stow-upland st
Raffe James, Bury st
Raffe James, Tavern st
Reddish Edward, Market place
Runneckles Robert, Bury st

BRICK AND TILE MAKERS.
Fison William L. Bury st [road
Hart John George & Co. Ipswich

BRICKLAYERS.
Andrew Joseph, Tavern st
Banyard Theodore, Regent st
Webb Richard (and mason), Bury st

BUILDERS.
(See also Carpenters.)
Blomfield William, Bury st
Dennis Charles, Bury st
Lyas William, Ipswich st
Revett Daniel, Bury st
Webb Richard, Bury st

BUTCHERS.
Abbott Frederick A. Ipswich st
Beaven Geo. William, Market place
Cuthbert John, Regent st
Cuthbert Thomas, Bury st
Halls Edward, Stow-upland st
Hayward George, Bury st

CABINET MAKERS.
Bailey William, Bury st
King William, Ipswich st
Payne James, Butter market
Read John, Ipswich st
Squirrell Robert, Market place

CARPENTERS.
Blomfield William, Bury st
Dennis Charles, Bury st
Lyas Ambrose, Church yard
Lyas William, Ipswich st
Pave Robert, Bury st
Rednell Abraham, Ipswich st
Revett Daniel (and smith), Bury st

CHINA, GLASS, &c. DEALERS.
Parmenter Isaac, Butter market
Reeve John, Market place

575

PIGOT'S DIRECTORY OF SUFFOLK (1839)
This page from a nine-teenth-century directory illustrates a typical entry for an English market town. The introductory section describes the current state of the local economy and provides some historical information. The names of the 'principal inhabitants' are followed by alphabetical lists of people engaged in various professions and trades. Such 'trade and commercial directories' do not record employees.

Universal British Directory, compiled largely by John Wilkes, was issued in five main volumes and 69 parts between 1790 and 1799. These soon gave way to the more detailed (and cheaper) directories that were produced by local publishers or printed as part of a national series such as that of James Pigot, whose first provincial directory was published in 1814, and who continued to publish until 1853, when the firm was taken over by Kelly's. Francis Kelly established his business in London and began to produce provincial directories in 1845. By the following decade, he had become the major publisher of directories over the south of England. Kelly's remained the best-known name in the business up to the middle years of the twentieth century.

Many of the medium-sized publishers were not active very long. Some catered for a particular market by printing specialized trade directories. The general trade directories conformed to a common style. The earliest arranged the names of local inhabitants in alphabetical order and gave their addresses. The later ones provided separate street sections with the names and occupations of the residents and classified entries of the various trades. Such directories provide an enormous amount of information, but even the best were far from comprehensive. The biggest firms employed full-time agents who visited houses to obtain information. Suspicion of the motives of the agents, simple annoyance at being pestered once a year for personal details, and absence from home account for the number of unrecorded householders in the street sections.

Directories did not claim to provide complete coverage like a census. Gore's Liverpool directory of 1851, for example, listed only 65 per cent of the householders that were recorded in the census of that year in those parts of the city which were dominated by court dwellings and multi-occupied houses. Even in smaller places, directories concentrated on the craftsmen and tradesmen and the professional inhabitants and neglected the labourers and servants. A study of Ashby de la Zouch, as revealed by White's directory of 1862 and the 1861 census returns, showed that tradesmen accounted for 33 per cent of the names listed in the directory but only 18 per cent of the householders in the census; no labourers or domestic servants were listed.

The addresses recorded in directories can often be used to quicken a search of a contemporary census return. With this in mind, it is useful to remember that the information collected for a directory was slightly out of date by the time it appeared in print. The maps and town plans that are contained in the best directories may also be used profitably alongside a census return. Of special value to the historian are the introductory sections on the history and topography of each settlement, for they provide details of land ownership and tenures and of townships, parishes, and manors at a time of considerable change. Some of the statements about the history of the place should be treated warily, but directories are a rich and accessible source which the family historian will often find rewarding.

Parish Registers

The most important source of genealogical information prior to the beginning of civil registration in 1837 and the census returns of 1841–91 is undoubtedly the parish register. Nor does this source cease to be useful during the reign of Victoria, particularly if a family remained in the same district for a long period of time; in such cases, it is possible to bypass the records of civil registration altogether, and often cheaper to do so. From 1 January 1813 the registers of the Church of England follow a standard format and are easy to use. In earlier times, they are far from straightforward. Considerable background knowledge is needed to use them effectively.

The system of parish registration of baptisms, marriages, and burials began in 1538, but only a minority of parishes have registers that go back that far. It seems that the normal practice at first was to record events on loose sheets, many of which were lost or destroyed in the course of time. In 1597 it was ordered that henceforth a special register should be kept and that previous records, where they survived, should be entered into this book. The minister and churchwardens were charged with signing each page as a true transcript. In many cases, ministers interpreted the instruction to mean that records should be copied only as far back as the beginning of the reign of Queen Elizabeth. It is common to find, therefore, that surviving registers begin in 1558 rather than 20 years earlier. The same Act, in 1597, ordered that in future a copy of the events registered during the past year should be sent

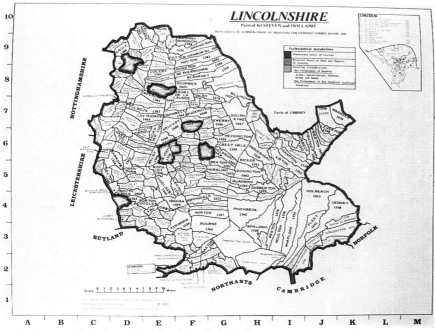

MAP OF THE PARISHES OF LINCOLNSHIRE

The Institute of Heraldic and Genealogical Studies, Northgate, Canterbury, has published a series of county maps which indicate the size and shape of ancient parishes and give the dates when their registers commence. The contrast between the shapes of the eastern fenland parishes and those of the rest of the county is immediately obvious. The map also identifies those parishes which formed part of separate jurisdictions.

© 1992. Trustees of the Institute of Heraldic and Genealogical Studies

to the bishop's office. These bishop's transcripts, as they are called, are kept at the archive offices which house the records of the ancient dioceses, e.g. Lichfield, Lincoln, or York, as distinct from the new dioceses which were created in the late nineteenth or twentieth centuries. They are invaluable where an original register has been lost or is inaccessible or difficult to read. On the whole, however, the original registers have been preserved better than the bishop's transcripts, especially in the earlier period of registration.

England and Wales had some 11,000 ancient parishes. These varied considerably in size, ranging from a few hundred acres to tens of thousands of acres. The largest ones were subdivided into chapelries, or chapels-of-ease, many of which acquired rights to conduct their own baptism, marriage, and burial services. Sometimes, these chapelries kept separate registers, but in other cases their records were copied each year into the parish register, usually in a separate section. This can cause a great deal of confusion when a search is made in a register. The family historian needs to become familiar with the administrative arrangements in the district that he is researching. Maps showing the ancient parish system are commonly available at record offices, and a series covering each county and giving the starting-date of every surviving register has been published by the Institute of Heraldic and Genealogical Studies, Canterbury.

Some important places today were small or non-existent at the time when parishes were created and may have formed part of a parish named after a place that is now insignificant. Indeed, new and growing towns may have spread over the borders of more than one parish. During the nineteenth century, many new parishes were created in the expanding towns and cities. The researcher who is working backwards in time and has become familiar with the structure of local parishes in the Victorian age therefore needs to adapt his searches to a different administrative framework in earlier periods. The standard reference work is F. A. Youngs, Jr., *Guide to the Local Administrative Units of England*. London and the major provincial cities such as Norwich and York had long been divided into numerous parishes, some of which disappeared when the population moved out of the ancient central areas and churches were closed. Tracing an ancestor in the capital city or in a great provincial centre can be a time-consuming business involving the search of numerous registers.

Locating the present whereabouts of a parish register is not a straightforward task, though a local record office will usually be able to advise. Some parishes deposited their registers for safe-keeping with record offices long before the measure of 1979 which insisted that this should be done unless a parish could prove that it had adequate facilities for storing and preserving such records. Only a minority of registers are still kept in parish churches; most are now deposited with the county or city record offices that are used by the modern dioceses. Before searching for an original register, however, it is worth consulting all the indexes at a reference library to see what is in print. Many parish registers have been published, at least in part, either

Quiet Please

Pencils only

privately or by a parish register society. Some of these societies are now more than a hundred years old and have an extensive series in print.

It is common policy in record offices for registers to be made available for study only on microfilm. A prior appointment has usually to be made in order to reserve a microfilm reader. The bishop's transcripts at the ancient diocesan record offices have also been placed on microfilm in many cases. This policy has become necessary because of the deteriorating condition of the documents through their unprecedentedly heavy use. One benefit arising from this policy has been that local record offices or libraries have sometimes obtained microfilm copies of bishop's transcripts that are held at other places, often far away.

The Church of Jesus Christ of Latter-Day Saints, commonly known as the Mormon Church, requires its members to trace their ancestors in order to baptize them by proxy. The Mormon Church has made a huge investment in transcribing records and in reproducing them on microfilm or microfiche. These records have been computerized as the International Genealogical Index, which is updated regularly and is available on microfilm. (The next updating will also be on disc.) The IGI, as it is universally known amongst genealogists, can be consulted by anyone, regardless of whether or not he or she is a member of the Mormon Church. The Mormons have constructed special buildings in various parts of Britain which are open to the public for

A County Record Office
This interior view of the Essex County Record Office at Chelmsford shows the typical facilities available to members of the public.

the purpose of genealogical research. The IGI and other records on microfilm may be consulted free of charge, or for a voluntary donation. Otherwise, microfilm copies of the IGI are available at public reference libraries and record offices and at the meeting-places of many of the various family history societies. The index is far from complete, partly because such an extensive programme takes time, but also because some bishops or parish priests have theological objections to baptism by proxy of people whose parents chose to baptize them according to the rites of the Anglican Church. It is important to remember that the information in the IGI must always be checked, for much of it has been gathered by untrained amateurs who may have made mistakes. Nevertheless, the IGI has been a fruitful source for many a family historian; it can save a lot of time and point one in the right direction.

The entries in the early parish registers are often disappointingly sparse. A record of baptism may simply give the date of the event, the name of the child, and the name of the father. The style of entries varies from register to register and over time in the same place. Nor should we expect improvements as time goes on; even if the form of entry improves for a short period, it usually lapses back into the meagre standards of an earlier age. Some registers were very well kept from the sixteenth century onwards; others have numerous gaps. If entries were made at the end of a week or a month, then names may have been misremembered or a space left blank. William Holland, the parson of Over Stowey, Somerset, in the early nineteenth century, appears to have written the entries in his register on Fridays or Sundays, and to have dated them according to the date of the writing, not that of the actual events. If a clerk was responsible for keeping the register, he may not have written it up until the end of the year. The register of St Peter's, Dorchester, for 1645 notes that: 'In twelve months there died 52 persons whose names are not inserted, the old clerk being dead who had the notes.'

A great deal of confusion is caused by the old custom of starting the official year not on 1 January but on 25 March (Lady Day). The entries for each year do not stop on 31 December but continue to the following Lady Day. All the dates between 1 January and 25 March therefore need to have another year added to them to convert them to modern reckoning. For example, a baptism recorded as taking place on 24 January 1694 needs to be noted as 24 January 1694/5, a method of notation that was occasionally used at the time. Such dates must be recorded carefully, for it may be assumed falsely that a baptism recorded on 21 February 1708 occurred before the marriage of the parents on 11 April 1708, whereas in fact the baptism was 10 months later. This method of recording was abandoned on 1 January 1752, and in the same year Britain fell into line with the rest of Europe by adopting the Gregorian calendar in place of the Julian. The old calendar, which did not have a leap year, was 11 days out by this time, so 14 September was decreed to follow 3 September. Minor genealogical problems are caused by the adjustment of birthdays to the new calendar, but they need not concern us seriously. It took a while for people to adjust their thinking to the new style. For years afterwards some fairs were held on the traditional days; in 1760, for example, a fair at Chapel-en-le-Frith was advertised for the Thursday before Old Candlemas and one at Belper for Old May Day. If the government's financial year still ends on 6 April, 11 days after Lady Day, it is not surprising that even after 1752 some parish registers continued to be written in the old manner until a new man took over or the clerk got in a hopeless muddle.

Such problems are minor compared with the difficulty of reading sixteenth- and seventeenth-century registers. There is no easy way round this; anyone seriously interested in searching the records of this period must acquire some competence in palaeography. Knowing the format of a document is half the battle. The early registers are simple in form and give only the barest of details. Although Latin was commonly used, this does not present much difficulty. Robertus and Henricus are readily identifiable as Robert and Henry, though Guillelmus may not be an obvious William. Fortunately, the surnames are given in their English form. The searcher quickly learns the few common phrases, e.g. *baptizatus erat, nupti erat, sepultus erat*, that were used to record baptisms, marriages, and burials. (Many English words are based on Latin originals, and so the meaning of *nupti* and *sepultus* may be guessed from 'nuptials' and 'sepulchre'.) A variety of Latin terms, e.g. *filius populi*, or the English 'base', 'bastard', etc., were used to record illegitimacies. Abbreviations may cause other difficulties and spellings reflect the way that the writer spoke. These difficulties must be faced, but they are not insurmountable.

Anyone addressed in the register as Mr or Mrs was of gentry rank; sometimes their entries are written in larger and bolder letters. Before the eighteenth century a clergyman was not normally styled Reverend, but noted as clerk, meaning cleric. Most entries record a person simply by his or her Christian name and surname. Sometimes, however, a great deal of extra information is provided, either on the whim of the person doing the recording or in response to some directive from the government or a bishop. Some parish registers are a valuable source of information about occupations, noting these when a man was married or buried or when he baptized a child. If such information is provided consistently over a period of years, it can be used to reconstruct the occupational structure of the entire parish in a way that is normally possible only with nineteenth-century census returns.

The baptism registers are not a record of actual births, but of the church ceremonies that followed. It has been commonly stated that baptism took place three days after a birth. William Shakespeare's baptism on 26 April 1564 has been widely accepted to mean that he was born (appropriately for the national bard) on 23 April, St George's Day, but in fact the interval between birth and baptism varied from time to time and from place to place. William Camden, Shakespeare's contemporary, wrote in *Remaines Concerning Britain* that 'our Ancestors in this Realm until later time baptized and gave names the very birth day or next day after'. In later times, it is

THE BAPTISM REGISTER OF
ST SIDWELL, EXETER
(1736/7)
The register starts at Ladyday (25 March), which was
the usual style until 1752.
The entries before Ladyday
were recorded under 1736;
afterwards they were noted
under 1737. The name of
the father, but not of the
mother, was given. Several
of the fathers were soldiers;
two were 'strangers' from
outside the parish. Illegitimate children were de-
scribed as 'base'.

safe to assume that the majority of baptisms took place within two or three weeks of the birth, though many examples can be quoted of even longer delays. The custom of private baptism at home was fashionable in the late seventeenth and eighteenth centuries, particularly in London. These private events were normally entered as such in the parish register. It cannot be assumed that the lack of an entry means that a child was not baptized. Carelessness on the part of whoever was responsible for the register is a more likely explanation. Such carelessness may mean that we can now proceed no further with a particular line.

Most marriages were performed in a parish church after the calling of banns, but even people of modest incomes sometimes preferred to marry by licence. The normal practice was for the bridegroom to apply to the chancellor or surrogate of the diocese in which he or his prospective wife lived and in which the marriage was to be celebrated and to make a formal statement, or 'allegation', upon oath, that there was no lawful impediment to the marriage. Licences were normally issued through diocesan consistory courts and were recorded in the bishop's register, though they can also be found in the records of certain peculiar jurisdictions. When the bride and groom lived in different dioceses, however, they had to apply to the Vicar-General of the Archbishop of the province, either Canterbury or York. If a parish register has subsequently been destroyed, the record of such a licence may be the only surviving evidence that a wedding took place. The marriage of William Shakespeare and Ann Hathaway, to quote a famous example, is proved by the licences issued by the consistory court of the Bishop of

THE MARRIAGE REGISTER OF ST SIDWELL, EXETER (1762)
Lord Hardwicke's Marriage Act had made this form of entry standard from 1754. The information provided by such registers is much fuller than that normally given in previous registers.

Burials 1743

March 25 Christopher Hooper +
        30 Ephraim Honley
April 1 Timothy Comyns
         James Jenkins
       3 Robert Redford
       4 Susanna Gill +
       8 James Warmley +
      12 Mary Daughter of Samuel Cane
      17 Elizabeth Tucker Widow
         David Gibbons executed et Anantra ———
      19 Eliz: Alston
         Mary, Wife of Samuel Cane
      24 Thomas Burless   +
      29 Mary Tout   +
May   1 Humphrey Gosling   +
       2 Susanna Rose Widow
       6 Joanna Penny   +
       7 John, Son of John Thomas
         Hannah Jewel
       8 Anne, Daughter of John Holloway
       9 Susanna Woodey   +
      11 John, Son of John Beerd
         John Goldsery
      13 Susanna, Wife of John Tucker
      14 Richard Jordain
         Mary Pearce   +
      15 John Burt
         James, Son of James Fox +
      16 Thomas Brock
      18 Jane Kendol   +
      25 Mary Drew   +
      26 Richard Percy
            Leskey   +
      27 William Stansfield Sol:
      31 ——— Burnet   +
         William Gater Minister.

THE BURIAL REGISTER OF
ST SIDWELL, EXETER (1743)
The register is a simple list
of names and dates of burial. When a child was buried
in this parish, the father's
name was also recorded.
As women were sometimes
noted as 'widow' or 'wife
of', those without such descriptions may have been
single. (Consistency was not
a strong point of the keepers
of the register, however.) An
unusual entry on this page
refers to an execution.

Worcester, but cannot be found in the parish registers of Stratford and the surrounding countryside. In Shakespeare's case, his bride was pregnant and the close season of Advent prevented the calling of banns on three successive Sundays.

Burial registers provide a fuller record of events than do those which record baptisms and marriages, but even they are incomplete. A family historian may occasionally find a tombstone in the churchyard but no equivalent entry in the burial register. Such omissions can have resulted only from the carelessness or oversight of the keeper of the register. Excommunicates and suicides were forbidden burial with Christian rites, though some were buried surreptitiously in a corner of the churchyard. The use of the word 'interred' in a burial register may suggest such an event, but usually indicates that the deceased was a Roman Catholic who did not wish to be buried according to the Anglican form of service. Most entries are straightforward, though modern readers may find curious the provision of the Acts of 1666 and 1678 that shrouds should be woollen and that the register should confirm that a person was buried 'in wool'.

Important changes in registration procedure took place during the Commonwealth. The Act which came into force on 29 September 1653 transferred responsibility to an elected officer, known as the Parish Register (*sic*). In practice, either the minister or the parish clerk was often elected as register, and some parishes simply ignored the legislation. The overall quality of parish registers during the Interregnum is poor, but in some parishes a new volume was purchased and the entries became fuller. The Act stipulated that births rather than baptisms should be recorded, but local practice varied substantially; some registers noted both events. The greatest change involved the marriage ceremony, which until 1657–8 could be solemnized by a JP after the reading of banns on three successive weeks in church, chapel, or market-place. Upon the Restoration of King Charles II in 1660, the Act was repealed and registration procedure reverted to the previous local practice.

In the later seventeenth and eighteenth centuries various attempts to improve the quality of registration were made by the central government or by the bishops of certain dioceses. In some parishes fuller information was provided after 1694, following the decision to tax entries, but elsewhere the form of entries did not improve. In the diocese of York, for a few years after 1777, some registers give remarkably full details. Thus, an entry in the Kirkburton register for 11 October 1777 records the baptism of Robert Hey, son of Abraham Hey of Thorncliff, clothier (the son of George Hey), and his wife Sarah, the daughter of John Sikes of Lepton, by Esther, the daughter of Abraham Hey of Thorncliff. Unfortunately, ministers and clerks soon got tired of providing such detailed genealogical information.

Lord Hardwicke's Marriage Act of 1753 brought about a standard form of entry for marriages. In order to prevent the laxity of clandestine marriages, the Act stated that every marriage must be preceded by the issue of a licence or the calling of banns, that the ceremony must be performed in the parish where at least one of the parties resided, and that a record must be made in a proper book kept for that purpose. The entries henceforth had to be signed

Page 5.

BAPTISMS solemnized in the Parish of *Esher* in the County of *Surry* in the Year 1814						
When Baptized.	Child's Christian Name.	Parents Name. Christian.	Surname.	Abode.	Quality, Trade, or Profession.	By whom the Ceremony was performed.
18 . March 27th No. 33.	Thomas Son of	Thomas & Grace	Smithers	Esher	Labourer	W Diggle Curate
April 3d No. 34.	Emma Stacey Robert	Thomas Alexander & Elizabeth	Roberts	Thames Ditton	Farmer	W Diggle Curate
April 8th No. 35.	John Son of	Thos & Sarah	Denham	Esher	Carpenter	W Diggle Curate
April 8th No. 36.	Ann Daughter of	Willm & Mary	Mansell Born Jan 6 1812	Esher	Shoemaker	W Diggle Curate
April 8th No. 37.	Jane Daughter of	Willm & Mary	Mansell	Esher	Shoemaker	W Diggle Curate
April 17th No. 38.	Eliza Daughter of	John & Louisa	Ride	Esher	Carpenter	W Diggle Curate
May 1st No. 39.	James Son of	Joseph & Elizabeth	Clark	Esher	Publican	W Diggle Curate
May 8th No. 40.	Francis Rose	a Negro		Esher		W Diggle Curate

b

THE NEW STYLE OF REGISTERS

The Baptism Register of Esher, Surrey (1814) (left) From 1 January 1813 all parish registers followed a standard form in bound volumes with printed sheets. They provide far more information than before.

The Marriage Register of Ewell, Surrey (1827) (opposite) Marriage entries in parish registers had been standardized since 1754, but from 1 January 1813 they were recorded in bound volumes in the manner illustrated here. It is always worth noting the names of the witnesses, who in this case were apparently related to the bride.

by the parties and by witnesses, in a bound volume of printed forms. The insistence on a licence or banns remained in force until 1836, when civil ceremonies conducted by a registrar were allowed.

Entries in the Church of England registers were finally standardized by an Act of 1812, which came into effect on 1 January 1813. From that time onwards, Anglican registers consist of bound volumes of printed forms; they are easy to use and much more informative than previous registers. A baptismal entry gives the name of the baptized child, the date of the baptism, the Christian names and surnames of the parents, their abode, and the occupation of the father. The burial register records the name of the deceased, his or her abode, the date of the burial, and his or her age. A marriage record notes the names of both partners, their parishes, the date of the wedding, and the names of the witnesses. If a family lived in a restricted area for a long period in the nineteenth century, and attended church rather than chapel, the family historian may well find all the genealogical details that he requires from a parish register without searching the records of civil registration. In the three centuries that preceded civil registration, parish registers are an essential source that cannot be bypassed.

Page 43.

Records of Protestant Nonconformity

On Sunday, 29 March 1851 a national census was taken of those who attended religious services that day. It revealed that in the country as a whole less than half the population went to any form of service and that in the great industrial cities the proportion fell to as low as 1 in 10. A further blow to the Established Church was the finding that about half of those who did meet for worship preferred a Nonconformist chapel. In some parts of Britain the proportion of Nonconformists to Anglicans was even higher, and nowhere in the country did it fall to below 1 in 3. The family historian clearly needs to be aware of the strength of the various Nonconformist sects in the nineteenth century and to consider whether a vital piece of information about an ancestor which does not appear in a parish register might be contained in the records of a chapel or meeting-house.

The term 'Nonconformist' was applied originally to those who refused to subscribe to the Act of Uniformity of 1662 and the other provisions of the 'Clarendon Code', after the Restoration of Charles II. The Old Dissenting sects of the later seventeenth century consisted of the Presbyterians, Independents (or Congregationalists), Baptists, and Quakers. Some of these terms were used loosely and, of course, congregations may have modified their beliefs over time. Thus, the Sheffield Dissenters were described either as Presbyterians or Independents in the late seventeenth century, but a split in 1715 led one group on to the road to Unitarianism, while the others remained fast in their beliefs but became known as Congregationalists.

Enquiries made by Bishop Compton in 1676 suggest that in Charles II's reign Protestant Dissenters formed only 4 per cent of the national population, though in some parishes the proportion was considerably higher. Even if this figure underestimates the true strength of Nonconformity, it shows that Dissenters were far fewer in number than in Victorian times. These early Dissenters often used the Church of England for their baptism, marriage, and burial services, so these events were recorded in the parish registers of the Anglican Church (with no mention of the fact that the participants were Dissenters). The separate registers that were kept by some seventeenth-century Nonconformist congregations were often a record of baptisms only. Unless an ancestor was a Quaker, the family historian is not often faced with the problem of finding alternative registration during the seventeenth century and much of the eighteenth.

The Old Dissenting sects continued to use the Established Church for services that involved registration long after Nonconformists had achieved freedom of worship in 1689. If a baptism of a child of a known Dissenting family cannot be found in an Anglican register, however, it is worth visiting Doctor Williams' Library, London, where a voluntary General Register of Births was opened for Dissenters on 1 January 1743. Births were registered from many parts of Britain, though clearly the register was most commonly

used by Londoners. It was closed in 1837 upon the commencement of civil registration.

The Society of Friends were the first Dissenters to keep registers systematically. George Fox's earliest converts were particularly numerous in Westmorland, Lancashire, and Yorkshire, but the movement soon expanded rapidly in London and the south-west, in Bristol and Norwich, and then in Scotland and Ireland. It achieved considerable success in America, where in 1681 William Penn founded the state of Pennsylvania. In England, the Quakers became the most numerous of all the Nonconformist sects in the late seventeenth century, but after Toleration in 1689 their membership gradually dwindled.

From their earliest days the Friends adopted a structure of monthly and quarterly meetings. Records of births, marriages, and burials were sometimes kept by particular meetings, but more often this task was the responsibility of the monthly meetings which may have been held at some distance from the local meeting-house. Most registers were started before 1670, though some entries are retrospective. The Society of Friends rejected the names of the days and months because these were derived from heathen gods. Sunday was referred to as the First Day, January as the First Month, and so on. This practice does not present undue difficulty to the genealogist, except that up to the change of calendar in 1752 March was the First Month, April the Second Month, etc. The form of entry in Quaker registers was not standardized until 1776, from which time duplicate entries were sent to the quarterly meetings. Membership lists are uncommon before the late eighteenth century; indeed, many meetings did not keep them until 1836.

Even the Quakers were sometimes prepared to use the Church of England for some of their vital events. Few Quaker marriages, but some births and many more burials, are recorded in parish registers. The first Quakers were often buried in gardens or orchards rather than the parish churchyard, but by the end of the seventeenth century most meeting-houses had a burial ground. The earliest graves were unmarked. It is rare to find headstones before 1850, when they were permitted by the Yearly Meeting, provided there was 'such an entire uniformity . . . as may effectually guard against any distinctions being made in that place between the rich and the poor'.

The best Nonconformist registers after those of the Quakers are the ones kept by the Moravians. Their earliest register is that of the Fetter Street congregation, London, which was begun in 1741, 13 years after three brethren had been sent to London and Oxford from Saxony by Count Zinzendorf. Moravian settlements at Fulneck, Yorkshire, Ockbrook, Derbyshire, etc. still

WESLEYAN CHAPEL, MELKSHAM, WILTSHIRE
The chapel was built in 1871–2 in the High Street, Melksham, by which time the Wesleyans had long become respectable. The neo-Gothic style of Anglican and Roman Catholic churches was still somewhat suspect, so this chapel was fronted with a classical pediment supported by four giant Corinthian columns.

survive, but the sect was always overshadowed by the Methodist denomination, with which it had many affinities.

Until 1742 John Wesley's preaching was largely confined to London and Bristol, but for the rest of his life he travelled incessantly over the whole of Britain. In 1744 circuits for Wesleyan preachers were established and the first national conference was held. The followers of George Whitefield had already broken away and had founded 31 societies by 1747. When Whitefield died in 1770 the leadership of his Calvinistic Methodists passed to the Countess of Huntingdon, but many of the societies drifted into Congregationalism. The break between the Wesleyan Methodists and the Church of England did not come until 1784. Further splits occurred when the Methodist New Connexion was founded in 1797, when the Primitive Methodists broke away in 1812, and when the Wesleyan Reform Union was established in 1849. At first, the rise of Methodism had little effect on parish registration, for like the older Dissenters most Methodists attended the local Anglican church for their baptism, marriage, and burial services. Very few Methodist registers date from before the 1790s and most begin in the second decade of the nineteenth century; even then, the majority are merely records of baptisms.

Lord Hardwicke's Marriage Act of 1753 brought to an end the practice of marrying simply by making a declaration before witnesses. This practice had allowed Nonconformists to celebrate marriages in their own chapels and meeting-houses. After 1753 all Nonconformists, except the Quakers, were expected to marry in the Church of England. Although many Roman Catholics defied the Act, the Protestant Dissenters seem to have complied with its terms.

The Nonconformists had a long battle to get their baptism or birth registers recognized by the State. Before the reign of Victoria no one could obtain a government post without producing proof of baptism in the Established Church. The beginning of civil registration changed the situation. In 1836, following the General Registration Act, a commission was set up to enquire into the 'State, Custody and Authenticity of Non-parochial registers'. The Commissioners approached the various dissenting bodies, asking them to send in their registers to the Registrar-General where they would be examined and, if approved, authenticated. Their suggestion that the registers should be deposited with the Registrar-General and made legal evidence was embodied in the Non-Parochial Registers Act of 1840. Some 856 volumes of Nonconformist registers were surrendered to the state for authentication. A second deposit of 'non-parochial' registers was catalogued in 1859. In all, some 7,000 volumes and files are now stored in the Public Record Office, where they may be consulted free of charge, under the reference RG. 4 to RG. 8 or on the microfilm at the Family Records Centre. No indexes are provided, so it is helpful to have some idea of the locality (and preferably the particular denomination) in which a birth, marriage, or death occurred. Most early registers were surrendered; many later ones have since been deposited in record offices; but others were lost when chapels closed.

Records of Roman Catholicism

Very few Catholic families can trace their descent in the male line from English Catholics who were living in the eighteenth century. Most are descended either from nineteenth-century immigrants from Ireland or continental Europe or from converts and those who married into Catholic families. During the later sixteenth, seventeenth, and eighteenth centuries English Catholics formed only a small, persecuted minority, though in certain rural areas, under the leadership of gentry families, they were much stronger than national figures imply.

Some of the earliest parish registers date from a time when England was still a Catholic country, but after the accession of Elizabeth in 1558 Roman Catholics were faced with the problem of complying with the law whilst at the same time worshipping as their consciences dictated. Most Catholics in

St Mary's Roman Catholic Church, Clapham

Our Lady of Victories was built between 1849 and 1851 when Clapham was one of the new, densely populated London suburbs that had mushroomed in the countryside south of the Thames. William Wardell, a young Catholic, was the architect. By the end of the century the church had to be enlarged to accommodate the growing population.

the sixteenth, seventeenth, and eighteenth centuries opted for an Anglican burial service but private baptism and marriage services. The fear of persecution meant that registers were rarely kept before the middle of the eighteenth century. When a register was started, retrospective entries were sometimes made. More registers were kept after 1791, but many do not begin until the early nineteenth century. At first, priests seem to have regarded these registers as their personal responsibility and took the registers with them when they moved. The areas that they served were in any case often large and bore no relationship to the Anglican parishes.

'Popish Recusants' were frequently presented before the ecclesiastical and civil authorities. Their names therefore appear in the records of archdeacons' courts and quarter sessions. These records are far from being comprehensive, for many an incumbent was prepared to turn a blind eye to Catholic practices. Two sets of returns for the years 1705 and 1706 for Derbyshire illustrate the difficulties. The earlier set is kept in the House of Lords, for that is where concern about the strength of Catholicism was expressed, leading to the decision to hold a national enquiry. The second set is housed at the Lichfield Joint Record Office, which holds the records of the diocese of Coventry and Lichfield. The differences between the two accounts are considerable and in some parishes the incumbents refused or neglected to provide the information. As no guide-lines were issued, the returns took a variety of forms. Some incumbents listed whole families, some husbands and wives only, and others just the heads of households.

By 1811 the total of English Catholics was somewhere in the region of 250,000. Already the greater part consisted of Irish immigrants, together with French *émigrés* and refugees. Between 1791 and 1814 large numbers of Catholic chapels were opened, mainly in the north. The Catholic Emancipation Act of 1829 allowed Catholics to worship as they pleased and led to the building of more churches and some new cathedrals.

Catholic Irish people began to emigrate to England in significant numbers during the first half of the eighteenth century, when they settled in certain parts of London and Liverpool. By the beginning of the nineteenth century Liverpool was the most favoured destination. The Catholic population of the city numbered 12,000 by 1821, 60,000 by 1832, and 80,000 by 1840. Some Catholic immigrants came from other parts of Lancashire, but the great majority were Irish. From Liverpool they soon spread to the industrial towns of south Lancashire, across the Pennines to Leeds, and south to the Potteries, the Staffordshire coalfield, and Birmingham. Irish navvies who worked on the railways in the boom years of the 1830s and 1840s sometimes settled far from their original bases. Meanwhile, the Irish colonies in London were growing rapidly. The great famine of 1845 forced many more Catholic Irish to emigrate. It has been estimated that three-quarters of the Catholic population in England by the middle of the nineteenth century was of Irish origin.

Catholic authorities were reluctant to deposit their registers alongside those of the Protestant Nonconformists, upon the start of civil registration, on the grounds that they were required for religious purposes and that extracts had to be certified by a priest. The northern registers were deposited, however, and these can now be consulted in the Public Record Office. In recent years, many Catholic registers and other records have been deposited in local archive repositories, such as the Lancashire Record Office.

Records of Jewish Congregations

European Jews belong to one of two main groups. Those whose ancestors lived in Spain are called Sephardim, from a medieval Hebrew word meaning Spaniards. Those whose ancestors inhabited the Rhine valley during the Middle Ages and later moved across Germany and into Poland and Russia are called Ashkenazim, from a medieval Hebrew word meaning Germans. Both communities belong to the main stream of Rabbinic Judaism and the differences between them are of Hebrew pronunciation, liturgical tradition, custom, temperament, and some minor points of religious practice rather than of belief.

The first Jewish immigrants were brought from Rouen by King William I, shortly after the Norman Conquest. By 1290, when they were expelled from England by Edward I, their estimated numbers were not more than 3,000, nearly all of whom were based in London or a few of the great provincial cities such as Lincoln or York. A small colony of Sephardic Jews eventually resettled in the capital from 1541 onwards, but it was not until the middle of the seventeenth century that Jews were formally readmitted into the country. By 1734 the total number of Jews in England was estimated at 6,000.

Most of the sixteenth- and seventeenth-century Jewish immigrants were Sephardic Jews, who came principally from Portugal. Many of them were wealthy merchants. During the eighteenth century other Sephardic Jews, from Italy, Morocco, Turkey, etc., settled in London and joined the Portuguese synagogue. Some eventually moved on to India, the West Indies, and the American colonies. The majority of English Jews, however, are of Ashkenazic origin, their ancestors coming from Poland, Germany, or Central Europe. Their native language was Yiddish, an offshoot of German written in Hebrew characters. Many of these were poor men who earned a living by travelling around the countryside, hawking jewellery and haberdashery, hoping to save enough to open a shop in a provincial town. Others practised skilled crafts, such as engraving. Perhaps half of the 6,000 English Jews in 1734 were Ashkenazim. Immigration in the nineteenth century altered this proportion considerably. By 1882 the Sephardic Jews of London were estimated at about 3,500 and the Ashkenazic at about 15,000, half the latter being immigrants or descendants of immigrants who came after 1800. Thousands of Ashkenazic Jews entered England to escape persecution in Central and Eastern Europe in 1848–50, 1863, and from the 1880s onwards,

JEWISH REFUGEES IN LONDON (1890) *(above)*

Refugees from Russia are seen here in the Poor Jews' Temporary Shelter, Leman Street, London.

THE UNITED WORKMEN'S AND WLODOWA SYNAGOGUE, HARE STREET, LONDON *(left)*

This synagogue in the East End of London was built by the voluntary labour of Jewish carpenters in the evenings after their day's work. The community was established in 1914 and the building was used from the 1920s.

until an Act of 1905 restricted the scale of immigration. Many of these poor immigrants flocked to the East End of London or to some of the burgeoning industrial cities, notably Leeds.

In his chapter on 'The Jews' in *Sources for Roman Catholic and Jewish Genealogy and Family History*, edited by D. J. Steel, Edgar R. Samuel makes the point that one of the principal difficulties in tracing an Ashkenazic Jewish ancestry is the variable nature of the surnames, which developed both through Anglicization and translation. For example, a Bristol Jew, Eliezer, the son of Jacob, who built a synagogue there in 1786, was known to the townsmen as Lazarus Jacobs. His descendants all called themselves Lazarus. Similarly, the descendants of David might be called Davis, and those of Moses, Moss. The Hebrew Zevi (a stag) was Germanized into Hirsch or Hirschel, then Anglicized into Hart, only to emerge finally as Harris.

Synagogue records have often been deposited in local record offices. Most early synagogues kept an accurate record of marriages and burials, but were less careful with births. The records of Ashkenazic synagogues are particularly difficult to use because they are written in Hebrew or Yiddish in a cursive script and because they record Hebrew or synagogical names, which do not always correspond with the English names that were used every day; nor do they note surnames. Specialist guidance is clearly needed here. Of course, many Jews appear in the ordinary parish registers of the Church of England, just like Protestant Nonconformists or Roman Catholics.

Probate Records

The numerous wills that survive from the Middle Ages were made mostly by members of aristocratic and gentry families or by rich town merchants. In some dioceses the wills of large numbers of middle-income and even quite poor testators were being registered in the late Middle Ages, but in general the practice of making a will did not become common amongst farmers and craftsmen until the sixteenth century. At all times, the poorer sections of society remained largely unrepresented. Even among the social groups that were most likely to make a will, however, many did not bother. Studies of the number of wills made in a parish compared with the number of entries for adult males in the burial register always demonstrate that making a will was a minority concern, usually in the order of 1 in 3 or 1 in 4. Very few wives made wills (for, according to the law, a married woman could do nothing without the consent of her husband), but many widows and spinsters did.

Families had other methods of transferring property, for example, helping sons to obtain a suitable property at the time of marriage and providing daughters with marriage portions. If the children were still minors a man might make provision for them in the event of his wife remarrying, otherwise the property would pass to her new husband during her lifetime and the children might be disadvantaged. If the children had already left home and everyone in the family knew what was to happen to the remainder of the patrimony then a will was unnecessary.

Until 1858 the responsibility for proving a will lay with the Church. Probate records before this date are therefore held at the ancient diocesan record offices, with the exception of those proved between 1653 and 1660, when the Prerogative Court of Canterbury (the PCC) was given sole jurisdiction throughout England and Wales. The probate records for these seven years are now housed at the Public Record Office, as are all those proved through the PCC between 1383 and 1858. Indexes of all PCC wills before 1700 have been published by the British Record Society and indexes of later material are being prepared. Elsewhere, the provision of indexes varies considerably in quality from one record office to another and from period to period. Thus, the indexes of wills proved through the diocese of York from 1389 to 1688 have been printed in several volumes of the Yorkshire Archaeological Society Record Series, but after 1688 one has to consult the typed index at the Borthwick Institute of Historical Research, York. Some other record offices still rely on handwritten indexes compiled a long time ago.

The family historian has to familiarize himself with another set of administrative units before he can find the probate records for his parish. Archivists will advise and maps may be available at record offices. The standard guidebooks are A. J. Camp's *Wills and Their Whereabouts* and J. S. W. Gibson's, *Wills and Where to Find Them*. The structure of the probate courts in the province of Canterbury was different in some respects from that of the province of York. In both provinces, however, the principle was that a higher court had to be used if a testator held property in more than one lower jurisdiction. Those with land or other goods in only one archdeaconry used the archdeacon's court, those with property in two archdeaconries went to the episcopal courts, those with possessions in two bishoprics had to go to the Archbishop's Prerogative Court, and finally those with property in the two provinces went to the senior court at Canterbury.

Many parishes (and sometimes scattered properties within a parish) belonged to peculiar jurisdictions, whose records are kept separately. These peculiars were often parishes whose tithes went to support a prebend at the cathedral and whose records were therefore proved by the Dean and Chapter. Other peculiars included parishes whose tithes had once belonged to the Knights Templar or the Knights Hospitaller and others which had been special liberties, e.g. a royal castle or a possession of an archbishop. Fortunately, nearly all these collections are housed alongside the main body of probate records in the archives of the ancient dioceses. Sometimes they may turn up elsewhere, e.g. in a solicitor's deposit at a local record office, when the rights of a peculiar had been purchased upon the dissolution of the original owning body.

Wills were originally proved by the Church. They usually began by committing the testator's soul to Almighty God and his or her body to burial in a church or churchyard. Only the richer members of a local society could

THE WILL OF WILLIAM BRAY OF UPMINSTER, ESSEX (1689)

This clergyman's will follows a standard form. It reads:

In the name of god Amen this Twentieth day of Aprill in the year of o[u]r Lord One thousand six hundred Eighty & Nine I William Bray of Upminster in the County of Essex Clerke being ill in body but of sound & p[er]fect minde & understanding doe make ordaine & declare this my last Will & Testament in manner & forme following. Imprimis I give devise & bequeath unto my loveing wife Jane Bray and to her heires & assignes forever all & every my messuages, Lands & tenem[en]ts whatsoever scituate lyeing & being in the severall p[ar]ishes of Hadfield & Dinting in the County of Derby And alsoe all that my Advowson in grosse donac[i]on, Presentac[i]on, right of Patronage & free disposic[i]on of the Rectory & p[ar]ish Church of Upminster in the County of Essex abovesaid. Item I give devise & bequeath unto my said loveing wife Jane Bray & to her heires & assignes all & every my messuages lands & tenem[en]ts whatsoever lyeing & being in the severall p[ar]ishes of Whittfield & Glossopp in the said County of Derby And alsoe all those my messuages lands & tenem[en]ts scituate lyeing and being in Wakefield in the County of Yorke which said p[re]misses in Wakefield now are or late were in the severall tenures or occupac[i]ons of Mary Browne widd[ow] Henry Sharpe Robert Shawe & Thomas Hayward or their assignes or undertenants to bee sold by her or her said heires or assignes for & towards the payment of my debts which said messuages Lands & tenem[en]ts in Whittfield, Glossopp & Wakefield I doe hereby charge with the payment of my said debts. Lastly all my goods chattells debts due to mee & all my other p[er]sonall Estate whatsoever I give & bequeath unto my above named loveing wife Jane Bray whom I doe hereby make the sole Executrix of this my last will & Testament And I doe hereby revoke all other wills by mee formerly made In Wittnes whereof I have hereunto sett my hand & seale the day & year above written.

Will. Bray

Signed sealed published & declared by the s[ai]d William Bray as for his last Will & Testam[en]t in the p[resen]ce of

Joseph Holt

Hen. Sedgwicke

Frances Sedgwicke

The Latin formula in the bottom right-hand corner is the clerk's note to the effect that probate was granted to Jane, the widow of William Bray, on 2 May 1689.

expect to be buried within the church. Most wills have a long preamble which follows one of the standard forms taken from books of advice on how to draw up a will. Before the Reformation a typical Catholic formula might read: 'I bequeath my soul to Almighty God, our Lady Saint Mary and all the Holy Company of Heaven . . .'. Later preambles express a belief in salvation and redemption through Christ, e.g. 'I commend my soul unto Almighty God my Maker and Redeemer by whose precious blood shedding I trust to be saved.'

After making provision for the payment of all debts and the funeral expenses, the testator proceeded to dispose of his or her worldly goods. Last wills were normally made shortly before death (as is evident from shaky signatures) and so a clause was often inserted to say that all previous wills were thereby annulled. If a dying person was too ill to make a will, then a nuncupative will, i.e. an oral statement attested by sworn witnesses, was accepted by the church court. If a person died intestate, the court had the power to grant letters of administration of the estate to those whom it considered legitimate administrators.

The will of John Burton of Totley, Derbyshire, made in 1571/2, illustrates many of the typical forms of the wills of that period:

In the name of god amen. In the year of our lord god 1571 and the xxviith day of februarie I John Burtone of totley in the p[ar]yshe of Dronfield Sycke of body and houlle of mynd and good of Remembrance macke my Testament and last will In this maner fowlowynge fyrst I geve my soule unto god almyghty my maker and Redymer and my body to by buryed In the parishe chyrchyarde of Saynt John Baptys at Drounfeld Ite[m] I geve and by queath my farme unto Joanne my wife to

197

have enjoy and Occupy at the pleasur of Mr John Barcar to brynge up my chyldren so lonnge as she keepth heere weadow and if it forton Joane my wife mary that then hear tearme of years to seace and then all the sayd tearm that I have to by to the bryngyne up of all my chyldren untyll my s[o]n andrew by at his age and able to occupy it him selfe and if she mary my son andrew to have all my tearme of years Item I geve and by queath unto my s[o]n andrew an Irne bund wayne and a plough youcke and all such thynges belonngynge unto husbandry also a great arcke a basket an ambry and a long boord also I geve and by queath unto my good measter Mr John Barcar

THE PROBATE INVENTORY OF GEORGE TAYLOR OF REIGATE, SURREY (26 DECEMBER 1695)
This extract from a yeoman's inventory reads:

Item In the Hall Chamber
One Feather bed, One bedstedle One Sett of Curtains and Valence mat and cord, £1. 15s., Item Four chaires, 6s., Item One old Cupboard and One old chest, 3s., Item one pair of Fire Irons and one pair of Andirons, 12s., Item One Stand & a voider, 1s.

Item In the back Chamber
Two Feather beds, Four bolsters Four Pillows Four blanketts One quilt One Rug, Two bedsteddles mats & cords, £5, Item Five Chests, One side board One Press, One Desk One Close stoole Two chairs and a cupboard, £1. 10s., Item One trundle bedstedle, 5s.

Item In the Hall
One drawing table & carpett Four joined stooles, Five turkey worked chaires and two stooles, £2, Item One little table & carpett, 3s., Item One Round table, 3s. 6d., Item Two cupboards One chair and three Cushoins, 18s.

xiiis iiiid desyryng hym to by good Measter unto my wife and Chyldren as I tryst he will also my mind and will is my wife to have the third part of al my goodes after the maner and custom and all the Residu of my goodes to by Equally divided Amonnge my Chyldren Also I macke Joane my wife my full exec[u]tor to Dyspose for the health of my soule as she thought best and p[ro]vide and sy that this my p[re]sent will by fully contented and fullfylled and also my will is that my uncle Thomas Burton Thomas Calton John owtrym and Robert Poynton by over syers of my Chyldren Thes by me Deats owynge unto my John Burton Willm Robynson xls Thomas Sayles xvs iiiid.

Great care has to be taken in interpreting words whose meaning seems obvious but which might have been used differently in the past. Cousin was used to denote a wide range of kinsmen, and even father, son, daughter, and brother may have been used for in-laws. Children who had already been provided for may not be mentioned in a will. Conversely, people who are mentioned may not have been alive by the time that a will was proved.

From the reign of Henry VIII onwards it was the practice of the church courts to insist that the executors appointed three or four local men to make 'a true and perfect inventory' of the personal estate of the deceased. This practice continued well into the eighteenth century, varying from one locality to another. Tens of thousands of inventories survive, covering most parts of the country. They are normally attached to the will or to the letters of administration where no will had been made. The appraisers, as the valuers were normally called, listed every piece of household furniture, room by room, and then perhaps the livestock and crops, the contents of a workshop, and all the bits and pieces that were valued together as 'huslement'. A family historian who finds an inventory of the possessions of a forebear gets a marvellous insight into the way of life and standard of living of his sixteenth-, seventeenth-, or eighteenth-century ancestor. Inventories have been widely used by social and economic historians and there is a vast literature concerning them, including numerous glossaries of the archaic and dialect words that were used.

On 12 January 1858 the State took over responsibility for proving wills through either the Principal Registry in London or the district offices in the rest of the country. Since 1874 the Principal Registry (Family Division) has been at Somerset House in the Strand, which is open to the public (free of charge and without the necessity of obtaining a ticket) between 10 a.m. and 4.30 p.m., Monday to Friday. This registry also receives copies of the wills proved in the district offices. The annual indexes of probates and of letters of administration (known as admons) for the whole of the country may be consulted here or in some of the larger municipal libraries which have printed copies. The indexes record the name of the testator, his or her address, the date and sometimes the place of death, the date of probate, the names of the executors or administrators, the value of the estate, and the name of the office in which the will was proved. A small charge is made for a registered copy of a will.

Manorial and Estate Records

The family historian will normally turn to manorial records only after he has made a thorough search of parish registers and wills. The chances of finding genealogical information in this source depend not only upon the survival of archives but on the size, the importance, and the length of life of the manor concerned. It is a common experience to find nothing of value, but sometimes manorial records will not only fill out the picture for the early modern period but will take the searcher back well into the Middle Ages. The records of the manor of Wakefield, to quote one outstanding example, provide continuous information from the thirteenth to the twentieth century.

A manor was sometimes coterminous with a parish, but very often it bore no relationship to the other unit. Manors varied in size from a few hundred to many thousands of acres. Some parishes contained two or three manors within their bounds, and some of these manors stretched over parts of neighbouring parishes as well. It is often difficult to establish the precise boundaries of a manor, many of which had numerous detached portions. Moreover, many manors contained large parcels of freehold land, whose owners made only a token recognition of the lord. Ownership of a manor did not necessarily mean that the lord owned most of the land, but only that he had certain customary rights, which varied from place to place.

Some manor courts ceased to function during the sixteenth and seventeenth centuries, but others continued to meet at regular intervals even into the nineteenth century. A handful, most famously that at the surviving open-field village of Laxton, meet at the present day. Manorial records are not always easy to trace, for if the ownership of a manor passed to someone who lived away then the records might have been moved out of the district. Many have been deposited at county and city record offices, while those of the numerous manors which belonged to the Crown or to the Duchy of Lancaster etc. will be found in the Public Record Office. Other manorial and estate records are kept in the British Library Department of Manuscripts. An archivist at the local record office will be the best person to give advice on the whereabouts of the records of individual manors.

Post-medieval manorial records are commonly listed in catalogues of archives under the heading 'estate papers'. The manor was indeed a unit of estate management and with the decline of manorial courts the records take the form of rentals, leases, surveys, and accounts. Even where courts continued to function, the term 'manorial court rolls' is rather misleading for the post-medieval period when stewards preferred to use bound volumes or sheets of paper.

Manorial courts were of two kinds. The court baron registered transfers of copyhold lands and the court leet saw to such day-to-day matters as the repair of hedges, the scouring of ditches, the rounding up of stray cattle, and

COURT ROLL OF THE MANOR OF OCKLEY, SURREY (1718)

Until 1733 manorial court rolls were often written in Latin. Family historians with little or no knowledge of Latin may nevertheless readily identify names amongst the jurors and officers of the manor. Names such as John, William, Edward, Lawrence, and Thomas can be easily recognized, and the surnames are in English.

the punishment of petty crime. A record of a meeting of a court leet commonly starts with a list of the ordinary members of the community who formed the jury, or 'homage', of the manor. Sometimes, all those freeholders who owed some form of allegiance to the manor are listed; many of them were absentee owners who never set foot in the district. The 'homagers' or 'jurymen' were the local inhabitants. After electing various officials, the jury agreed by-laws, known as 'paines' from the penalties which were imposed for their non-observance. Offenders against previous laws were fined and their names recorded.

A family historian may well find his ancestor serving on the manorial jury or being brought before the court for a specified offence. The records of the court baron will be of more use than those of the court leet in searching for genealogical information and for noting the transfer of copyhold property. The descent of a family holding can sometimes be traced over several generations. Dates of death are often given or can be inferred and family relationships are sometimes stated or can be deduced. The term 'copyhold tenure' is derived from the custom whereby a tenant held a copy of the entry in the manorial court rolls which recognized his possession of a holding according to agreed terms. Each manor had its own customs regarding the ways that holdings could be transferred. Copyhold tenure began tc give way to leaseholding during the sixteenth century, but it was not legally abolished until 1922.

The records of manorial courts baron are often difficult to interpret. Even scholars who have considerable experience may be misled by forms which are frequently complicated and sometimes downright ambiguous. The indispensable guide is P. D. A. Harvey's *Manorial Records*. The transfers or conveyances recorded by a court may represent either sales, mortgages, or inheritance through entails, endowments, or trusts. These observations apply equally to the deeds that are kept in family or solicitors' collections in local record offices or registries of deeds. Such deeds are usually even more difficult to understand because of the long-winded forms of expression that were used from the sixteenth to the nineteenth centuries. Nevertheless, the difficulties should not be overstated. Manorial records can be a mine of genealogical information, going back well before the beginning of parish registration of baptisms, weddings, and burials.

A survey of a manor is of special value, particularly if it is accompanied by a map. Surveys become more common in the post-medieval period and often signify a change of ownership; a new lord was understandably keen to know exactly what he had purchased or inherited, often with a view to increasing the entry fines and rents. A survey might name each tenant, describe his buildings, give the acreage and use of every part of the holding, and record the conditions of tenure. In most cases, surveys will give a good indication of who was living in a particular place at a certain point in time, but they must not be regarded as comprehensive lists of the inhabitants of a particular community. As we have already noted, a manor was not necessarily the same unit as a parish; householders who were tenants of another manor will not be listed alongside their neighbours. Moreover, a farmer might have held only part of his land from a particular manor; the acreage that is recorded may not have been the only land that he farmed. A more serious problem is that tenants may have sublet their land to others who were

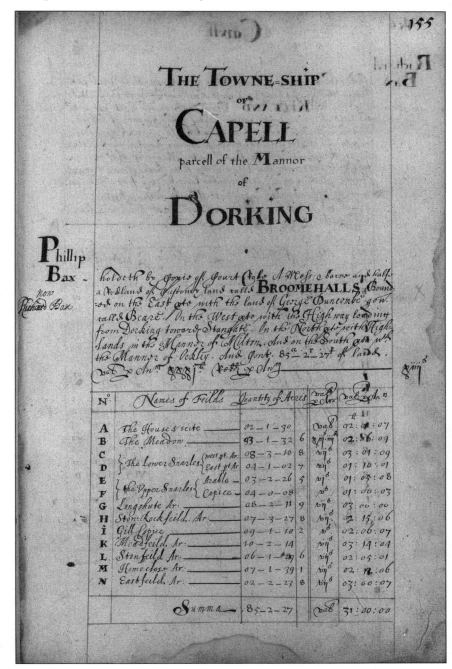

Survey of the Township of Capel in the Manor of Dorking, Surrey (1649)

Manorial surveys give many details of property leased by the lord to his tenants. In Capel, Phillip Bax held a messuage called Broomehalls, with 85 acres 2 roods 27 perches of land, at an annual rent of 14 shillings. The fields are listed by name, size, and value. A marginal comment inserted later notes that Richard Bax was the tenant.

not recorded. The family historian can therefore be easily misled. He will usually be grateful for getting at least part of the picture.

Rentals are less informative than surveys and their survival is often patchy. They give the names of the tenants of the estate and the rents that were due each year, at Lady Day and Michaelmas, or Christmas and Mid-

summer. However, they too may record the names of absentee tenants
rather than the subtenants who actually lived there and farmed the land.
Leases may be found amongst manorial and estate records or amongst solicitors' collections and private deposits. Those which were granted for three
lives (the common method in western parts of England) are particularly
useful to the family historian, for the lives that were entered were commonly
those of the parents and the eldest son. A good run of leases will help the
searcher to trace the descent of a property.

Manors were not just rural institutions. In many towns, they existed
alongside the borough; elsewhere, corporations had acquired the manorial
rights. In Sheffield, the Dukes of Norfolk continued to hold manorial courts
well into the nineteenth century, though many aspects of local government

RECORDS OF THE MANOR OF HAM, SURREY

Succession to Property (1775)
Manorial court records sometimes provide a great deal of genealogical information if the succession to a property is not straightforward. This entry informs us that Thomas Twibell had died several years previously and had been succeeded as tenant by John Cross. John Wright, the son and only heir of Ann Wright (the youngest daughter and heir of John Cross), was admitted as tenant in 1775. He immediately let the property to Ann Horne, the wife of Thomas Horne of London, gentleman. Her complicated family history is set out at some length.

were the responsibility of an independent Town Trust, while in neighbouring Doncaster the mayor and corporation had acted as lords of the manor since the Middle Ages. The records of Doncaster corporation therefore include numerous rentals and leases.

Enclosure Awards, Tithe Awards, and Land Tax Assessments

In many parts of the country the family historian may find rich information about an ancestor amongst the records of parliamentary enclosure, but this is not a source that is available everywhere, nor is it one where the information is set down in a consistent manner. About 6 million acres of open fields, commons, and wastes were enclosed by some 4,000 private Acts of Parliament, the great majority between 1750 and 1850. The many other manors and parishes which had been enclosed privately by agreement in earlier times have no such records. An Act of Parliament was necessary only when agreement could not be reached amicably. W. E. Tate's *Domesday of English Enclosure Acts* gives a list of the places that were enclosed by the parliament-

ary process and some record offices have published catalogues of the awards that are available for particular counties.

Whereas a local historian will be interested in the whole process of enclosure and the effects that it had on his particular community, the initial interest of the family historian will be concentrated on the legal document known as the award, which was drawn up after all claims had been considered and a thorough survey had been made. In many places, only the commons and wastes were enclosed; in such cases the award will specify only the allotments of former common land that were distributed amongst those who had previously enjoyed common rights. In those parts of England, notably much of the Midland Plain, where the arable land was still farmed on a communal system in open fields, an award will cover all the land in the parish. Similar comprehensive awards are found in cases where only the commons and wastes were enclosed but where the opportunity was taken at the same time to convert tithe payments to a fixed sum. A schedule lists the owners and tenants of every piece of property that is covered by the award. These properties are shown on an accompanying map.

If tithe payments were not altered at the time of enclosure the family historian whose ancestors were country-folk at the beginning of Victoria's reign should look for a tithe award. These were made in the years following the Tithe Commutation Act of 1836. Three copies of each award were made;

FIELD PATTERNS, PADBURY, BUCKINGHAMSHIRE
The rectangular fields are the product of the enclosure award of 1796. The hedgerows overlie the ridge-and-furrow patterns of former open-field agriculture. In *Medieval England: an aerial survey* M. W. Beresford and J. K. S. St Joseph have shown that the pattern of ridge-and-furrow seen here matches that of strips depicted on a map of 1591. The lane to the right of centre follows the line of an old field way, which in 1591 was named Stighegate.

C.C.—London: Printed and Published (By Authority,) by

LANDOWNERS.	OCCUPIERS.	Numbers referring to the Plan.	NAME AND DESCRIPTION OF LANDS AND PREMISES.	STATE OF CULTIVATION.	QUANTITIES IN STATUTE MEASURE			Amount of Rent-Charge apportioned upon the several Lands, and Payable to the Rector.		
					A.	R.	P.	£	s.	d
Braithwaite John Hall Richard	Kinch Thomas	148	Well field	Pas	1	2	23			
		151	Tenements				14			
		130	Part of Long Meadow	Pas	1	1	24			
					3	-	21 X		15	6
Butler Cornelius	Bruty William	209	Gallows field	Ara	4	1	13			
		209a	Do	Ara	7	3				
		215	Plantation	Plant						
					12	-	22 Y	3	12	-
Butler James	Himself	105a	Piece by New Road	Pas		3	-			
		226	Garden	Ara	1	1	16			
					2	-	16 X		15	-
Copland John	Moss James (Exors of)	101	Lower Brick field	Pas	1	2	2		8	6
	Scott Charles	102	Upper Do	Pas	1	1	29		5	
	Himself	229	Garden				11			
		230	Do			2	13			
						2	24 X			
Copland John Junr	Himself	332	Part of Friars place	Pas		1	28			
		333	Part of pasture	Pas		1	6			
		337		Pas	1	-	26			
					1	3	12 Y		10	6
	Miller John	331	Skyblue	Pas	2	-	31		12	
	Moss Thomas	336	Part of Long Meadow	Pas	1	2	18		9	

one was deposited in the parish chest and should now be in a local record office, a second went to the bishop and should be kept in the archives of the ancient diocese, and a third went to the central government and should now be in the Public Record Office's store at Ashridge. The national reference work is R. J. P. Kain and H. C. Prince, *Tithe Surveys of England and Wales*, but catalogues for some counties are available at local record offices. About 2 out of every 3 parishes or townships have a tithe award. Most were drawn up by 1841 and all were completed by 1860. There is nothing comparable until the Inland Revenue house surveys of 1910–13, when detailed descriptions and valuations of each house in the country were made and the names of owners and tenants (but not necessarily occupants) were recorded. These are kept in the Public Record Office at Kew under IR.58 and IR.121–35.

Tithe awards list the owners and each of the occupiers of every piece of property. The properties are described as house, cottage, garden, orchard, field, etc. and their size is recorded. Tithe awards are a valuable source of information about field names; some even say what crop was being grown at the time of the survey. The large-scale maps which accompany the awards are often the earliest detailed maps available for a particular parish. They can be used with the 1841 and 1851 census returns to build an accurate picture of a place in the middle years of the nineteenth century. Six-inch ordnance

TITHE AWARD, CHELMSFORD, ESSEX (1843) The award is arranged by landowners' names in alphabetical order, followed by the names of the actual occupiers of each piece of property. The numbers in the third column relate to an accompanying map. The award is also an important source for field names, land use, field sizes, and values.

survey maps are not usually available until the 1870s, though a pilot survey was carried out in Yorkshire 20 years earlier.

The family historian who becomes deeply interested in the history of the places where his ancestors lived will need to examine the enclosure and tithe awards in much greater detail than the researcher who at this stage is merely trying to find out where exactly his ancestor resided. Part of this deeper interest will lead the historian to the land tax assessments of that period. Here again, however, the beginner will find much that is immediately useful.

The land tax was introduced in the late seventeenth century, but the chances of assessments surviving before 1780 are very hit and miss. These assessments take the form of annual lists of the names of the proprietors of land in each parish and (at least in theory) the names of the actual occupiers. Assessments were organized on a county, hundred, and parish basis, so the returns may be found amongst quarter sessions records, in estate and family archives, or in parish collections. The duplicate returns that were made each year between 1780 and 1832 and deposited amongst quarter sessions records have the best chance of survival. The only record that covers almost the whole of England and Wales in a uniform way is that for the year 1798, which is contained in 121 volumes in class IR.23 at the Public Record Office, Kew. After 1798 standard printed forms were used. The reliability of land tax assessments has been hotly debated, but the family historian will find them a useful source for the period immediately before civil registration and the census returns, when parish registers are at their least reliable. By using a series of assessments a family historian can see who occupied a property over time and he can identify the year when the name of a head of household was replaced by a different one.

Poor Law Records

The Tudor monarchs made the ecclesiastical parishes (or their subdivisions, known as townships) responsible for certain civil functions, notably the relief of the poor. The Elizabethan Acts of 1598–1601 formed the basis of the Poor Law until the 1834 Poor Law Amendment Act created unions of parishes to serve in their place. Unpaid Overseers of the Poor were chosen at a yearly meeting of parishioners about Easter. They normally served for one year and were responsible for raising taxes (the 'poor rates' or 'assessments'), relieving the poor, and keeping accounts which had to be presented at the end of their period of office. Men were expected to serve without payment for loss of earnings, and they were responsible for their conduct to the Justices of the Peace. Records concerning the operation of the Poor Law are therefore normally found at county record offices, either amongst the deposited parish records or amongst the records of the quarter sessions.

The Elizabethan Poor Law aimed to relieve the 'deserving poor', to provide work, and to discipline the idle. Begging was punished by whipping,

ACCOUNTS OF THE
OVERSEERS OF THE POOR,
MITCHAM, SURREY (1663)
(left and opposite)
The accounts of William
Greene, esquire, and Jeffry
Phillips begin by noting income received from be-
quests and 'assessments'
(poor rates), amounting to
£59. 15s. 6d. The 'disburse-
ments' include the payment
of rents and pensions and
the additional sums that
were paid to needy individuals. Elizabeth Smyth was
maintained at four different
places during the year. Extra
payments were made for
washing her linen, remov-
ing her goods and lumber,
providing her with shoes
and mending them twice,
bleeding her when she was
ill, and giving her small
sums of money that added
up to 3s. 7d. Ten widows
were provided with coats at
the parish charge. The
names of those parishioners
who were present at the
passing of the accounts are
given at the end.

unless the JPs granted a special dispensation. The problem for the Overseer
was how to define the 'deserving poor'. Overseers were responsible to the
local rate-payers, who were anxious to keep the rates low, but they were the
ones who had face-to-face contact with the poor who were requesting relief.
The Overseer knew full well that if he turned down a request the person
seeking relief might appeal to the nearest JP. He was therefore frequently
faced with a dilemma. Some quarter sessions records include petitions, such

as that of Elizabeth Hepworth of Owlerton in the parish of Sheffield, a widow for 11 years, who claimed that she 'has had no relief all that time but what she earned by her hard labour without being chargeable to her neighbours . . . now of great age being 69 years old and much weakened with bodily infirmities being disenabled to work for a livelihood is driven into great distress and want'. The JPs ordered the parish overseers to pay her 6*d*. a week maintenance. Overseers were not always as tight-fisted as they appear to have been in this case and often showed compassion for the poor. For example, many parishes did not take up the 'badging' powers of 1697, which allowed these local authorities to insist that poor people in receipt of charity should wear a letter P, or some similar distinguishing mark, on their apparel. Generally speaking, most parishes looked after those whom they considered their own 'deserving poor'.

All parishes had the problem of finding homes for poor orphans and finding employment for the children of parents who were in receipt of poor relief. The Acts of 1598–1601 empowered overseers to bind such children as apprentices and to pay their premiums from the parish rates. The Overseer had the often difficult task of finding a master. The 1697 Act imposed a £10 penalty on anyone who refused, without good reason, to accept a pauper child into his home and workplace, though anyone who felt aggrieved could petition the JPs. Quarter sessions depositions, where they survive, record many distressing cases.

The Act of Settlement of 1662 gave statutory authority to the previous practice of many parishes throughout England in stating that poor people were the responsibility of the parish where they were last legally settled. In the first place, a person was legally settled in the parish where he or she was born. However, if work was obtained in another parish for more than a year, or if an apprenticeship was served elsewhere, or if a family moved to a new parish and resided there unchallenged by the Overseer for more than a year, then the new place of residence became the legal settlement. When a woman

AN APPRENTICESHIP INDENTURE FOR A POOR CHILD, BETCHWORTH, SURREY (1790)
The churchwardens (Thomas Russell and James Roberts) and overseers of the poor (Benjamin Risbridger and John Felton) of the parish of Betchworth, in the presence of two JPs, apprenticed a poor child (Joseph, the son of Thomas Chart) to Joseph Chart, a peruke-maker and hairdresser of Dorking, until he was 21, according to the standard terms.

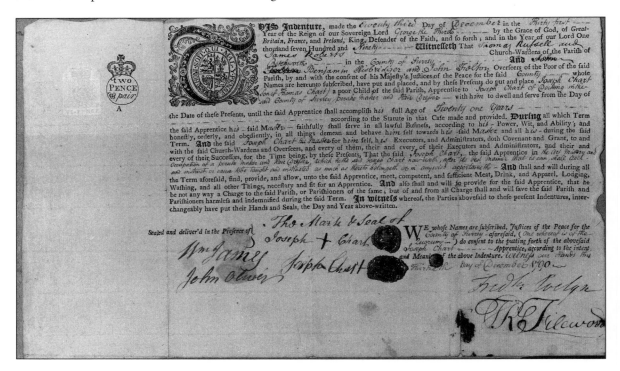

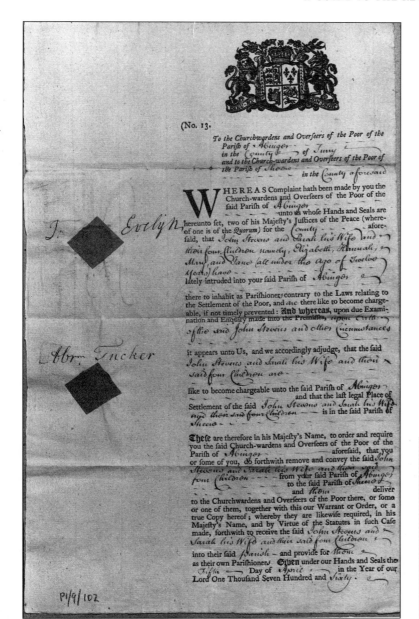

REMOVAL ORDER, ABINGER TO SHERE, SURREY (1760)

John and Sarah Stevens and their four children had recently arrived in the parish of Abinger. Fearful that the family would become a burden on the poor rates, the overseers applied to the Justices of the Peace to have them removed to Shere, their last legal place of settlement. The standard removal order authorized this procedure.

married, she became the responsibility of her husband's parish. A parish would often allow newcomers within their boundaries only if the parish where the immigrants were legally settled would issue a certificate to this effect. An Act of 1691 defined the various ways in which a certificate could be obtained. Such settlement certificates may survive among the parish records that have been deposited at a local record office.

Settlement disputes formed a major part of the business at meetings of the quarter sessions. Both sides in a dispute employed learned counsel to argue their case. Parishes thought it was worth their while to do so, for losing a case might mean that they were saddled with maintaining a poor family for ever. In 1701 Richard Gough remembered the salutary experience of the case of Humphrey Beddows, a lame man who was born in the parish of Cardington and who settled in Myddle upon his marriage to Mary Davis. The parish officers complained to the local JP, who issued a 'warrant of disturbance'. Sometime later, Beddows fell ill and was removed to Cardington, but the officers there claimed that he was legally settled in Myddle. By this time, the warrant had been lost, so the removal order by which Beddows was sent back to Myddle was confirmed. 'This was the first contest that we had and thus we lost it,' commented Gough, 'but thanks be to God we never lost any afterwards.' The consequences for the parish of Myddle were considerable. Beddows's daughter Elizabeth, 'an idle, wanton wench', gave birth to a child and claimed that she was married to a soldier. The father was apprehended, escaped, and was recaptured, and after two cases argued by learned counsel before the JPs, the family was removed to Condover, where the husband was legally settled. Beddows's son was another cause of trouble. He was twice set apprentice, but each time ran away; he ended up in the House of Correction. Beddows's mother-in-law, Sina Davis, 'a crafty, idle, disembleing woman', who pretended to be lame and who 'went hopping with a staffe when men saw her, butt att other tymes could goe with it under her arme', had maintenance from the parish for many years, and her blind son Andrew received from the parish £3 per annum for 40 years or more. It was clearly worth while for a parish to try to persuade the JPs to take a poor family off their hands and pass them on to others.

Quarter sessions records are kept in county record offices. Some of the earliest ones have been published by the relevant county record society. The formal business of the courts is recorded in the indictment and order books, but these are in the form of brief minutes. Where depositions and petitions survive, the detail is much more human and vivid. Few counties have quarter sessions records from the sixteenth century—Essex is exceptional in having rich material—but most have records dating at least from the second half of the seventeenth century. The JPs had a lot of other business to see to, of course, including disputes concerning highways and bridges, licensing alehouses, regulating inland trade, punishing those who broke the law, and so on. An ancestor might appear in the quarter sessions records under any of these headings.

Those records which deal with the poor are the ones which provide the greatest amount of genealogical material. When a poor person was examined by a JP, a careful note was kept of his or her movements over the previous years, in order to establish where responsibility for maintenance lay. These settlement depositions may survive either amongst quarter sessions records or amongst the collections of individual parishes. An example from Yorkshire at the end of the eighteenth century reads as follows:

West Riding of Yorkshire. The Voluntary Examination of Robert Townsend of Sheffield in the said Riding taken on Oath this 3 Day of December in the Year of our Lord 1798 before us two of his Majesty's Justices of the Peace in and for the said Riding, as touching his last Place of legal Settlement.

This Examinant saith and deposeth, that he is about Forty nine Years of Age, was born in the Army when his father then served as he has been informed and believes

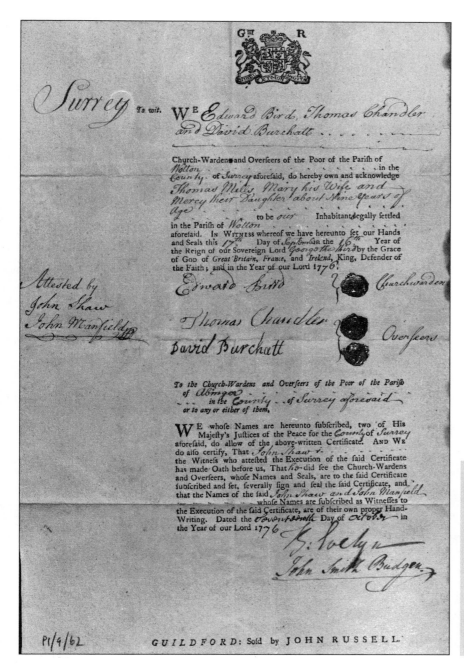

SETTLEMENT CERTIFICATE, WOTTON, SURREY (1776)

The churchwardens and overseers acknowledged that Thomas and Mary Mills, and their 9-year-old daughter Mercy, were the responsibility of the parish of Wotton. The overseers of Abinger would not have allowed the Mills family to settle without this certificate.

the same to be true, but both his Father and Mother died before this Examinant had any knowledge of them, that when he was about Fifteen years of age he was sent to sea but in what capacity he does not know previous to which Time he traveled up and down the Country wit, Hawker and Pedlar this Examinant says that he was about Four or five years upon the seas that the Ship in which he went out in was lost and that this Examinant and some other of the Ship Crew was taken up and Landed at Park Gate [near Liverpool] he then went to Manchester and worked as a Day Labourer there and in the Neighbourhood for about four years he then went to Hoyland in the County of York and worked with several People as a Day Labourer for about Five years he then went to Sheffield and worked in different branches of business till the year 1791 when he went to Bolton upon Dearne in the said Riding when he served with different Masters for about half a year when he intermarried with Rachael Hague whose legal settlement was at Bolton aforesaid soon after this Examinant returned to Sheffield where he has resided ever since.
(Sheffield Archives, PR9/93/32)

Information obtained from quarter sessions and parish records can sometimes be pieced together to reconstruct events in the history of a pauper family over a long period of time. William Peace of Hunshelf, Yorkshire, was described as a labourer when he appeared before the magistrates at Pontefract quarter sessions in 1752 for stealing beef, as a result of which he

HUGH MYDDLETON SCHOOL, CLERKENWELL, LONDON (1906)

Few old photographs are more evocative of the past than scenes like this. Where they survive, school records can be of great value to the family historian. In particular, admission registers from 1870 onwards can give not only the name of a child and the date of admission, but the father's name and address (sometimes the mother's name also), the child's date of birth, the name of his or her previous school, and the date of leaving. Some registers go on to record when a child left school and the destination.

was whipped. On 8 June 1752 an order was issued by the JPs for his removal from the township of Penistone to the township of Hunshelf, with his wife, Ann, and daughter Jemmy. Penistone and Hunshelf were in the same ecclesiastical parish, but were separate townships, or civil parishes. William Peace remained the responsibility of Hunshelf township until he died in 1768, though he normally managed to maintain himself. Ann received a total of £192. 16s. 0d. in relief from 1783 until her death in 1812, when her funeral expenses were met by the township. Their daughter Jemmy married M. Walker and had 10 children. In 1794 Walker was charged at the quarter sessions meeting held at Sheffield with stealing three-pennyworth of goods from Joseph Wood's warehouse. He was ordered to be transported to Botany Bay, but never reached there and probably died in the bulks.

Dr Keith Snell has emphasized the significance of settlement from the point of view of poor families, who treated proof of a claim on 'their' parish much as a family heirloom. Details of the family's settlement were carefully preserved and repeated to children from an early age. Certificates acknowledging settlement (or apprenticeship indentures) were passed from father to son; receipts of rent paid in excess of £10 per annum were produced decades later in evidence; and details of old removal cases affecting the family were told during examinations. The knowledge of the law possessed by some pauper families rivalled that of the lawyers who were consulted in parochial settlement disputes. The law was seen by the poor as a guarantee of parish relief during a period of poverty; this was some compensation for the restrictions imposed on their freedom of movement.

Military Records

A great deal of information about men who served in the armed forces can be obtained from the Family Records Centre, 1 Myddelton Street, London EC1, and the Public Record Office at Kew. The regimental registers that are kept at the Family Records Centre record the births, marriages, and deaths of soldiers who were stationed in the United Kingdom upon the occasion of these events during the period 1761–1924; the marriage records also note the names, births, and baptisms of any children who were born to the marriage. For those who were serving overseas at the time of births, marriages, and deaths, the searcher has to turn instead to the Army Register Book (1881–1959) or to similar books for the Royal Navy (1837–1959) and the Royal Air Force (1918–59). Since 1959 the entries for all three forces are recorded together. Certified copies of these entries may be obtained at the same cost as the ordinary birth, marriage, and death certificates.

The Public Record Office issues a number of useful leaflets on the military and naval records in its custody at Kew. If the name of the regiment in which an ancestor served is known, a great deal of time is saved in searching a mass of material. The Army and Navy records which provide genealogical information are many and varied. They include the muster rolls of each regiment, which give place of birth, age on enlistment, and often the trade of the recruit. The earliest rolls are those of the Royal Artillery, which start in 1719. Certificates of baptism survive for officers from 1755. For all ranks, there are the chaplains' returns of 1796–1800, which register births, baptisms, marriages, and deaths abroad; these returns have a comprehensive index. The original registers of births, baptisms, marriages, and deaths, which were kept by regiments both at home and abroad between 1790 and 1924, are also housed at Kew. The records of service in the Royal Artillery between 1756 and 1917 give the places of birth, marriage, discharge, or death. Records pertaining to widows' pensions, 1735–1912, include proof of marriage and often sworn statements regarding the date and place of birth. The Chelsea Hospital registers record baptisms (1691–1812), marriages (1691–1765), and burials (1692–1856). Other records include casualty returns (1809–57), which give name, rank, place of birth, trade on enlistment, details of the casualty, and the next of kin.

The naval records that are held at Kew begin with the ships' musters, which start in 1680, become fuller from 1696, and are more or less complete from 1740 onwards. These list everyone who was serving on board, and give the ages and places of birth of the ratings. Dates and places of birth of seamen are also given in the Description books from the 1790s. Other useful records may be listed briefly. Lieutenants' passing certificates, which were issued from 1789 onwards, are accompanied by certificates of baptism. Certificates of service survive for ratings from 1802 to 1894. Bounty papers from 1675 to 1822 give the names and addresses of recipients of bounty. Pensions records include details of service and place of birth, and the marriage certificates of widows. The Greenwich Hospital records include registers of baptisms (1720–1856), marriages (1724–54), and burials (1705–1857), and the entry book of pensioners who resided there at some time between 1704 and 1869.

If the name of the regiment in which an ancestor served is known, it may be worth while to contact the appropriate regimental museum. Even if no further genealogical information is forthcoming, the museum will be able to provide a great deal of background information about the life of a soldier and the campaigns in which an ancestor might have been involved.

Adult males throughout Britain were liable for service in the local defence force, or militia, when occasion arose. Lists of names, known as muster rolls or militia returns, were drawn up from time to time, from the sixteenth to the nineteenth centuries. Most of the Tudor and Stuart ones are kept in the Public Record Office at Kew, though some are found in local record offices. The indispensable guides are Jeremy Gibson and Alan Dell, *Tudor and Stuart Muster Rolls: A Directory of Holdings in the British Isles* and Jeremy Gibson and Mervyn Medlycot, *Militia Lists and Musters, 1757–1876: A Directory of Holdings in the British Isles.*

The early Tudor rolls are valuable in proving the existence of a surname within a particular locality before the beginning of parish registration. A number of muster rolls have been printed by county record societies. The most famous is that for Gloucestershire in 1608, which has been published as *Men and Armour for Gloucestershire in 1608*. This is arranged on a parish basis and records 19,402 individuals by name, approximate age, and occupation. The occupations have been analysed by A. J. and R. H. Tawney in their article 'An Occupational Census of the Seventeenth Century'. The surnames (which are indexed alphabetically) can be analysed in the same way as those in the printed hearth tax returns for various other counties. The pattern of migration into Gloucestershire is clear from the numerous surnames of Welsh or Welsh Border origin, compared with the insignificant number of northern locative names. The large number of distinctive regional surnames that appear in the list include Aly (6), Baddam (14), Berrowe (11), Cloterbrooke (28), Eddon (12), Millard (25), Nelme (36), Pegler (35), Sly (12), Tylladam (12), and Wollams (8). Their original homes may well be found in or close to Gloucestershire.

The militia was re-established in 1757, when it was ordered that each parish should provide for training a number of able-bodied men aged 18 to 50. Lists of all men within this age-range (which was lowered to 45 in 1762) were therefore drawn up from time to time, so that ballots could be held. From 1806 onwards the age of each man in the lists was recorded. As the militia was the responsibility of the Lord-Lieutenants of the counties, these records tend to be found in local rather than central record offices. The muster rolls or enrolment books are of limited use as they only give the names of those who were balloted for service. In many parts of the country, however, there are complete lists of all those who were balloted. Good collections survive for Cumberland, Dorset, Hertfordshire, Kent, Lincolnshire, Northamptonshire, and the city of Bristol, and elsewhere for various hundreds or wapentakes and for individual parishes. The best lists are both thorough and informative. Those for Dorset in the 1790s, for example, record not only a man's name, but also his occupation, any infirmity, height, marital status, and number of children aged under 10, and they distinguish the 'young men' of the parish from the rest. On the other hand, although the various Militia Acts from 1758 onwards always stipulated that the lists must record the names of all men in the appropriate age-range, it is clear that this did not always happen. Those who were exempted on account of their occupation, infirmity, etc. were sometimes not included and others may have been left off through carelessness or perhaps bribery.

The best of the eighteenth-century militia lists, compiled under the Act of 1757, are those for Hertfordshire (1758–65), which are gradually being published by the Hertfordshire Family and Population History Society, and a series of six for Northamptonshire, covering the period 1762–86, the fullest of which has been published under the title *Northamptonshire Militia Lists, 1777*. This has an analysis of the recorded occupations and an alphabetical index of surnames. The index notes numerous names that were common in the county but rare or absent beyond, names such as Ager (12), Allibone (5), Beeby (14), Blencowe (20), Buswell (26), Chater (9), Clever (21), Cunnington (14), Dunkley (60), Essam (8), Henson or Hemsman (39), Iliff (10), Judkins (14), Labram (9), Linnell (31), Mobbs (12), Peach (18), Pettifer (20), Pratt (22), Satchel (20), Tarry (25), Treadgold (7), Vann (18), and Wooding (19), many of them with alternative spellings. The list provides a springboard for further research into the homes of these family names.

The 'Defence Lists' of 1798 and 1803–4, i.e. the *Posse Comitatus* lists of 1798 and the *Levée en Masse* lists of 1803–4, are similar in appearance to the militia ballot lists. Their purpose was to organize a reserve defence force at the time of war with revolutionary France. Parish constables were ordered to record the names of all able-bodied men aged 15–60, who were not already serving with the yeomanry, volunteers, or the militia. In 1803 the instruc-

TRADE UNION RECORDS
The membership lists of Trade Unions can help to locate an ancestor in a particular job and place. This membership certificate of the Durham Miners' Association has been signed by the General Secretary in anticipation of his accepting a new member.

tions were to list all men aged 17–55. Buckinghamshire is the only county with a complete return. This valuable document has been edited by F. W. Beckett and published as *The Buckinghamshire Posse Comitatus, 1798*. The editor has analysed the occupations of the 23,500 or so men who are listed, and the surnames are indexed alphabetically. They too are a rich source for discovering the distinctive local names of the county. These include Allnutt (16), Anstee or Anstiss (31), Badrick (20), Boddy or Bodily (40), Cooling (14), Dancer (21), Deeley (19), Dormer (20), Ginger (34), Gomme (29), Grace (61), Grimsdale (18), Gurney (80), Illing (13), Munday (46), Neighbour (21), Oxlade (16), Peppitt (12), Plumridge (28), Puddifoot (15), Seabrook (18), Showler (27), Shrimpton (33), Stallwood (23), Stuchbury (13), Syred (35), Tappin (22), Theed (9), Verney or Varney (39), and Wooster (20). In all, 771 Buckinghamshire men who appear in the list of 1798 possessed one or other of these 30 names, whereas in neighbouring Northamptonshire 21 years earlier only 7 of these surnames were recorded, and even they were shared by only 14 men.

Apprenticeship and Freemen Records

Individual apprenticeship indentures survive in their thousands in miscellaneous collections all over the country, but there is no national collection except Crisp's Bonds at the library of the Society of Genealogists, which lists about 18,000 apprentices between 1641 and 1888. The Inland Revenue records at the Public Record Office for the period 1710–1811 are worth consulting for various trades. For example, anyone who has an ancestor who was a framework knitter in Nottinghamshire, Leicestershire, or Derbyshire might find this source rewarding, but those with an ancestor who was a Hallamshire cutler will find nothing of value here. The records provide the name, place of residence, and trade of the master, the name of the apprentice, and, until 1752, the name of the apprentice's father. Indexes compiled for the Society of Genealogists cover apprentices up to 1774 and masters up to 1762. Some local indexes have been published by record societies, e.g. in Surrey, Sussex, and Wiltshire.

In those parts of the country where a particular group of trades was dominant a record of all apprentices and freemen of a trade company might be preserved. The records of the Cutlers' Company of Hallamshire from the incorporation of the company in 1624 have been printed. They note the name of the apprentice, his father's name, occupation, and residence, the master's name, trade, and residence, the year when the apprenticeship began, its length, and the date of entry into the freedom of the company. Sons of freemen of the company had an automatic right of entry without the necessity of a formal apprenticeship. Anyone with an ancestor in this district should certainly consult this source, for even in the seventeenth century over half the local work-force were employed in the cutlery and allied trades.

Another type of freedom allowed a man to enjoy the privileges of one or other of the major cities and corporate towns. These included the right to practise a trade and the right to vote. The sons of other freemen and those who had completed an indentured apprenticeship in one of the recognized local trades formed the main body of the freemen, but others had purchased their freedom or had been honoured by such an award. The municipal authorities kept a register (or a series of rolls) of those who had been admitted into freedom. These records are normally kept in local record offices, but many have appeared in print. Some cover a long period from the Middle Ages to modern times. A good example is M. M. Rowe and A. M. Jackson's *Exeter Freemen, 1266–1967*. By the eighteenth century such records are far less valuable to the historian.

At their most complete, the rolls record the date of admission, the name of the freeman, the name and residence of his father, and (where an apprenticeship had been served) the name and trade of the master. The evidence provided by the rolls has been used to study urban occupations and the

HOGARTH: 'INDUSTRY AND IDLENESS' (1747)
This preparatory sketch for *The Fellow 'Prentices at their Looms* shows two apprentices in the weaving trades under the supervision of their master.

Alston Yearly Friendly Society, Alston N.W.A.

social and geographical background of freemen, but the reliability of freemen's rolls has been questioned by historians and it should be borne in mind that they cover only a proportion of the local population. Neverthe-less, a family historian might strike lucky and the source should certainly be consulted.

Hearth Tax and Protestation Returns

The various hearth tax returns of the 1660s and 1670s and the protestation returns of 1641–2 can be of great value to the family historian who is having difficulty in tracing his ancestors in the seventeenth century. They locate certain people at particular points in time, and by demonstrating the distri-bution patterns of surnames within a county they suggest which parish re-gisters might be profitably consulted in the search for an individual event. The family historian who does not know where to search for an ancestor in the late seventeenth or early eighteenth century might well find a lead from these sources. Thus, an eighteenth-century Lincolnshire family whose sur-name was recorded in such forms as Edenborough or Eddingborrow (which appear to have been derived from Edinburgh) can be traced back to Thomas Edenborough, who married Frances Thorp at Heckington in 1701. A poss-ible line of enquiry to an earlier generation is suggested by the appearance of the name James Edenborow in the hearth tax return for Orston, Notting-hamshire, in 1664. Orston lies on the road from Nottingham to Grantham, near the Lincolnshire border. The Jacob Ettenborow who paid tax on one hearth at nearby Scarrington in 1674 may have been the same person. An obvious task is to search the parish registers of Orston and Scarrington to see whether James was Thomas's father.

The hearth tax was payable on the number of chimneys possessed by each house in England and Wales during the years 1662–88. It formed a major part of the government's revenue during the reigns of Charles II and James II, but was abolished after the Glorious Revolution deposed King James. The tax was collected at a county level, so occasionally a return may survive at a local record office. Thus, the original return for the West Riding of Yorkshire for Lady Day 1672 is kept at Wakefield Library, but the edited version which was forwarded to London is housed at the Public Record Office. Selected returns for various counties have appeared in print, with full indexes. Family

THE HEARTH TAX RETURN FOR BROOKLANDS, SURREY (MICHAELMAS 1662)

This return is unusual in having only one person with one hearth. Were there other people who were exempted on grounds of poverty? It lists the heads of household and the number of hearths for which they were chargeable. Richard Lucas, who signed the return, was no doubt the local constable. A transcription reads:

A List of the Firehearths Taken Att Micklemas 1662

	Hearths
Cha. Bickerstafe Esqr.	22 paid
Mr More	14 paid
Will. Woodman	6 paid
John Cosham	6 paid
John Worthington Clarke	5 paid
John Woodman	3 paid
Tho. Chillman	3 paid
John Bridger	8 paid
Canticke Dove	1 paid
Will. Mercy	3 paid
Rob. Stanton	6 paid
Ralph Woodman	7 paid
John Rumings	3 paid
John Hard	2 paid
Tho. Saker	2 paid
Widd. Tichburne	3 paid
Tho. Lucas	3 paid
Will. Ware	2 paid
Edward Arther	2 paid
Anthony Beach	2 paid
John Allin	4 paid
Rich. Lucas	3 paid

Richard Lucas

history societies are conscious of the need to publish the best returns for their area, but at the moment only a minority of counties have anything in print.

The returns that were made to central government are kept in the Public Record Office at Kew, in the Exchequer division, under the call number E.179. No county has a complete set of returns for the whole period; indeed, in some counties, such as Wiltshire, the searcher is likely to be disappointed. The indexes note the length of each return, and this information is usually a good guide to which list is the fullest. A dedicated researcher will consult each of the returns that is available.

The collectors of the tax divided each county into its respective hundreds or wapentakes. These were then arranged by township, sometimes in alphabetical order. The family historian's task is eased if he has some grasp of the administrative structure of the county that he is interested in. Townships were the smallest units of local government from the Middle Ages until the nineteenth century. They were often identical with the ecclesiastical parishes, but in those parts of the country where parishes were large they formed subdivisions of the ecclesiastical units.

The entries for each township reflect the way in which the collector (assisted by the constable) toured the township to inspect each property. In estate villages, the name of the squire heads the list. Such men were given their titles or were addressed as 'Mr'. Here, as elsewhere, 'Mr' and 'Mrs' signified gentry status; the majority of people were recorded simply by their Christian name and their surname. Only the head of household was recorded; if this was a woman she was often named as Widow instead of by her first name. The number of hearths in the house was noted alongside the name. Those who were exempted from payment of the tax were recorded as 'poor' in the margin or were listed together at the end of each township's return. Unfortunately, in many cases the exempted poor were numbered but not named, or were simply not recorded.

Even though no single return is likely to be complete, collectively the records of the hearth tax are a major source of genealogical information for the third quarter of the seventeenth century. The protestation returns of 1641–2 can also yield rich pickings, where they survive in the library of the House of Lords. They list all males aged 18 and over who were called upon to subscribe to an Oath of Protestation of loyalty to king, Church, and Parliament shortly before the Civil War. The surviving lists appear to be remarkably comprehensive and include the names of the few individuals (determined recusants) who refused to take the oath. As they do not give the names of widows, they do not provide as full a record of local surnames as do the later hearth tax returns; such surnames might well be continued by males who at that time were under the age of 18 but whose fathers had died.

The returns for some counties or hundreds are missing. There is nothing for the counties of Leicestershire and Norfolk, or for the Yorkshire wapentakes of Staincross or Strafforth and Tickhill, for example. A full list of the

PRISON RECORDS

Where prison records survive they can be most informative. An unusually detailed collection was begun in 1859 by Robert Evan Roberts, the Governor of Bedford Gaol, who was concerned that habitual offenders were getting light sentences because their previous history was not known to the court. The photographing of prisoners did not become standard practice nationally until after 1870.

This committal record of 1861 gives far more information about William Flint than could normally be found for a law-abiding citizen. The nature of his offence indicates the harshness of the law at the time.

places for which returns survive are given in the appendix to the Fifth Report of the *Historical Manuscripts Commission* (1876), pages 120–34, which may be consulted in a good reference library. The returns for some counties, such as Nottinghamshire and Lincolnshire, have been published with an index.

Lay Subsidies and Poll Taxes

Earlier taxation lists are much less complete than those of the seventeenth century. The reliability of these lists and the proportion of the population who were exempt from taxes are a matter for continued debate amongst historians. From the point of view of the family historian, however, they may at least provide early evidence for a family name in a particular area and may well offer some clues to the homes of many distinctive surnames.

Lay subsidies are so-called because the clergy was exempt from such taxes. The subsidies that were collected between 1290 and 1334 are sometimes referred to as the tenths and fifteenths because of the practice of taxing one-tenth of the value of movable property of those who lived within a city, borough, or royal demesne and one-fifteenth of those who lived elsewhere. The names of taxpayers and the amount raised are arranged in the records under the vills (or townships) and boroughs. These returns are kept in the Exchequer division (E.179) of the Public Record Office, but some have been printed by record societies. Thus, in 1926 the Dugdale Society published *The Lay Subsidy Roll for Warwickshire of 6 Edward III (1332)*. The entry for the township of Wylye reads:

William son of Nicholas, 3*s.* 4*d.*, Wife of Thomas Daubeney, 3*s.* 6*d.*, Thomas Hiche, 2*s.* 0*d.*, William le Reue, 2*s.* 0*d.*, Executors of Robert le Clerke, 1*s.* 4*d.*, Thomas le Walshe, 1*s.* 6*d.*, Stephen le Whyte, 3*s.* 6*d.*, Peter the smith, 1*s.* 0*d.*, Peter le Reue, 1*s.* 0*d.*, Richard de Kereslee, 4*s.* 0*d.*, Thomas Henry, 1*s.* 4*d.*, John de Morton, 2*s.* 0*d.*, Wife of Stephen atte Welle, 2*s.* 4*d.*, Nicholas le Walshe, 2*s.* 0*d.*, John atte Grene, 3*s.* 0*d.*, William the clerk, 1*s.* 0*d.*, Robert Lemon, 1*s.* 0*d.*

All the various categories of surname are represented here, at the period when some surnames were becoming hereditary.

From 1334 onwards the returns no longer give the names of the taxpayers. In the sixteenth century a fresh attempt was made to increase revenue by a new tax on either land or goods. Large numbers of people were exempt and many others managed to avoid payment. In southern and Midland England the lay subsidy of 1523 appears to be the fullest, but in the north and in Wales that of 1543 is the best. Some of the later subsidies are as detailed as these. A good idea of the range of returns available for this period can be obtained from *Early Tudor Craven: Subsidies and Assessments, 1510–1547*, edited by R. W. Hoyle.

An alternative method of taxation used by central government in medieval times was the poll tax, levied in 1377 on all over 14, in 1379 on all over 16, and in 1381 on all over 15. It is again debatable how many people evaded the tax and how many were exempt from payment, but generally the poll tax returns list far more people than do the lay subsidies. The returns of 1379, when payment was graded according to wealth, are usually the best for the family historian. They are kept with the lay subsidies under E.179 in the PRO and so far few have appeared in print. The returns of 1379 for the West Riding were published by the Yorkshire Archaeological and Topographical Association in 1882. They are an invaluable guide to the range of surnames that were just being formed at that time. In the thinly populated Pennine township of Langsett, for example, the following people were recorded:

Villata de Langside: Adam Cutter Cecilia *uxor ejus*, iiijd., Johanna *filia ejus*, iiijd., Willelmus Swan Johanna *ux. ejus*, iiijd., Agnes *filia*, iiijd., Henricus Draper, iiijd.,

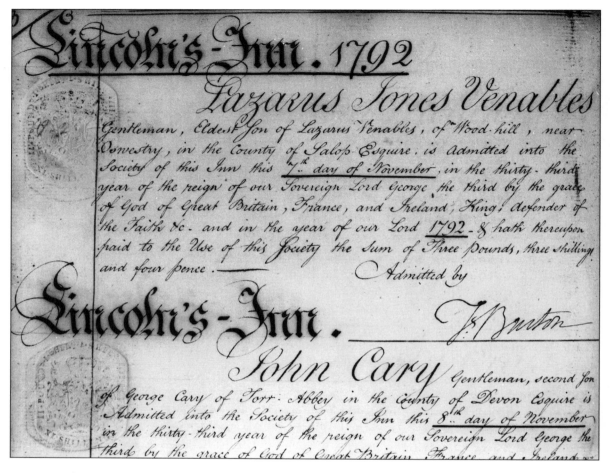

Lincoln's Inn. 1792

Lazarus Jones Venables

Gentleman, Eldest Son of Lazarus Venables, of Wood-hill, near Oswestry, in the County of Salop Esquire, is admitted into the Society of this Inn this 7th day of November, in the thirty-third year of the reign of our Sovereign Lord George the third by the grace of God of Great Britain, France, and Ireland, King, defender of the Faith &c. and in the year of our Lord 1792 & hath thereupon paid to the Use of this Society the Sum of Three Pounds, three Shilling and four pence. ——— Admitted by

Lincoln's-Inn.

J. Burton

John Cary Gentleman, second Son of George Cary of Torr-Abbey in the County of Devon Esquire is Admitted into the Society of this Inn this 8th day of November in the thirty-third year of the reign of our Sovereign Lord George the third by the grace of God of Great Britain, France, and Ireland &c.

Emma Draper, iiijd., Willelmus Drak' Agnes *ux. ejus*, iiijd., Robertus Sylbot Johanna *ux. ejus*, iiijd., Johannes Preest Matilda *ux. ejus*, iiijd., Agnes *filia*, iiijd., Adam Hatter Cecilia *ux. ejus*, iiijd., Elias del Strete Elena *ux.*, Berker, vjd., Johannes Sylbot Johanna *ux.*, Bakester, vjd., Robertus Amias Agnes *ux.*, iiijd., Adam de Sowthagh' Matilda *ux.*, iiijd., Alicia Robynwyf', Webster, vjd., Willelmus de Hatyrlay Elena *ux.*, Mercer, xijd., Johanna *ancilla*, iiijd., Amicia Hattirslay, Marschall', vjd., Alicia *ancilla*, iiijd., Johannes de Swyndene Cristiana *ux.*, iiijd., Johanna de Swyndene junior Matilda *ux.*, iijd., Johanna Hattirslay mayden iiijd., *Summa* ixs.

The Latin forms—*uxor ejus* for 'his wife', *filia* for 'daughter', *ancilla* for 'servant'—do not present too much difficulty; nor do the Roman numerals. Married couples and single people each paid at the basic rate of 4*d*., but craftsmen and traders were assessed at 6*d*. or 1*s*. Amongst the locative surnames recorded here is that of Hattersley, which originated across the Pennines and has since become common a few miles to the south, in and around Sheffield.

The revolt of 1381 convinced the government that personal taxation was extremely unpopular. There are therefore no comparable records for the fifteenth century, which is a difficult period for genealogical research. The poll tax was revived in 1641 and levied on seven occasions between 1660 and 1697. These returns may be found in the PRO or in local record offices. Some of the lists are long and detailed; the numbers who evaded payment were probably fewer than those who did not pay when the tax was revived in the late 1980s.

Reading Old Documents

The documents of the last 200 years are not usually difficult to read, unless the scribe has an idiosyncratic style. Words are normally spelt the same way as at present and letters are formed in a recognizable manner. The family historian who gets back to the sixteenth and seventeenth centuries, however, is faced with real problems of interpretation. The script is likely to be radically different from modern styles and much of it may be in Latin. The beginner has every reason to feel daunted by the sheer difficulty of reading a document, let alone understanding the information that it contains.

These are difficulties which must be admitted and faced honestly. There is no easy way out of the problem. Nevertheless, all hope should not be abandoned immediately. What seems impossible to read at first sight might be transcribed with practice. Several manuals provide guidance for the beginner. They include L. C. Hector, *The Handwriting of English Documents*, H. E. P. Grieve, *Examples of English Handwriting, 1150–1750*, C. T. Martin, *The Record Interpreter*, F. G. Emmison, *How to Read Local Archives, 1500–1700*, and K. C. Newton, *Medieval Local Records: A Reading Aid*. In addition to these, a number of similar guides are available from record offices, such as the *Borthwick Wallets* by A. Rycraft.

It is certainly possible with patience to teach oneself how to read Tudor and Stuart documents. The old adage 'practice makes perfect' is particularly appropriate here. Photocopies of documents should be obtained, if that is allowed, so that they can be examined at leisure. The trick is to recognize strange forms of letters in words which are obvious and to try these in the words that are proving difficult. It will be an encouragement to remember that even experienced researchers sometimes cannot read all the words in a document. Do not be embarrassed to ask for help; a fresh eye can often see the answer immediately and the helper will be pleased if he can read something that you cannot.

Half the battle is knowing what to expect. Wills can be read easily if the common form of the preamble is known and the usual way of proceeding is understood. That strange squiggle at the beginning of a probate inventory is soon recognized to be an abbreviated form of the Latin word *Imprimis*, meaning firstly. That list of names at the beginning of a manorial court roll will be seen to be a record of the jurors, whose first job will have been to choose the officers for the coming year. The more one knows about the ways that documents were drawn up and what they are likely to record, the easier is the task of deciphering the handwriting.

The ways in which documents written in Latin were set out are illustrated in a useful introductory guide, E. A. Gooder, *Latin for Local History*. Words that commonly appear in the records are translated in R. E. Latham (ed.), *Revised Medieval Latin Word List* and J. L. Fisher, *A Medieval Farming Glossary of Latin and English Words*. The beginner will therefore find plenty of guidance and can take heart that others have faced the same difficulties but have emerged triumphant.

SIXTEENTH- AND SEVENTEENTH-CENTURY HANDWRITING

Some of the variety of forms of letters used by legal scribes is well illustrated by this extract from A. Wright, *Court Hand Restored* (5th edition, 1818).

SELECT BIBLIOGRAPHY

ANDERSON, M., *Family Structure in Nineteenth Century Lancashire* (Cambridge: Cambridge University Press, 1971).

ARMSTRONG, W. A., 'The Flight from the Land', in G. E. Mingay (ed.), *The Victorian Countryside*, i (London: Routledge & Kegan Paul, 1981).

BAINES, D., *Emigration From Europe, 1815–1930* (London: Macmillan, 1991).

BANKS, E., and BROWNELL, E. E. *Topographical Dictionary of 2885 English Emigrants to New England, 1620–1650* (New York: New York Public Library, 1912).

BECKETT, F. W. (ed.), *The Buckinghamshire Posse Comitatus, 1798*, Buckinghamshire Record Society series, no. 25 (Aylesbury: Buckinghamshire Record Society, 1973).

BECKETT, J. V., *The Aristocracy in England, 1660–1914* (London: Blackwell, 1986).

—— and FOULDS, T., 'Beyond the Micro: Laxton, the Computer and Social Change over Time', *Local Historian*, 16(8) (1985).

BEIER, A. L., *Masterless Men: The Vagrancy Problem in England, 1560–1640* (London: Methuen, 1965).

—— and FINLAY, R. (eds.), *London, 1500–1700: The Making of the Metropolis* (London: Longman, 1986).

BELL, R., *The Book of Ulster Surnames* (Belfast: Blackstaff Press, 1980).

BERTHOFF, R. T., *British Immigrants in Industrial America, 1790–1850* (Cambridge, Mass.: Harvard University Press, 1953).

BEWICK, T., *My Life* (London: Folio Society, 1981).

BOAL, F. W., and DOUGLAS, J. N. H. (eds.), *Integration and Division: Geographical Perspectives on the Northern Ireland Problem* (London: Academic Press, 1982).

BOULTON, J., 'Neighbourhood Migration in Early Modern England', in Clark and Souden (eds.), *Migration and Society in Early Modern England*.

BRADLEY, L., *A Glossary for Local Population Studies* (Nottingham: Department of Adult Education, University of Nottingham, 1971).

BUCKHATZSCH, E. J., 'Places of Origin of a Group of Immigrants into Sheffield, 1625–1799', *Economic History Review*, 2nd ser., 2 (1950).

BURNETT, J., 'The Autobiography of the Working Class', *Labour History Review*, 55, pt. 1 (1990).

CAFFYN, L., *Workers' Housing in West Yorkshire, 1750–1920* (London: HMSO, 1986).

CAMP, A. J., *Wills and Their Whereabouts*, 4th edn. (Chichester: Phillimore, 1974).

CARTER, W. F. (ed.), *The Lay Subsidy Roll for Warwickshire of Edward III (1332)* (Oxford: Dugdale Society, 1926).

CAUNCE, S., *Amongst Farm Horses: The Farm Lads of East Yorkshire* (Gloucester: Alan Sutton, 1991).

CHARTRES, J., and HEY, D. (eds.), *English Rural Society, 1500–1800: Essays in Honour of Joan Thirsk* (Cambridge: Cambridge University Press, 1990).

CHAYTOR, M., 'Household and Kinship: Ryton in the Late Sixteenth and Early Seventeenth Centuries', *History Workshop*, 10 (Autumn 1980).

CLARK, P., and SOUDEN, D. (eds.), *Migration and Society in Early Modern England* (London: Hutchinson, 1987).

COLDHAM, P. W., *The Complete Book of Emigrants in Bondage, 1614–1775* (Baltimore: Genealogy Publications, 1987).

COLWELL, S., *Tracing Your Family Tree* (London: Faber, 1984).

COX, J., and PADFIELD, T., *Tracing Your Ancestors in the Public Record Office*, 4th edn. (London: HMSO, 1990).

CRESSY, D., *Coming Over: Migration and Communication between England and New England in the Seventeenth Century* (Cambridge: Cambridge University Press, 1987).

—— 'Kinship and Kin Interaction in Early Modern England', *Past and Present*, 113 (Nov. 1986).

CURRER-BRIGGS, N. *Worldwide Family History* (London: Routledge & Kegan Paul, 1982).

—— and GAMBIER, R., *Debrett's Guide to Tracing Your Ancestry* (London: Webb and Bower, 1990).

DICKINSON, W., 'On the Farming of Cumberland', *Journal of the Royal Agricultural Society*, 13 (1852), 219–20.

EARLE, P., *The Making of the English Middle Class: Business, Society and Family Life in London, 1660–1730* (London: Methuen, 1989).

EMMISON, F. G., *How to Read Local Archives, 1500–1700* (London: Historical Association, 1967).

ERICKSON, C., *Emigration from Europe, 1815–1914* (London: Adam and Charles Black, 1976).

EVERITT, A., *Landscape and Community in England* (London: Hambledon Press, 1985).

FERGUSON, J. P. S., *Scottish Family Histories* (Edinburgh: National Library of Scotland, 1986).

FIDLON, P. G., and RYAN, R. J. (eds.), *The First Fleeters* (Sydney: Australian Document Library, 1981).

FILBY, P. W., and MEYER, M. K. (eds.), *Passenger and Immigration List Index*, 6 vols. (Detroit, Mich.: Gale Research, 1981–5).

FINBERG, H. P. R., 'The Gostwicks of Willington', *Bedfordshire Historical Record Society*, 36 (1956).

FINLAY, R. A. P., *Population and Metropolis: The Demography of London, 1580–1650* (Cambridge: Cambridge University Press, 1981).

FISHER, J. L., *A Medieval Farming Glossary of Latin and English Words* (London: Standing Conference for Local History, 1980).

FITZHUGH, T. V., *The Dictionary of Genealogy* (Sherborne: Alphabooks, 1985).

—— *How to Write a Family History* (Sherborne: Alphabooks, 1988).

FORSTER, K. A., *Pronouncing Dictionary of English Place-Names* (London: Routledge & Kegan Paul, 1981).

GELLING, M., *Signposts to the Past* (London: Dent, 1978).

GIBSON, J. S. W., *Guides for Genealogists, Family and Local Historians* (various pamphlets, Federation of Family History Societies).

—— *Wills and Where to Find Them* (Chichester: Phillimore, 1974).

—— and DELL, A., *Tudor and Stuart Muster Rolls: A Directory of Holdings in the British Isles* (Birmingham: Federation of Family History Societies, 1989).

—— and MEDLYCOT, M., *Militia Lists and Musters, 1757–1876: A Directory of Holdings in the British Isles* (Birmingham: Federation of Family History Societies, 1989).

GILLEN, M., *The Founders of Australia: A Biographical Dictionary of the First Fleet* (Sydney: Library of Australian History, 1988).

GINTER, D., *A Measure of Wealth: The English Land Tax in Historical Analysis* (London: Hambledon, 1992).

GOODER, E. A., *Latin for Local History* (London: Longman, 1978).

GOODY, J., THIRSK, J., and THOMPSON, E. P. T. (eds.), *Family and Inheritance: Rural Society in Western Europe, 1200–1800* (Cambridge: Cambridge University Press, 1976).

GOUGH, Richard, *The History of Myddle*, ed. D. Hey (Harmondsworth: Penguin, 1980).

GRIEVE, H. E. P., *Examples of English Handwriting, 1150–1750* (Chelmsford: Essex Record Office, 1978).

GUPPY, H. B., *Homes of Family Names in Great Britain* (London: Harrison, 1890).

HAMILTON-EDWARDS, G., *In Search of Ancestry* (Chichester: Phillimore, 1983).

—— *In Search of Army Ancestry* (Chichester: Phillimore, 1977).

—— *In Search of Scottish Ancestry* (Chichester: Phillimore, 1988).

—— *In Search of Welsh Ancestry* (Chichester: Phillimore, 1986).

HANKS, P., and HODGES, F., *The Oxford Dictionary of Surnames* (Oxford: Oxford University Press, 1989).

HARVEY, P. D. A., *Manorial Records* (London: British Records Association, 1984).

HARVEY, R., *Genealogy for Librarians* (London: Bingley, 1983).

HATCHER, J., *Plague, Population and the English Economy, 1348–1530* (London: Macmillan, 1977).

HATLEY, V. A. (ed.), *Northamptonshire Militia Lists, 1777*, Northamptonshire Record Society series, no. 25 (Northampton: Northamptonshire Record Society, 1973).

HAWKINGS, D., *Bound for Australia* (Chichester: Phillimore, 1987).

HECTOR, L. C., *The Handwriting of English Documents* (London: Arnold, 1979).

HEY, D., *Family History and Local History in England* (London: Longman, 1987).

HIGGS, E., *Making Sense of the Census*, Public Record Office Handbooks, no. 23 (London: HMSO, 1989).

HOLDERNESS, B. A., 'Personal Mobility in Some Rural Parishes of Yorkshire, 1777–1822', *Yorkshire Archaeological Journal*, 42 (1970).

HOLMES, C., *John Bull's Island: Immigration and British Society, 1871–1971* (London: Macmillan, 1988).

HONE, N. J., *The Manor and Manorial Records* (London: Methuen, 1906).

HORN, J. P. R., 'Moving on in the New World: Migration and Out-Migration in the Seventeenth Century Chesapeake', in Clark and Souden (eds.), *Migration and Society in Early Modern England*.

HOSKINS, W. G., *Local History in England*, 3rd edn. (London: Longman, 1984).

—— *The Midland Peasant: The Economic and Social History of a Leicestershire Village* (London: Macmillan, 1957).

HOYLE, R. W. (ed.), *Early Tudor Craven: Subsidies and Assessments, 1510–1547*, Yorkshire Archaeological Society Record series, no. 145 (Leeds: Yorkshire Archaeological Society, 1987).

HUMPHREY-SMITH, C. R. (ed.), *A Genealogist's Bibliography* (Chichester: Phillimore, 1981).

—— (ed.), *The Phillimore Atlas and Index of Parish Registers* (Chichester: Phillimore, 1984).

HUNTER, J., *South Yorkshire: The History and Topography of the Deanery of Doncaster*, 2 vols. (London: Nichols, 1828–31).

IREDALE, D., and BARRETT, J., *Discovering Your Family Tree* (Princes Risborough: Shire, 1985).

JENKINS, D., *The Agricultural Community in South-West Wales at the Turn of the Twentieth Century* (Cardiff: University of Wales Press, 1971).

KAIN, J. P., and PRINCE, H. C., *Tithe Surveys of England and Wales* (Cambridge: Cambridge University Press, 1985).

KETTLE, A. J. (ed.), 'A List of Families in the Archdeaconry of Stafford', *Collections for a History of Staffordshire*, 4th ser., 8 (1976).

KIRK, R. E. G., and KIRK, E. F. (eds.), *Returns of Aliens Dwelling in the City and Suburbs of London from the Reign of Henry VIII to that of James I* (London: Huguenot Society, 1900–8).

KUSSMAUL, A., *Servants in Husbandry in Early Modern England* (Cambridge: Cambridge University Press, 1981).

LASLETT, P., *Family Life and Illicit Love in Earlier Generations* (Cambridge: Cambridge University Press, 1977).

LATHAM, R. E., *Revised Medieval Latin Word List* (London: British Academy, 1965).

LAWTON, R., 'Population Movements in the West Midlands, 1841–1861', *Geography*, 42 (1958).

MACFARLANE, A., *A Guide to English Historical Records* (Cambridge: Cambridge University Press, 1983).

McKINLEY, R. A., *A History of British Surnames* (London: Longman, 1990).

—— *Norfolk and Suffolk Surnames in the Middle Ages* (Chichester: Phillimore, 1975).

—— *The Surnames of Lancashire* (London: Leopard's Head Press, 1981).

—— *The Surnames of Oxfordshire* (London: Leopard's Head Press, 1977).

—— *The Surnames of Sussex* (London: Leopard's Head Press, 1988).

MACLYSAGHT, E., *The Surnames of Ireland* (Dublin: Irish Academic Press, 1980).

MANDER, M., *Tracing Your Ancestry* (Newton Abbott: David and Charles, 1976).

MARKWELL, F. C., and SAUL, P., *The Family Historian's Enquire Within* (London: Federation of Family History Societies, 1988).

MARSHALL, J. D., and WALTON, J. K., *The Lake Counties from 1830 to the Mid-Twentieth Century* (Manchester: Manchester University Press, 1981).

MARSHALL, L. M. (ed.), 'The Bedfordshire Hearth Tax Returns, 1671', *Bedfordshire Historical Record Society*, 16 (1934).

MARTIN, C. T., *The Record Interpreter* (Dorking: Kohler and Coombes, 1982).

MEEKINGS, C. A. F. (ed.), *Dorset Hearth Tax Assessments, 1662-1664* (Dorchester: Dorset Natural History and Archaeological Society, 1951).

—— (ed.), *Surrey Hearth Tax, 1664* (Guildford: Surrey Record Society, xvii, 1940).

MILLER, E., and HATCHER, J., *Medieval England: Rural Society and Economic Change, 1086–1348* (London: Longman, 1978).

MOODY, D., *Scottish Family History* (London: Batsford, 1988).

MORGAN, T. J., and MORGAN, P., *Welsh Surnames* (Cardiff: University of Wales Press, 1985).

NEWTON, K. C., *Medieval Local Records: A Reading Aid* (London: Historical Association, 1971).

NORTON, J. E., *Guide to the National and Provincial Directories of England and Wales, excluding London, Published before 1856* (London: Royal Historical Society, 1950).

O'DAY, A. (ed.), *H. Heinrick: A Survey of the Irish in England (1872)* (London: Hambledon Press, 1990).

PALGRAVE-MOORE, P., *How to Locate and Use Manorial Records* (Norwich: Elvery Dower, 1985).

PELLING, G., *Beginning Your Family History*, 4th edn. (London: Federation of Family History Societies, 1987).

PHYTHIAN-ADAMS, C. V., *Desolation of a City: Coventry and the Urban Crisis of the Late Middle Ages* (Cambridge: Cambridge University Press, 1979).

—— *Rethinking Local History* (Leicester: Leicester University Press, 1987).

PINE, L. G., *The Genealogist's Encyclopedia* (Newton Abbott: David and Charles, 1969).

PLOMER, W. (ed.), *Kilvert's Diary, 1870–1879* (Harmondsworth: Penguin, 1977).

PORTEOUS, J. D., *The Mells: Surname Geography, Family History* (Saturna Island, Canada: Saturnalia, 1988).

PRIOR, M., *Fisher Row: Fishermen, Bargemen and Canal Boatmen in Oxford, 1500–1900* (Oxford: Oxford University Press, 1982).

RAFTIS, J. A., *Tenure and Mobility: Studies in the Social History of an English Village* (Toronto: Pontifical Institute of Medieval Studies, 1964).

RAMSKER, C. A., 'Pre-Register Genealogy and a Lost Place-Name', *Local Historian*, 10(5) (1973).

RAVENSTEIN, E. G., 'The Laws of Migration', *Journal of the Statistical Society*, 48, pt. 2 (1885).

RAZI, Z., *Life, Marriage and Death in a Medieval Parish: Economy, Society and Demography in Halesowen, 1270–1400* (Cambridge: Cambridge University Press), 1980.

REANEY, P. H., *Dictionary of British Surnames* (London: Routledge & Kegan Paul, 1958).

—— *The Origin of English Surnames* (London: Routledge & Kegan Paul, 1967).

REDMONDS, G., *Yorkshire, West Riding: English Surname Series*, i (Chichester: Phillimore, 1973).

RIDEN, P., *Record Sources for Local History* (London: Batsford, 1987).

ROGERS, C. D., *The Family Tree Detective*, 2nd edn. (Manchester: Manchester University Press, 1983).

—— *Tracing Missing Persons* (Manchester: Manchester University Press, 1986).

ROWE, M. M., and JACKSON, A. M., *Exeter Freemen, 1266–1967*, Devon and Cornwall Record Series, extra series, no. 1 (Exeter: Devon and Cornwall Record Society, 1973).

SANDERS, P., *The Simple Annals: The History of an Essex and East End Family* (Gloucester: Alan Sutton, 1989).

SCHOFIELD, R. S., 'Age-Specific Mobility in an Eighteenth Century English Parish', in Clark and Souden (eds.), *Migration and Society in Early Modern England*.

—— 'Dimensions of Illiteracy, 1750–1850', *Explorations in Economic History*, 10 (1973).

SHAW, G., and TIPPER, A., *British Directories: A Bibliography and Guide to Directories Published in England and Wales (1850–1950) and Scotland (1773–1950)* (Leicester: Leicester University Press, 1988).

SILL, M., 'Mid-Nineteenth Century Labour Mobility: The Case of the Coal Miners of Hetton-le-Hole', *Local Population Studies*, 22 (1979).

SINCLAIR, C., *Tracing Your Scottish Ancestors: A Guide to Ancestry Research in the Scottish Record Office* (Edinburgh: HMSO, 1990).

SLACK, P., *The Impact of Plague in Tudor and Stuart England* (Oxford: Oxford University Press, 1990).

SMITH, J., *Men and Armour in Gloucestershire in 1608* (Gloucester: Sutton, 1980).

SNELL, K., *Annals of the Labouring Poor* (Cambridge: Cambridge University Press, 1985).

SPUFFORD, M., *Contrasting Communities* (Cambridge: Cambridge University Press, 1974).

STEEL, D. J., *Discovering Your Family History* (London: British Broadcasting Corporation, 1986).

—— *General Sources of Births, Marriages and Deaths before 1837* (Chichester: Phillimore, 1976).

—— (ed.), *Sources for Roman Catholic and Jewish Genealogy and Family History* (Chichester: Phillimore, 1974).

—— and TAYLOR, L. (eds.), *Family History in Focus* (Guildford: Lutterworth, 1984).

STEPHENS, W. B., *Sources for English Local History* (Cambridge: Cambridge University Press, 1981).

TATE, W. E., *Domesday of English Enclosure Acts*, ed. M. E. Turner (Reading: University of Reading, 1978).

—— *The Parish Chest* (Cambridge: Cambridge University Press, 1963).

TAWNEY, A. J., and TAWNEY, R. H., 'An Occupational Census of the Seventeenth Century', *Economic History Review*, 5 (1934–5).

THOMAS, B., 'The Migration of Labour into the Glamorganshire Coalfield, 1861–1911', *Economica*, 30 (1930).

THOMPSON, F. M. L., *The Rise of Respectable Society: A Social History of Victorian Britain, 1830–1900* (London: Fontana, 1988).

THRUPP, S. L., *The Merchant Class of Medieval London, 1300–1500* (Ann Arbor, Mich. University of Michigan Press, 1962).

VEREY, D. (ed.), *The Diary of a Cotswold Parson: Reverend F. E. Witts, 1783–1854* (Gloucester: Alan Sutton, 1986).

WAGNER, A., *English Genealogy* (Chichester: Phillimore, 1983).

WATKINS-PITCHFORD, W. (ed.), *The Shropshire Hearth Tax Roll of 1672* (Shrewsbury: Shropshire Archaeological and Parish Register Society, 1949).

WEBSTER, W. F. (ed.), *Nottinghamshire Hearth Tax, 1664-1674* (Nottingham: Thoroton Society Record Series, xxxvii, 1988).

WEINSTOCK, M. M. B. (ed.), *Hearth Tax Returns, Oxfordshire, 1665* (Oxford: Oxfordshire Record Society, XXI, 1940).

WEST, J., *Town Records* (Chichester: Phillimore, 1983).

WHITE, G. P., *A Handbook of Cornish Surnames* (Redruth: Dyllansow Truran, 1984).

WHITE, M. B., 'Family Migration in Victorian Britain: The Case of Grantham and Scunthorpe', *Local Population Studies*, 41 (1988).

WHITEMAN, A. (ed.), *The Compton Census of 1676*, Records of Social and Economic History, NS, no. 10 (Oxford: British Academy, 1986).

WITHYCOMBE, E. G., *The Oxford Dictionary of English Christian Names* (Oxford: Oxford University Press, 1977).

WOODWARD, D., 'The Impact of the Commonwealth Act on Yorkshire Parish Registers', *Local Population Studies*, 14 (Spring 1975).

WRIGHTSON, K., 'Critique: Household and Kinship in Sixteenth Century England', *History Workshop*, 12 (Autumn 1981).

—— *English Society, 1580–1680* (London: Hutchinson, 1982).

WRIGLEY, E. A., and SCHOFIELD, R. S., *The Population History of England, 1541–1871: A Reconstruction* (Cambridge: Cambridge University Press, 1981).

YOUNGS, F. A., *Guide to the Local Administrative Units of England*, 2 vols. (London: Royal Historical Society, 1980–91).

Index of Surnames

Abbott 81
Abd(e)y 48, 50
Ackworth 50
Acton 121
Adney 50
Adwick 47
Ager 220
Albury 50
Allibone 220
Allison 40
Allnutt 44, 221
Alvey 48
Aly 219
Ambler 47, 50
Ami(a)s 118, 228
Anderton 38
Anestey, Anstee,
   Anstiss 47, 221
Answer 22
Appleby 48, 50
Appleyard 44
Appowell 47
Arden 15, 16
Arkell 102
Armitage 50
Aselby 47
Ash 38
Ashburne 50
Aspinall, Aspinhalgh
   19, 65
Assheton 125
Aston 31
Atkin 59
Attwood 161
Atwell 30, 227
Audley 16

Baddows 214
Badrick 221
Bagshaw 33, 48, 55, 56
Bailey 29, 33
Baker 33, 38
Balcock 15
Bamford, Bamforth
   44, 48

Banks 29
Barber 33
Barker 33
Barley 22
Barlow 22, 33
Barnes 33
Barnesdale 47
Barnett 22
Barnsley 38, 47
Barraclough 47
Barrowcliffe 47, 50
Bateman 29
Bates 38
Batty 24
Baugh 82
Bax 203
Baxter 28
Beddowes 82, 214
Bee 48
Beeby 220
Beeley 48
Bellamy 48
Benbridge 47, 65
Bennett 33
Berkeley 15, 16
Bernard 22
Berrowe 219
Bessiker 50
Best 83
Bevan 25, 43
Beverly 50
Bickerstaff 44, 47,
   50
Bilcleft 51
Biles 46
Billinghurst 50
Bingley 38
Birch 38
Blakeway 82
Blanksby 33
Blatherwick 48
Blaxland 20
Blencowe 220
Blessed 28
Blonk 48

Bloxham 45
Blythe 83
Boddy 22
Bodely 22
Bolsover 22
Bond 29
Boon 34
Boot 49
Borradell 50
Boswell 34
Bough 82
Boulter 81
Bowditch 46
Bowen 82
Bowser 22
Brabazon 34
Brace 43
Bradbury 38
Bradley 33
Bradshaw 33
Bray 196
Brayne 81, 82, 118
Breakespeare 42
Brearley 47
Bremner 34
Brewster 28
Bridgeman 29
Briggs 33
Brighton 65
Bristow 18, 48
Broadbent 31, 50, 65
Broadhead 21, 30, 47
Broadwood 13
Brookes 33
Broomhead 22, 23,
   47
Brotherton 50
Brown(e) 33, 82
Buchan 156
Buchingham 48
Bullas 33
Bullivant 48
Bulmer 50
Burgin 34
Burnett 22

Burton 197
Buscough 50
Busli 17, 26
Buswell 220
Butler 29
Butterworth 48
Buxton 48, 50
Bywater 30

Calton 38, 44, 48
Camsall 47
Carlyll 65
Carpenter 34
Caunt 49
Cavendish 132
Cawood 50, 60
Cawthorne 47
Chadwyk 65
Champion 59
Chappel 38
Chater 220
Chidlow 82
Chitty 50
Chugg 50
Clegg 47, 48
Clerke 227
Clever 220
Cloterbrooke 219
Clotworthy 46, 47
Clough 29
Coldwell 30
Coleman 29
Collinson 24
Cooling 221
Corbett 82
Corfield 82
Corin 38
Cornish 50
Cornwallis 3
Cornwell 50
Costedel 29
Cotman 29
Cottam 49
Cottingham 50
Crapper 56, 57

Index

ILLUSTRATION SOURCES